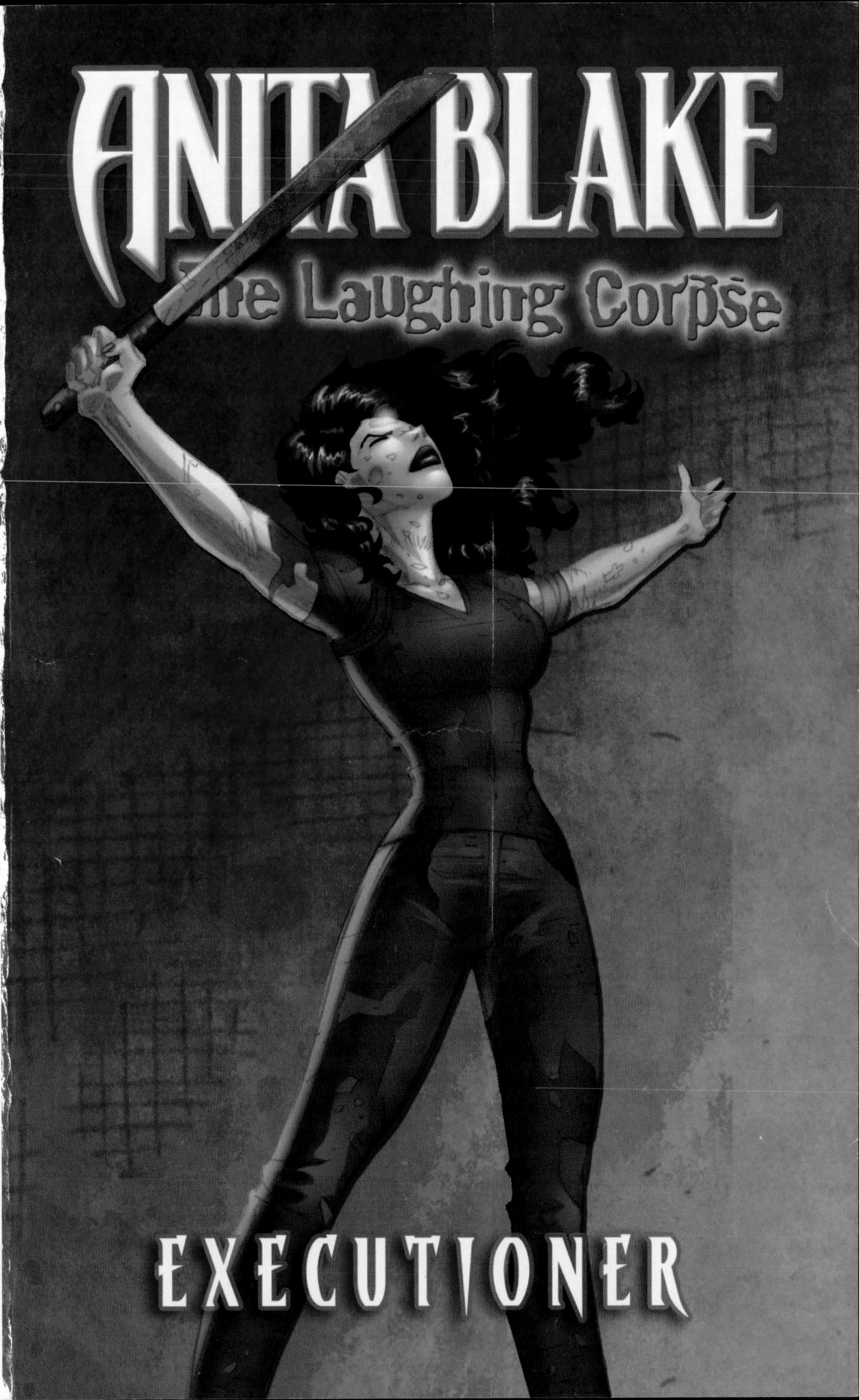
ANITA BLAKE
The Laughing Corpse
EXECUTIONER

ANITA BLAKE
The Laughing Corpse
EXECUTIONER

WRITER . . . . LAURELL K. HAMILTON

ADAPTATION . . . . JESS RUFFNER-BOOTH

ART . . . . RON LIM

COLORS . . . . LAURA VILLARI

LETTERS . . . . BILL TORTOLINI

COVER ART . . . . HARVEY TOLIBAO & BRETT BOOTH

WITH LAURA VILLARI AND JESS RUFFNER-BOOTH

EDITOR . . . . MICHAEL HORWITZ

SENIOR EDITOR . . . . RALPH MACCHIO

SPECIAL THANKS TO JONATHON GREEN, MELISSA MCALISTER,
ANN TREDWAY, CARRI CLEAVELAND & MARK PANICCIA

COLLECTION EDITOR . . . . CORY LEVINE

ASSISTANT EDITOR . . . . ALEX STARBUCK

ASSOCIATE EDITOR . . . . JOHN DENNING

EDITORS, SPECIAL PROJECTS. . . . . JENNIFER GRÜNWALD & MARK D. BEAZLEY

SENIOR EDITOR, SPECIAL PROJECTS . . . . JEFF YOUNGQUIST

SENIOR VICE PRESIDENT OF SALES . . . . DAVID GABRIEL

SENIOR VICE PRESIDENT OF STRATEGIC DEVELOPMENT . . . . RUWAN JAYATILLEKE

EDITOR IN CHIEF . . . . JOE QUESADA

PUBLISHER. . . . . DAN BUCKLEY

ANITA BLAKE, VAMPIRE HUNTER: THE LAUGHING CORPSE BOOK 3 — EXECUTIONER. Contains material originally published in magazine form as ANITA BLAKE, VAMPIRE HUNTER: THE LAUGHING CORPSE — EXECUTIONER #1-5. First printing 2010. Hardcover ISBN# 978-0-7851-3634-7. Softcover ISBN# 978-0-7851-3529-6. Published by MARVEL WORLDWIDE, INC., a subsidiary of MARVEL ENTERTAINMENT, LLC. OFFICE OF PUBLICATION: 417 5th Avenue, New York, NY 10016. © 2009 and 2010 Laurell K. Hamilton. All rights reserved. Hardcover: $19.99 per copy in the U.S. (GST #R127032852). Softcover: $16.99 per copy in the U.S. (GST #R127032852). Canadian Agreement #40668537. All characters featured in this issue and the distinctive names and likenesses thereof, and all related indicia are trademarks of Laurell K. Hamilton. No similarity between any of the names, characters, persons, and/or institutions in this magazine with those of any living or dead person or institution is intended, and any such similarity which may exist is purely coincidental. Marvel and its logos are TM & © Marvel Characters, Inc. **Printed in the U.S.A.** ALAN FINE, EVP - Office of the President, Marvel Worldwide, Inc. and EVP & CMO Marvel Characters B.V.; DAN BUCKLEY, Chief Executive Officer and Publisher - Print, Animation & Digital Media; JIM SOKOLOWSKI, Chief Operating Officer; DAVID GABRIEL, SVP of Publishing Sales & Circulation; DAVID BOGART, SVP of Business Affairs & Talent Management; MICHAEL PASCIULLO, VP Merchandising & Communications; JIM O'KEEFE, VP of Operations & Logistics; DAN CARR, Executive Director of Publishing Technology; JUSTIN F. GABRIE, Director of Publishing & Editorial Operations; SUSAN CRESPI, Editorial Operations Manager; ALEX MORALES, Publishing Operations Manager; STAN LEE, Chairman Emeritus. For information regarding advertising in Marvel Comics or on Marvel.com, please contact Ron Stern, VP of Business Development, at rstern@marvel.com. For Marvel subscription inquiries, please call 800-217-9158. **Manufactured between 4/12/10 and 5/12/10 (hardcover), and 4/12/10**

EXECUTIONER

The morally absent and mob-connected businessman Harold Gaynor offered vampire hunter and animator Anita Blake one million dollars to raise a three-centuries-old corpse. She turned him down, but a visit from Harold's bodyguard made it clear he won't take no for an answer.

Anita found another enemy in Dominga Salvador, a voodoo priestess who wanted more than Anita was willing to give in exchange for helping her find a missing boy. Dominga promised that something would come to hurt Anita when she least expects it. The boy's corpse was discovered, mutilated by what Anita believes to be a superhumanly strong zombie. Anita swore to find the undead killer and the mysterious animator powerful enough to raise it.

After discovering the truth behind Gaynor's checkered past and investigating another grisly murder scene left in the zombie's wake, Anita met with John Burke to examine the personal effects of his brother, an animator like Anita, for any clues as to who raised the zombie. They found a gris-gris, a voodoo charm that enables a less powerful necromancer to borrow the power of a much greater one. Anita tracked the gris-gris back to Dominga Salvador, and when she presented it to the elder priestess the charm began to crawl towards the source of its power!

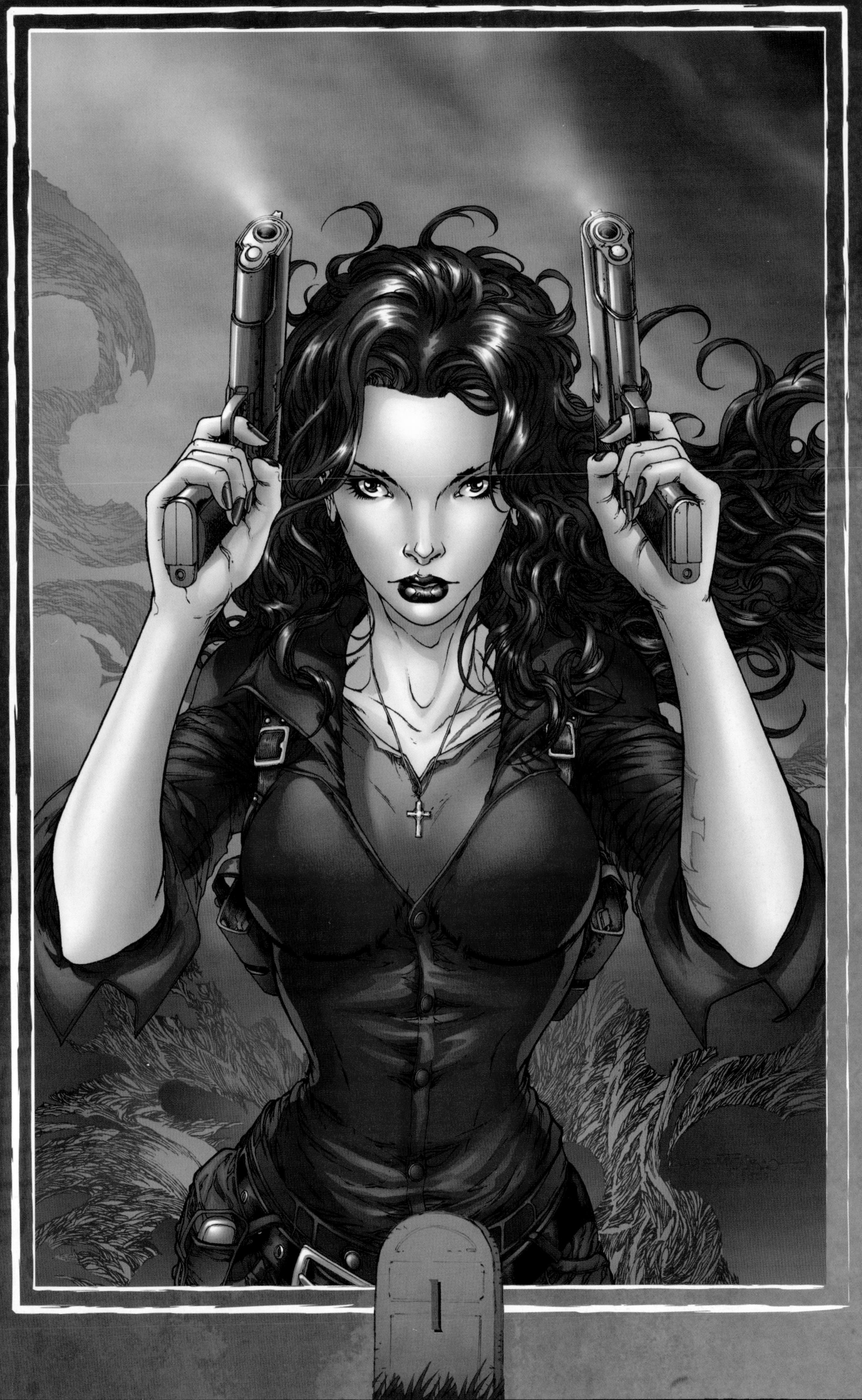
I

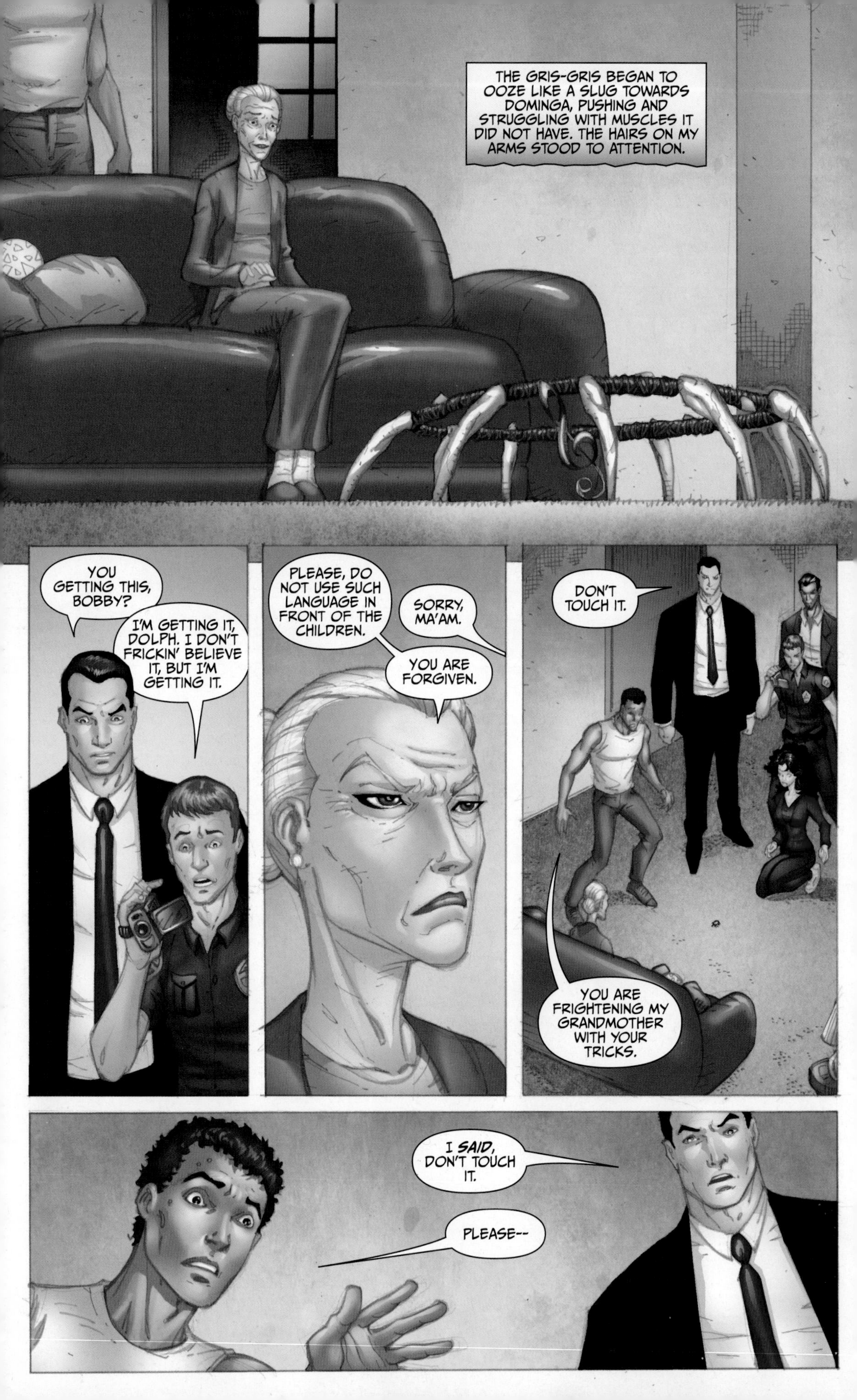

THE GRIS-GRIS BEGAN TO OOZE LIKE A SLUG TOWARDS DOMINGA, PUSHING AND STRUGGLING WITH MUSCLES IT DID NOT HAVE. THE HAIRS ON MY ARMS STOOD TO ATTENTION.
YOU GETTING THIS, BOBBY?
I'M GETTING IT, DOLPH. I DON'T FRICKIN' BELIEVE IT, BUT I'M GETTING IT.
PLEASE, DO NOT USE SUCH LANGUAGE IN FRONT OF THE CHILDREN.
SORRY, MA'AM.
YOU ARE FORGIVEN.
DON'T TOUCH IT.
YOU ARE FRIGHTENING MY GRANDMOTHER WITH YOUR TRICKS.
I *SAID*, DON'T TOUCH IT.
PLEASE--

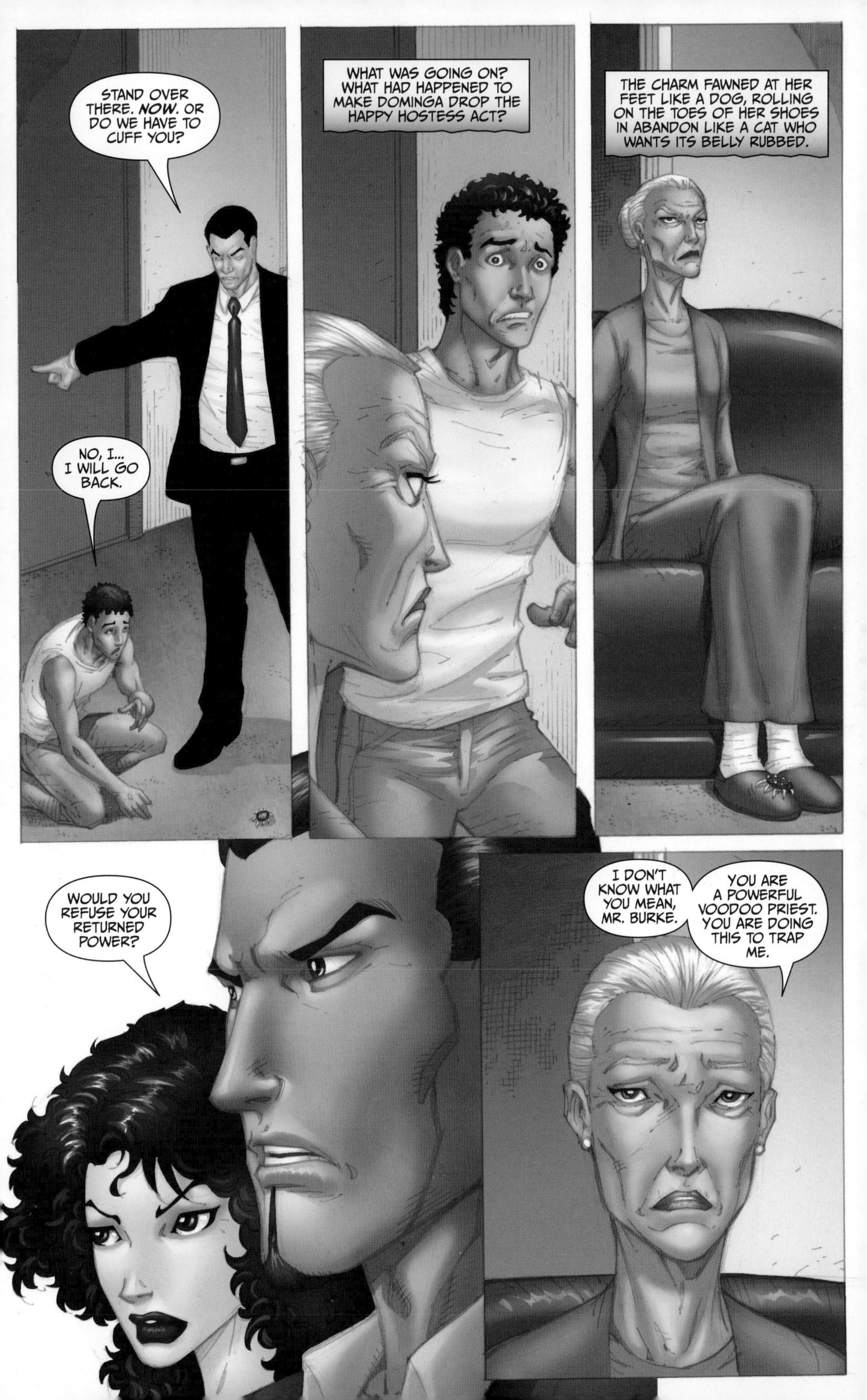
STAND OVER THERE. *NOW*. OR DO WE HAVE TO CUFF YOU?
NO, I... I WILL GO BACK.
WHAT WAS GOING ON? WHAT HAD HAPPENED TO MAKE DOMINGA DROP THE HAPPY HOSTESS ACT?
THE CHARM FAWNED AT HER FEET LIKE A DOG, ROLLING ON THE TOES OF HER SHOES IN ABANDON LIKE A CAT WHO WANTS ITS BELLY RUBBED.
WOULD YOU REFUSE YOUR RETURNED POWER?
I DON'T KNOW WHAT YOU MEAN, MR. BURKE.
YOU ARE A POWERFUL VOODOO PRIEST. YOU ARE DOING THIS TO TRAP ME.

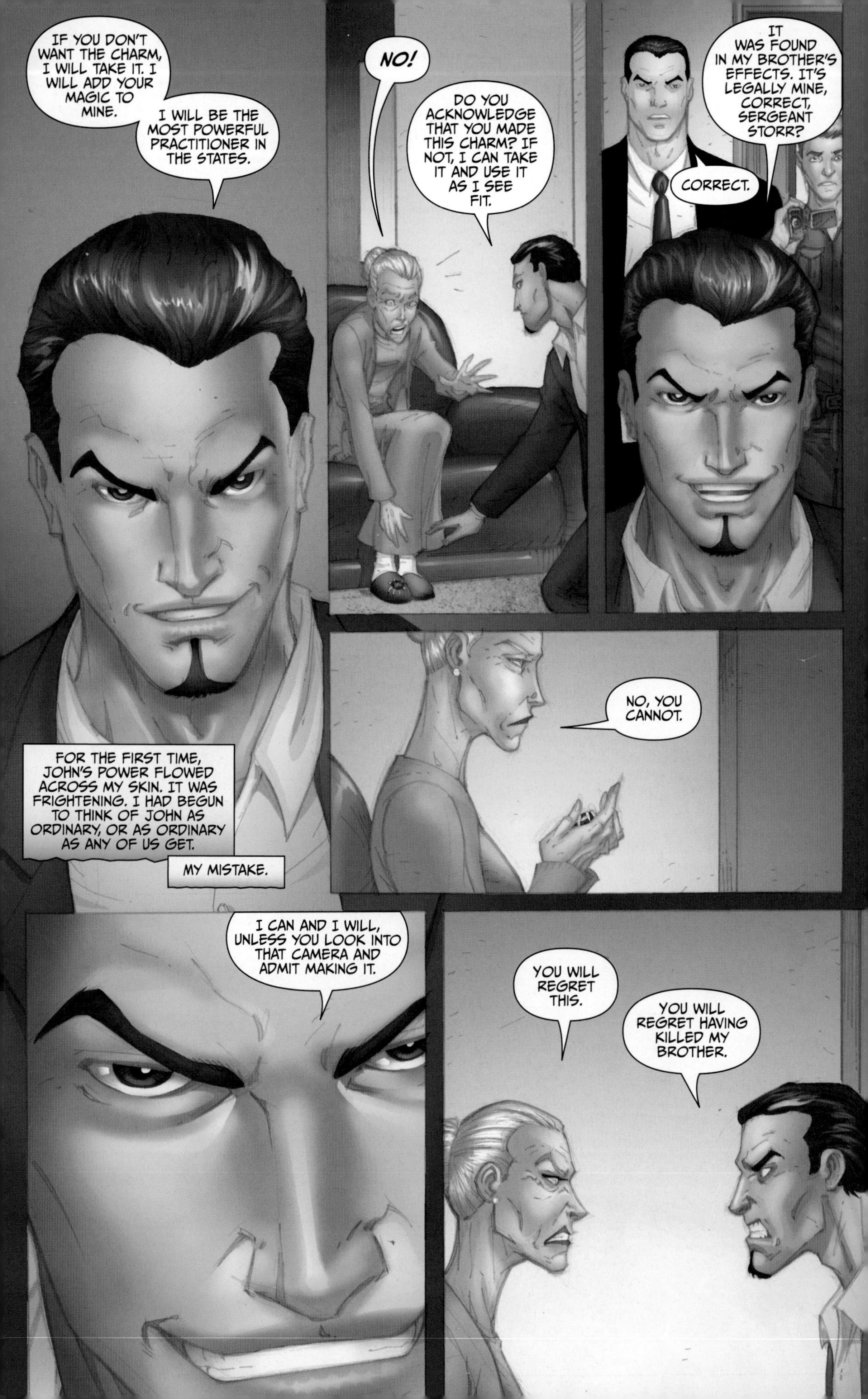
IF YOU DON'T WANT THE CHARM, I WILL TAKE IT. I WILL ADD YOUR MAGIC TO MINE.
I WILL BE THE MOST POWERFUL PRACTITIONER IN THE STATES.
NO!
DO YOU ACKNOWLEDGE THAT YOU MADE THIS CHARM? IF NOT, I CAN TAKE IT AND USE IT AS I SEE FIT.
IT WAS FOUND IN MY BROTHER'S EFFECTS. IT'S LEGALLY MINE, CORRECT, SERGEANT STORR?
CORRECT.
FOR THE FIRST TIME, JOHN'S POWER FLOWED ACROSS MY SKIN. IT WAS FRIGHTENING. I HAD BEGUN TO THINK OF JOHN AS ORDINARY, OR AS ORDINARY AS ANY OF US GET.
MY MISTAKE.
NO, YOU CANNOT.
I CAN AND I WILL, UNLESS YOU LOOK INTO THAT CAMERA AND ADMIT MAKING IT.
YOU WILL REGRET THIS.
YOU WILL REGRET HAVING KILLED MY BROTHER.

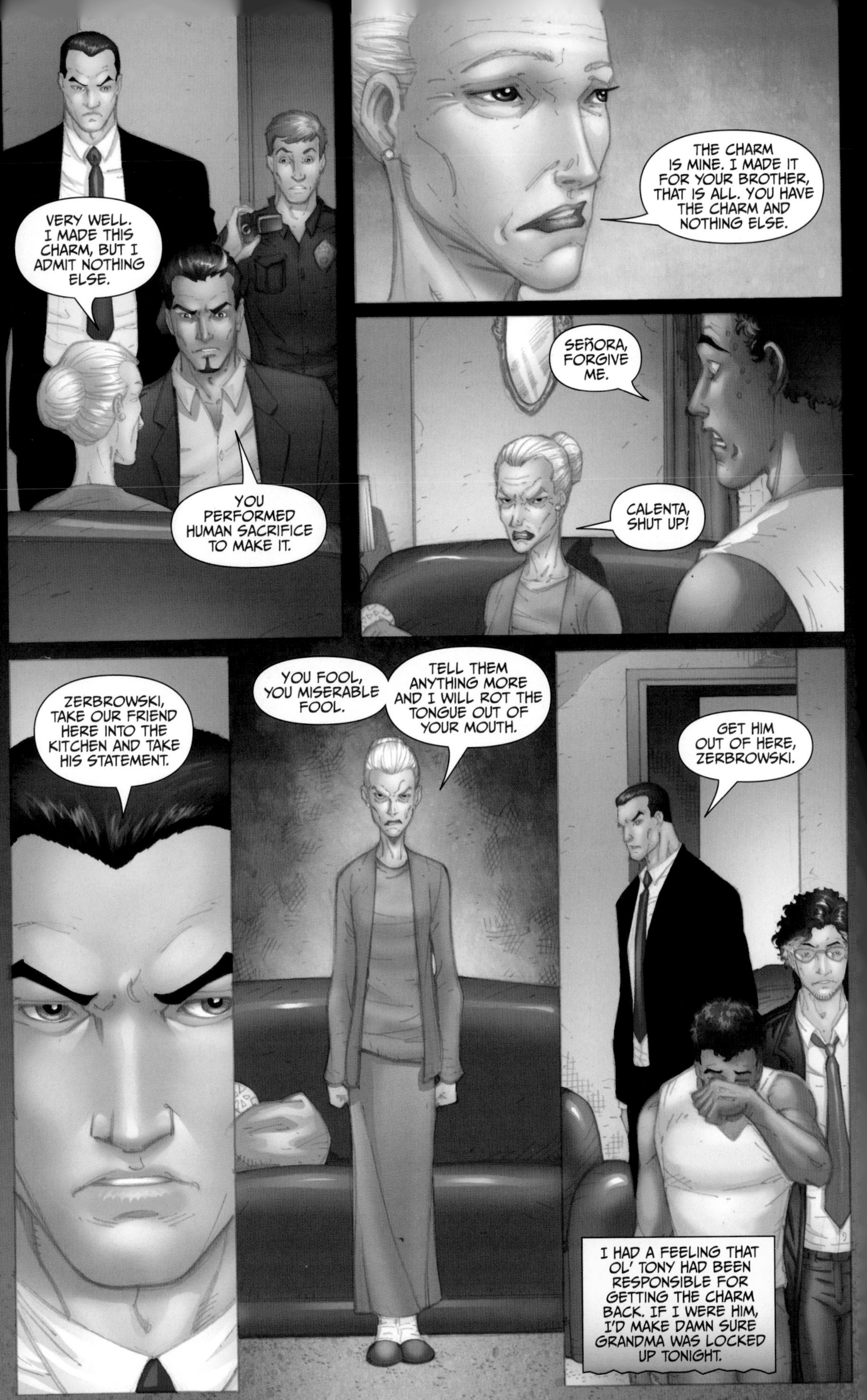
VERY WELL. I MADE THIS CHARM, BUT I ADMIT NOTHING ELSE.
YOU PERFORMED HUMAN SACRIFICE TO MAKE IT.
THE CHARM IS MINE. I MADE IT FOR YOUR BROTHER, THAT IS ALL. YOU HAVE THE CHARM AND NOTHING ELSE.
SEñORA, FORGIVE ME.
CALENTA, SHUT UP!
ZERBROWSKI, TAKE OUR FRIEND HERE INTO THE KITCHEN AND TAKE HIS STATEMENT.
YOU FOOL, YOU MISERABLE FOOL.
TELL THEM ANYTHING MORE AND I WILL ROT THE TONGUE OUT OF YOUR MOUTH.
GET HIM OUT OF HERE, ZERBROWSKI.
I HAD A FEELING THAT OL' TONY HAD BEEN RESPONSIBLE FOR GETTING THE CHARM BACK. IF I WERE HIM, I'D MAKE DAMN SURE GRANDMA WAS LOCKED UP TONIGHT.

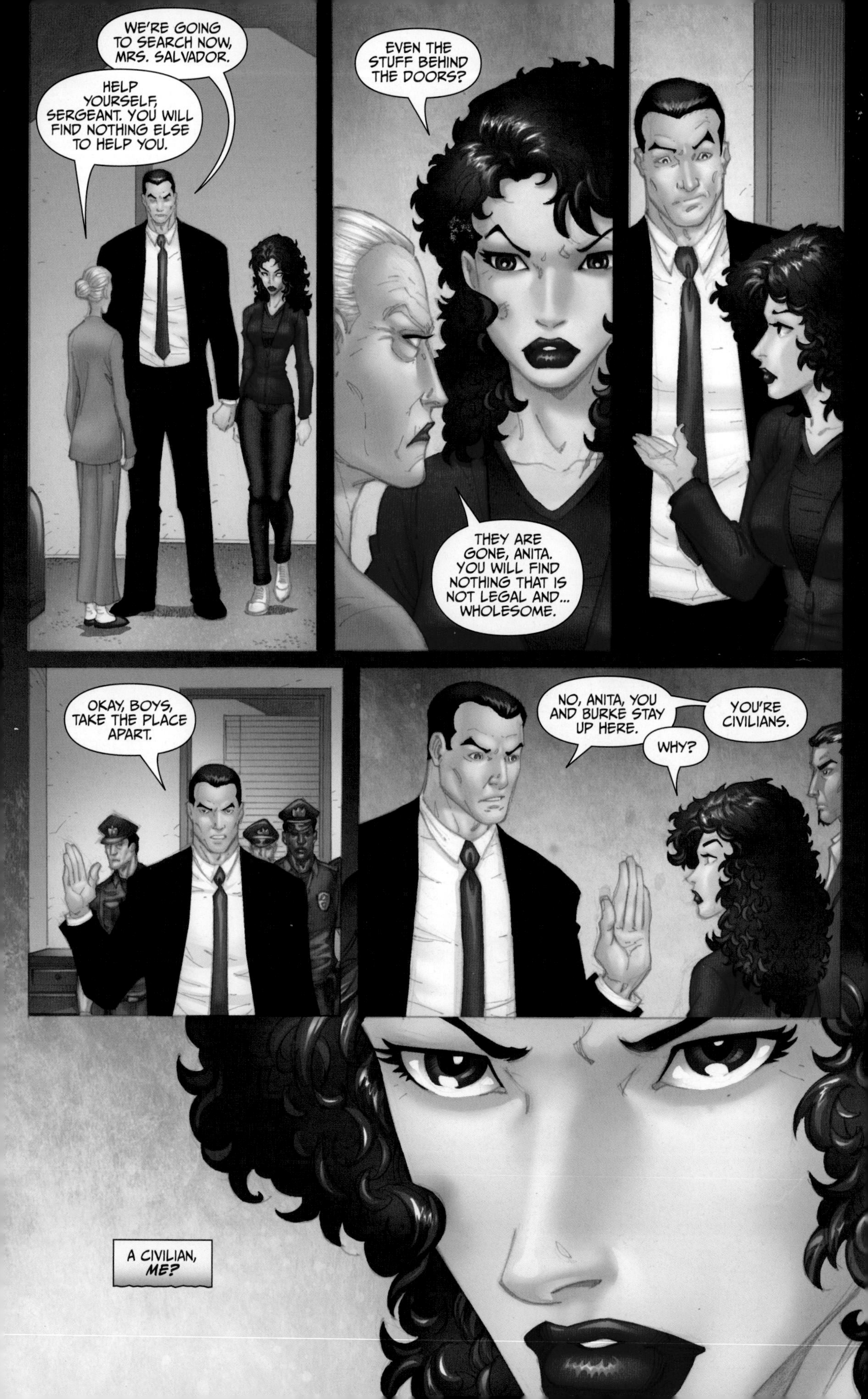
WE'RE GOING TO SEARCH NOW, MRS. SALVADOR.
HELP YOURSELF, SERGEANT. YOU WILL FIND NOTHING ELSE TO HELP YOU.
EVEN THE STUFF BEHIND THE DOORS?
THEY ARE GONE, ANITA. YOU WILL FIND NOTHING THAT IS NOT LEGAL AND... WHOLESOME.
OKAY, BOYS, TAKE THE PLACE APART.
NO, ANITA, YOU AND BURKE STAY UP HERE.
WHY?
YOU'RE CIVILIANS.
A CIVILIAN, *ME?*

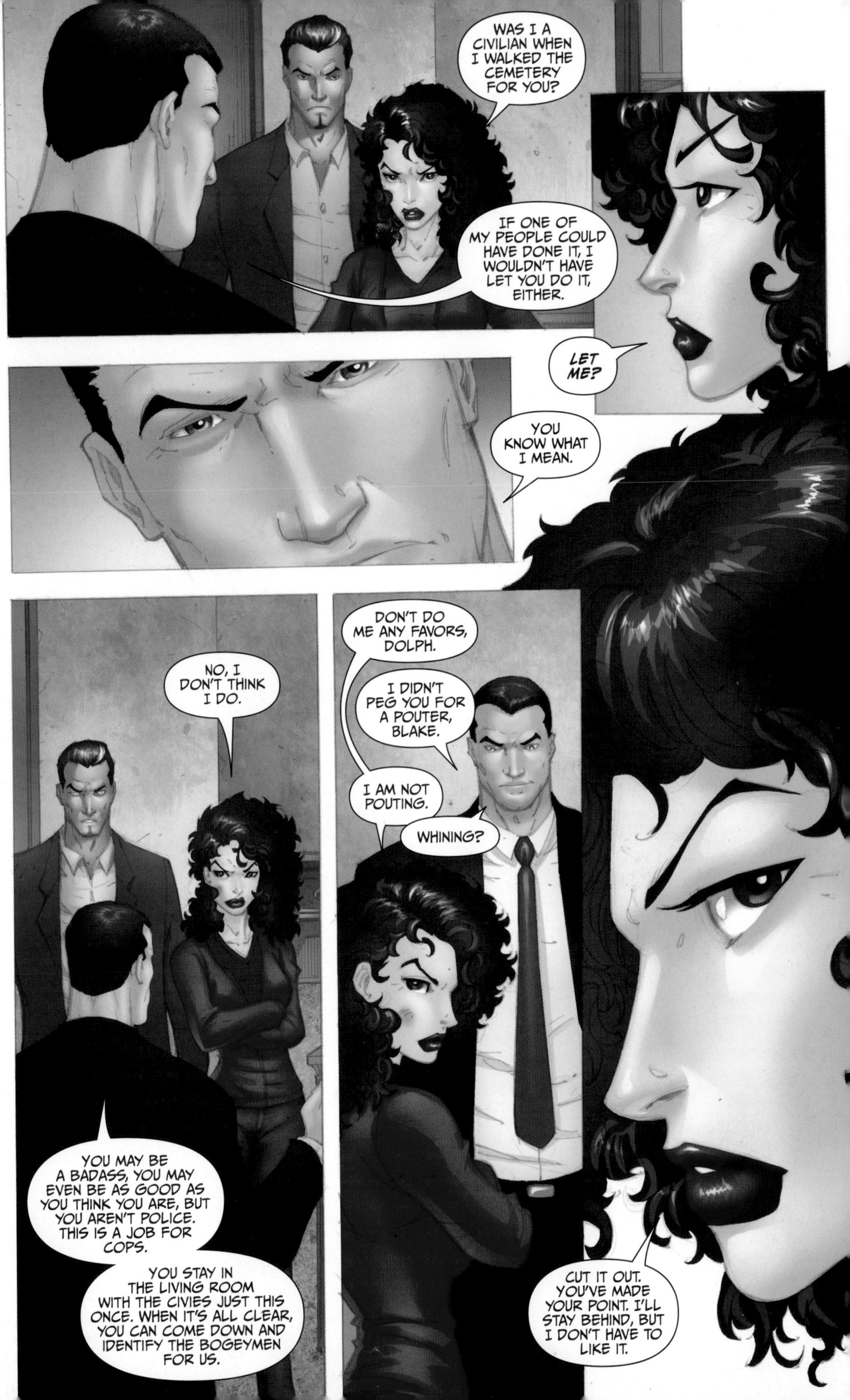
WAS I A CIVILIAN WHEN I WALKED THE CEMETERY FOR YOU?
IF ONE OF MY PEOPLE COULD HAVE DONE IT, I WOULDN'T HAVE LET YOU DO IT, EITHER.
LET ME?
YOU KNOW WHAT I MEAN.
NO, I DON'T THINK I DO.
YOU MAY BE A BADASS, YOU MAY EVEN BE AS GOOD AS YOU THINK YOU ARE, BUT YOU AREN'T POLICE. THIS IS A JOB FOR COPS.
YOU STAY IN THE LIVING ROOM WITH THE CIVIES JUST THIS ONCE. WHEN IT'S ALL CLEAR, YOU CAN COME DOWN AND IDENTIFY THE BOGEYMEN FOR US.
DON'T DO ME ANY FAVORS, DOLPH.
I DIDN'T PEG YOU FOR A POUTER, BLAKE.
I AM NOT POUTING.
WHINING?
CUT IT OUT. YOU'VE MADE YOUR POINT. I'LL STAY BEHIND, BUT I DON'T HAVE TO LIKE IT.

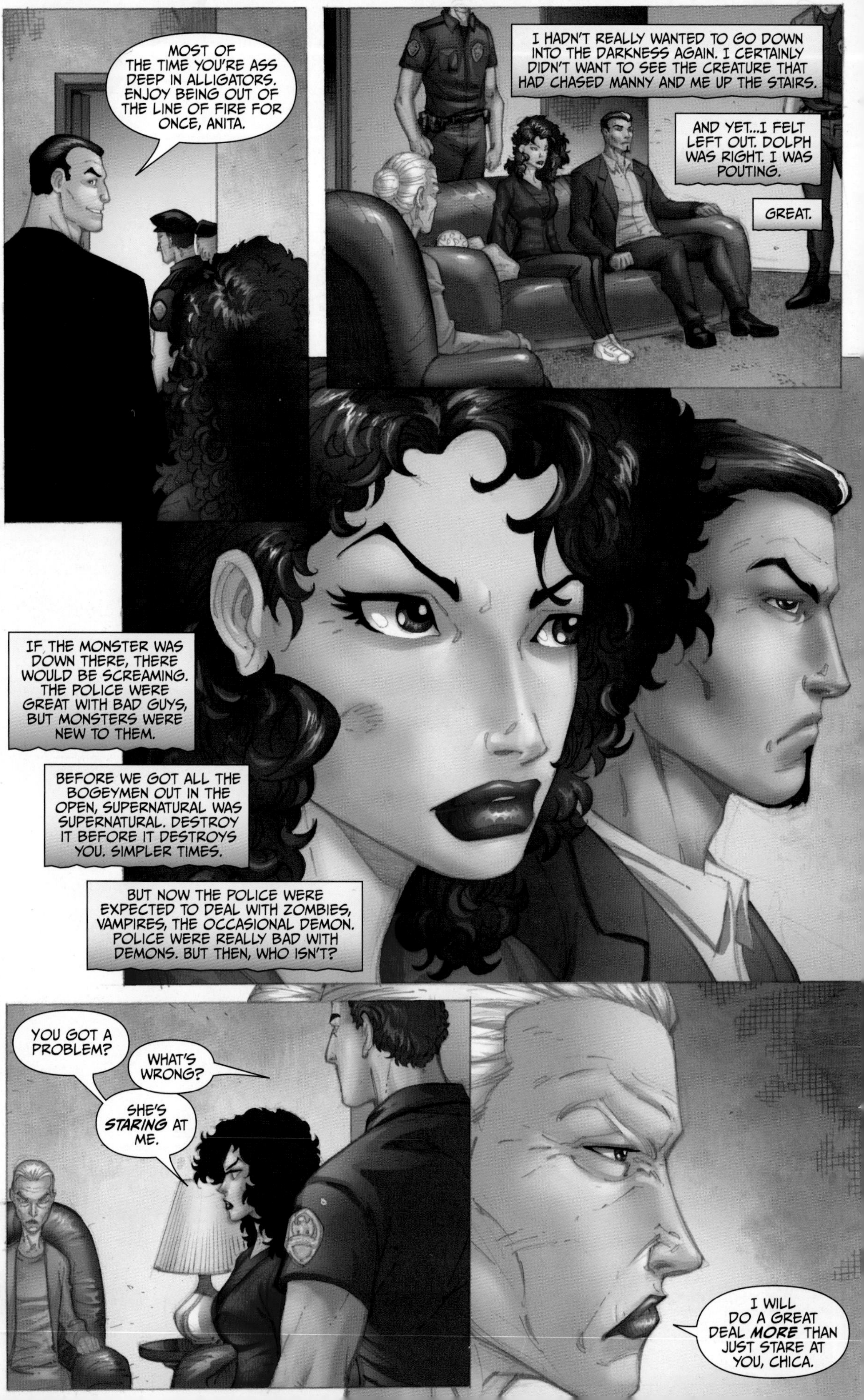
MOST OF THE TIME YOU'RE ASS DEEP IN ALLIGATORS. ENJOY BEING OUT OF THE LINE OF FIRE FOR ONCE, ANITA.
I HADN'T REALLY WANTED TO GO DOWN INTO THE DARKNESS AGAIN. I CERTAINLY DIDN'T WANT TO SEE THE CREATURE THAT HAD CHASED MANNY AND ME UP THE STAIRS.
AND YET...I FELT LEFT OUT. DOLPH WAS RIGHT. I WAS POUTING.
GREAT.
IF THE MONSTER WAS DOWN THERE, THERE WOULD BE SCREAMING. THE POLICE WERE GREAT WITH BAD GUYS, BUT MONSTERS WERE NEW TO THEM.
BEFORE WE GOT ALL THE BOGEYMEN OUT IN THE OPEN, SUPERNATURAL WAS SUPERNATURAL. DESTROY IT BEFORE IT DESTROYS YOU. SIMPLER TIMES.
BUT NOW THE POLICE WERE EXPECTED TO DEAL WITH ZOMBIES, VAMPIRES, THE OCCASIONAL DEMON. POLICE WERE REALLY BAD WITH DEMONS. BUT THEN, WHO ISN'T?
YOU GOT A PROBLEM?
WHAT'S WRONG?
SHE'S *STARING* AT ME.
I WILL DO A GREAT DEAL *MORE* THAN JUST STARE AT YOU, CHICA.

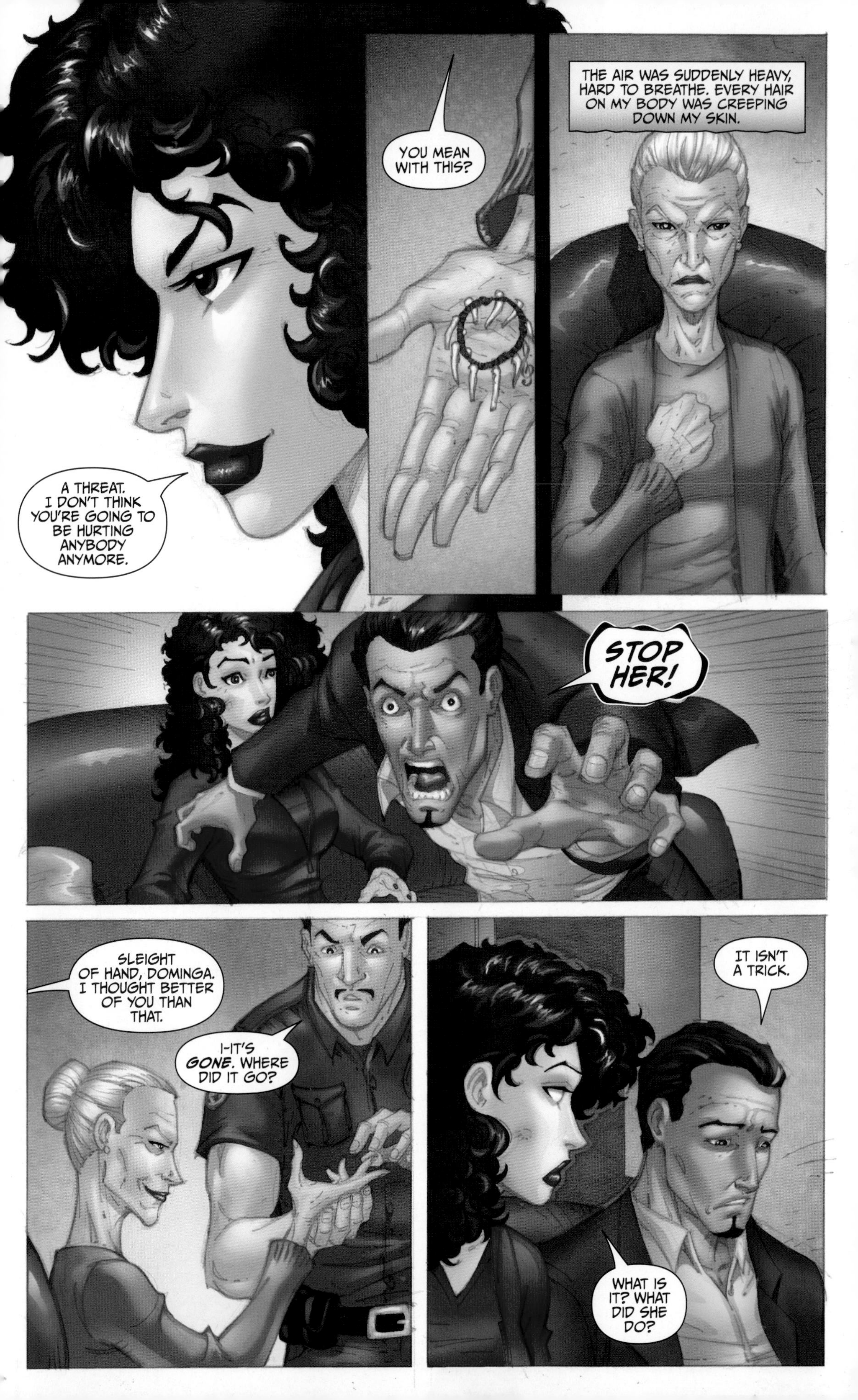
A THREAT. I DON'T THINK YOU'RE GOING TO BE HURTING ANYBODY ANYMORE.
YOU MEAN WITH THIS?
THE AIR WAS SUDDENLY HEAVY, HARD TO BREATHE. EVERY HAIR ON MY BODY WAS CREEPING DOWN MY SKIN.
STOP HER!
SLEIGHT OF HAND, DOMINGA. I THOUGHT BETTER OF YOU THAN THAT.
I-IT'S GONE. WHERE DID IT GO?
IT ISN'T A TRICK.
WHAT IS IT? WHAT DID SHE DO?

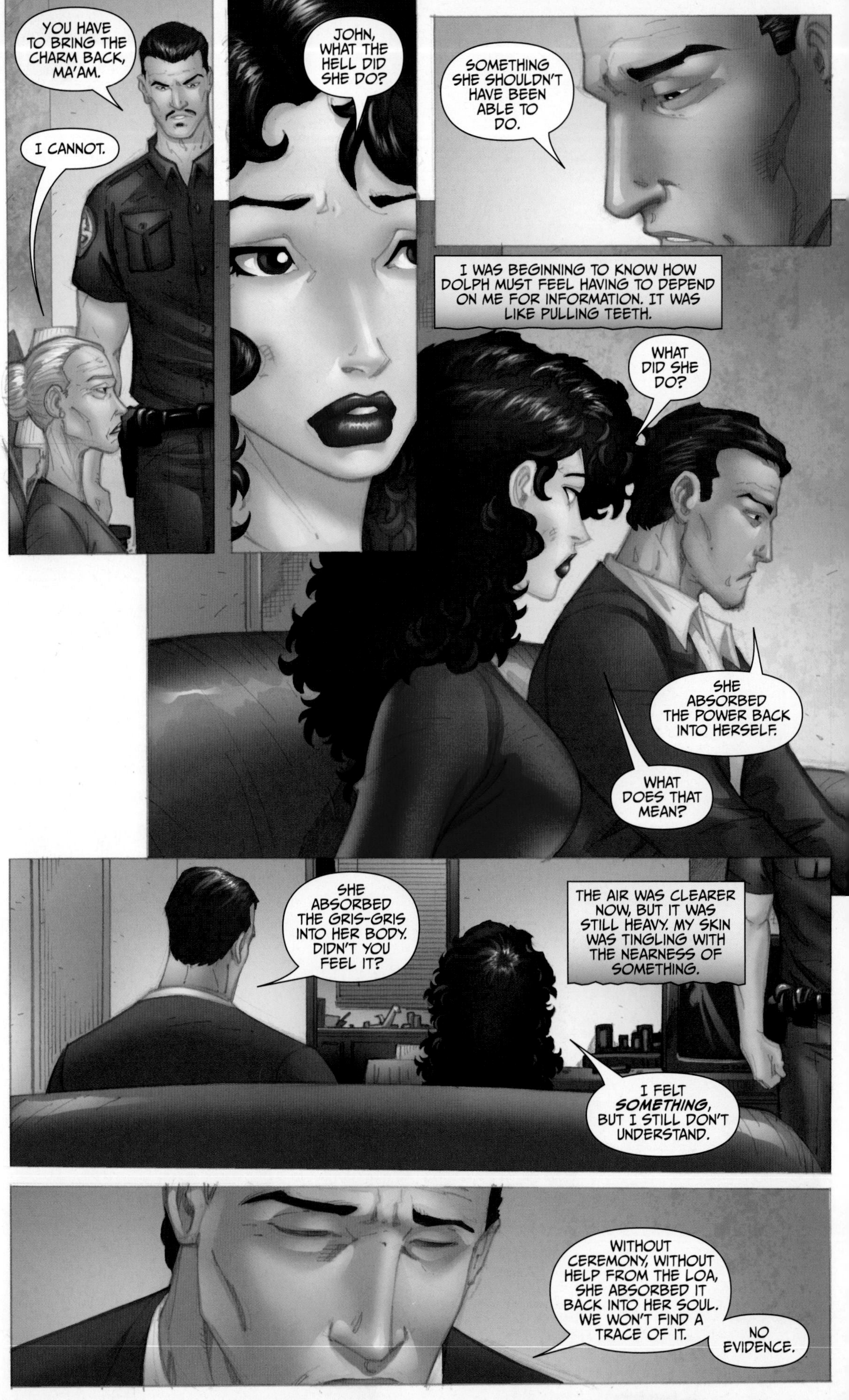
YOU HAVE TO BRING THE CHARM BACK, MA'AM.
I CANNOT.
JOHN, WHAT THE HELL DID SHE DO?
SOMETHING SHE SHOULDN'T HAVE BEEN ABLE TO DO.
I WAS BEGINNING TO KNOW HOW DOLPH MUST FEEL HAVING TO DEPEND ON ME FOR INFORMATION. IT WAS LIKE PULLING TEETH.
WHAT DID SHE DO?
SHE ABSORBED THE POWER BACK INTO HERSELF.
WHAT DOES THAT MEAN?
SHE ABSORBED THE GRIS-GRIS INTO HER BODY. DIDN'T YOU FEEL IT?
THE AIR WAS CLEARER NOW, BUT IT WAS STILL HEAVY. MY SKIN WAS TINGLING WITH THE NEARNESS OF SOMETHING.
I FELT *SOMETHING*, BUT I STILL DON'T UNDERSTAND.
WITHOUT CEREMONY, WITHOUT HELP FROM THE LOA, SHE ABSORBED IT BACK INTO HER SOUL. WE WON'T FIND A TRACE OF IT.
NO EVIDENCE.

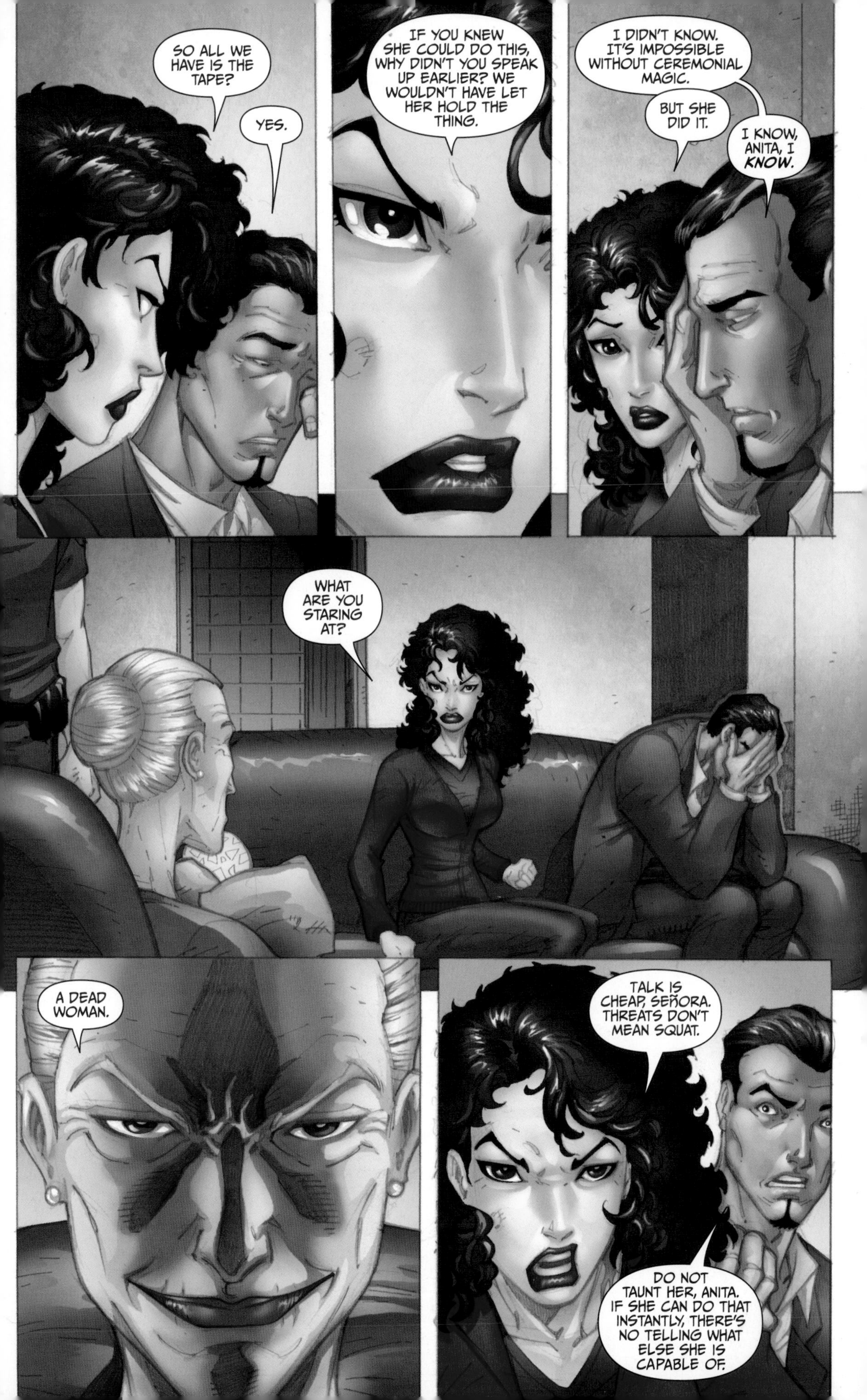
SO ALL WE HAVE IS THE TAPE?
YES.
IF YOU KNEW SHE COULD DO THIS, WHY DIDN'T YOU SPEAK UP EARLIER? WE WOULDN'T HAVE LET HER HOLD THE THING.
I DIDN'T KNOW. IT'S IMPOSSIBLE WITHOUT CEREMONIAL MAGIC.
BUT SHE DID IT.
I KNOW, ANITA, I *KNOW*.
WHAT ARE YOU STARING AT?
A DEAD WOMAN.
TALK IS CHEAP, SEÑORA. THREATS DON'T MEAN SQUAT.
DO NOT TAUNT HER, ANITA. IF SHE CAN DO THAT INSTANTLY, THERE'S NO TELLING WHAT ELSE SHE IS CAPABLE OF.

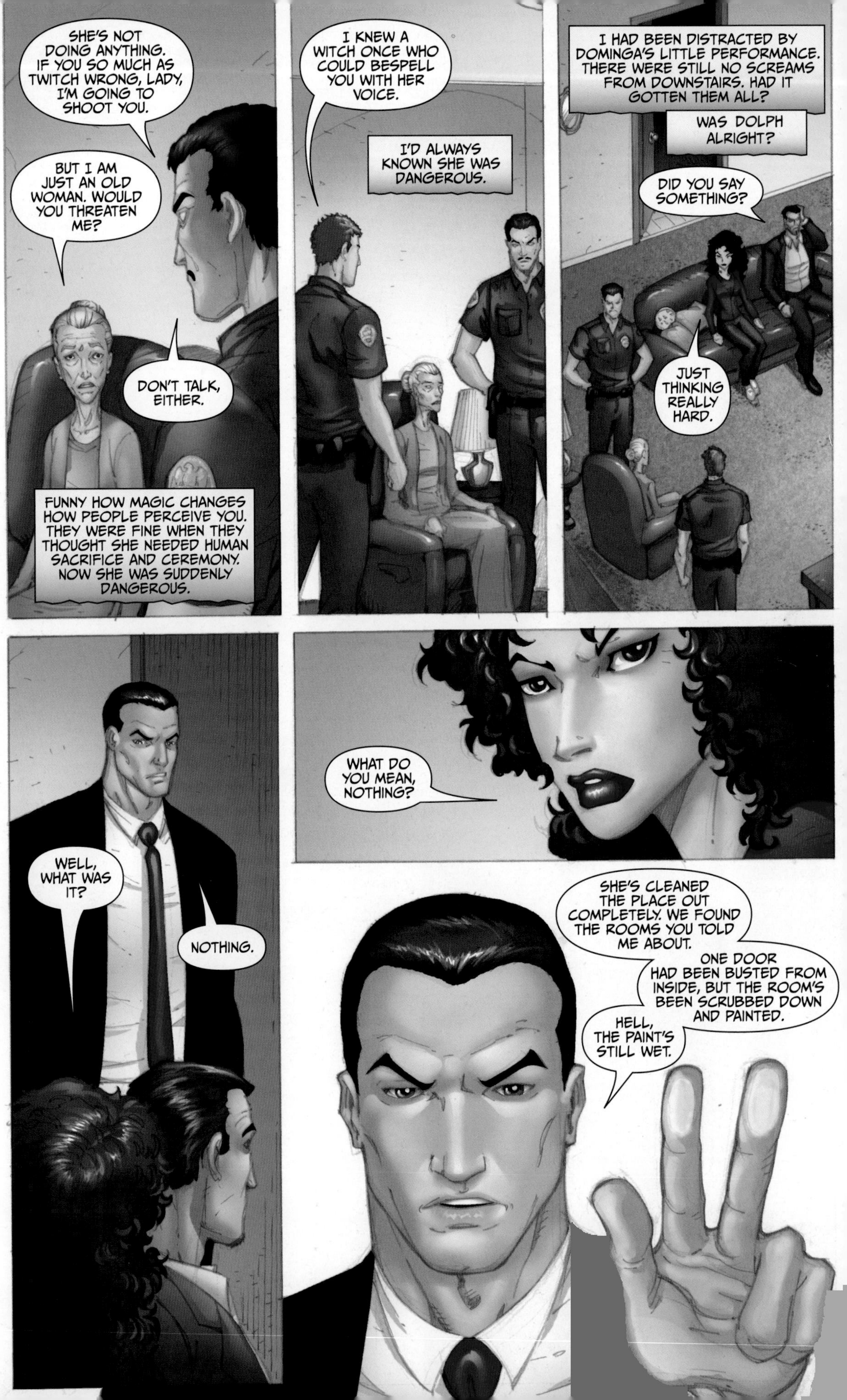
SHE'S NOT DOING ANYTHING. IF YOU SO MUCH AS TWITCH WRONG, LADY, I'M GOING TO SHOOT YOU.
BUT I AM JUST AN OLD WOMAN. WOULD YOU THREATEN ME?
DON'T TALK, EITHER.
FUNNY HOW MAGIC CHANGES HOW PEOPLE PERCEIVE YOU. THEY WERE FINE WHEN THEY THOUGHT SHE NEEDED HUMAN SACRIFICE AND CEREMONY. NOW SHE WAS SUDDENLY DANGEROUS.
I KNEW A WITCH ONCE WHO COULD BESPELL YOU WITH HER VOICE.
I'D ALWAYS KNOWN SHE WAS DANGEROUS.
I HAD BEEN DISTRACTED BY DOMINGA'S LITTLE PERFORMANCE. THERE WERE STILL NO SCREAMS FROM DOWNSTAIRS. HAD IT GOTTEN THEM ALL?
WAS DOLPH ALRIGHT?
DID YOU SAY SOMETHING?
JUST THINKING REALLY HARD.
WELL, WHAT WAS IT?
NOTHING.
WHAT DO YOU MEAN, NOTHING?
SHE'S CLEANED THE PLACE OUT COMPLETELY. WE FOUND THE ROOMS YOU TOLD ME ABOUT.
ONE DOOR HAD BEEN BUSTED FROM INSIDE, BUT THE ROOM'S BEEN SCRUBBED DOWN AND PAINTED.
HELL, THE PAINT'S STILL WET.

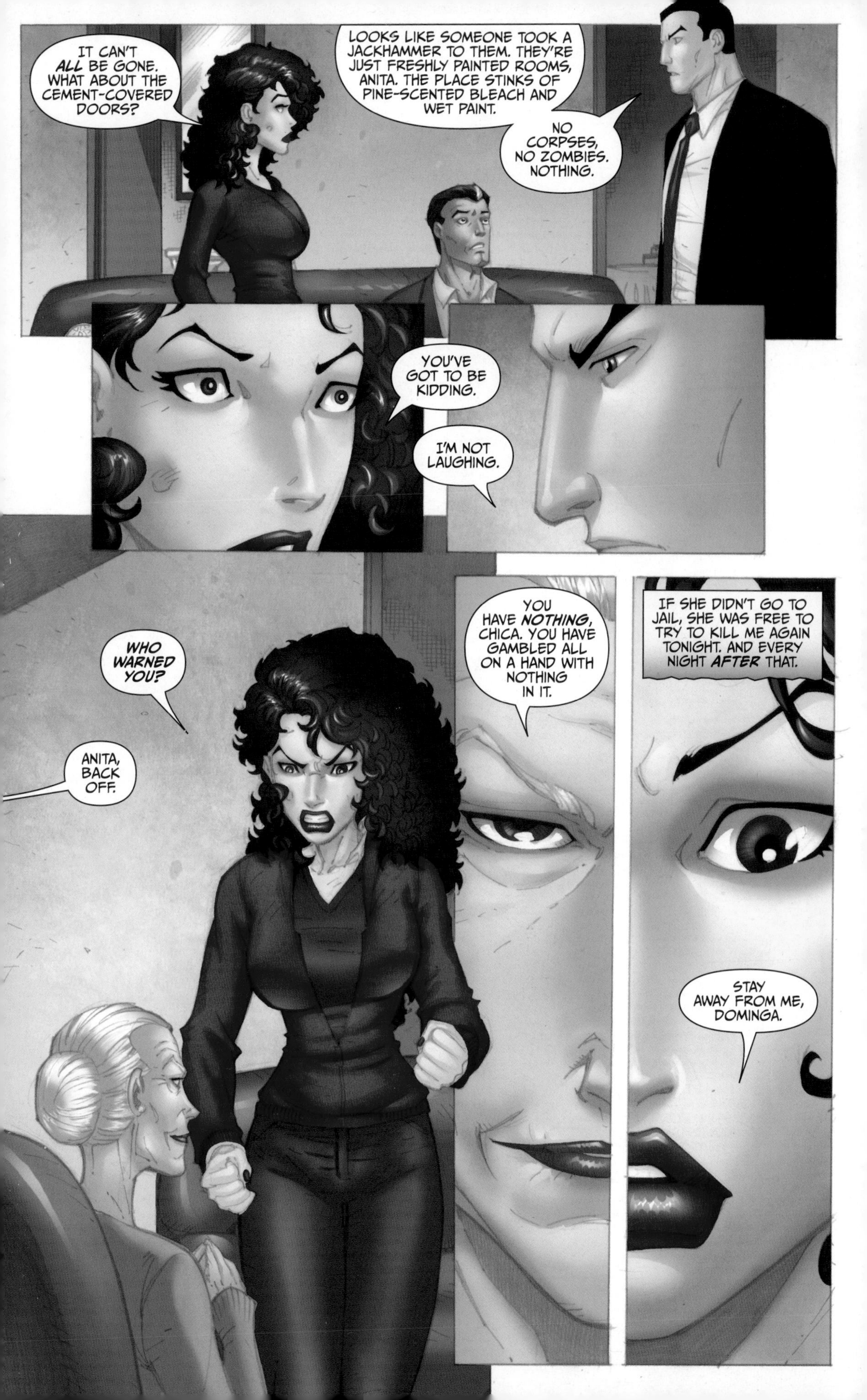
IT CAN'T ALL BE GONE. WHAT ABOUT THE CEMENT-COVERED DOORS?
LOOKS LIKE SOMEONE TOOK A JACKHAMMER TO THEM. THEY'RE JUST FRESHLY PAINTED ROOMS, ANITA. THE PLACE STINKS OF PINE-SCENTED BLEACH AND WET PAINT.
NO CORPSES, NO ZOMBIES. NOTHING.
YOU'VE GOT TO BE KIDDING.
I'M NOT LAUGHING.
WHO WARNED YOU?
ANITA, BACK OFF.
YOU HAVE NOTHING, CHICA. YOU HAVE GAMBLED ALL ON A HAND WITH NOTHING IN IT.
IF SHE DIDN'T GO TO JAIL, SHE WAS FREE TO TRY TO KILL ME AGAIN TONIGHT. AND EVERY NIGHT AFTER THAT.
STAY AWAY FROM ME, DOMINGA.

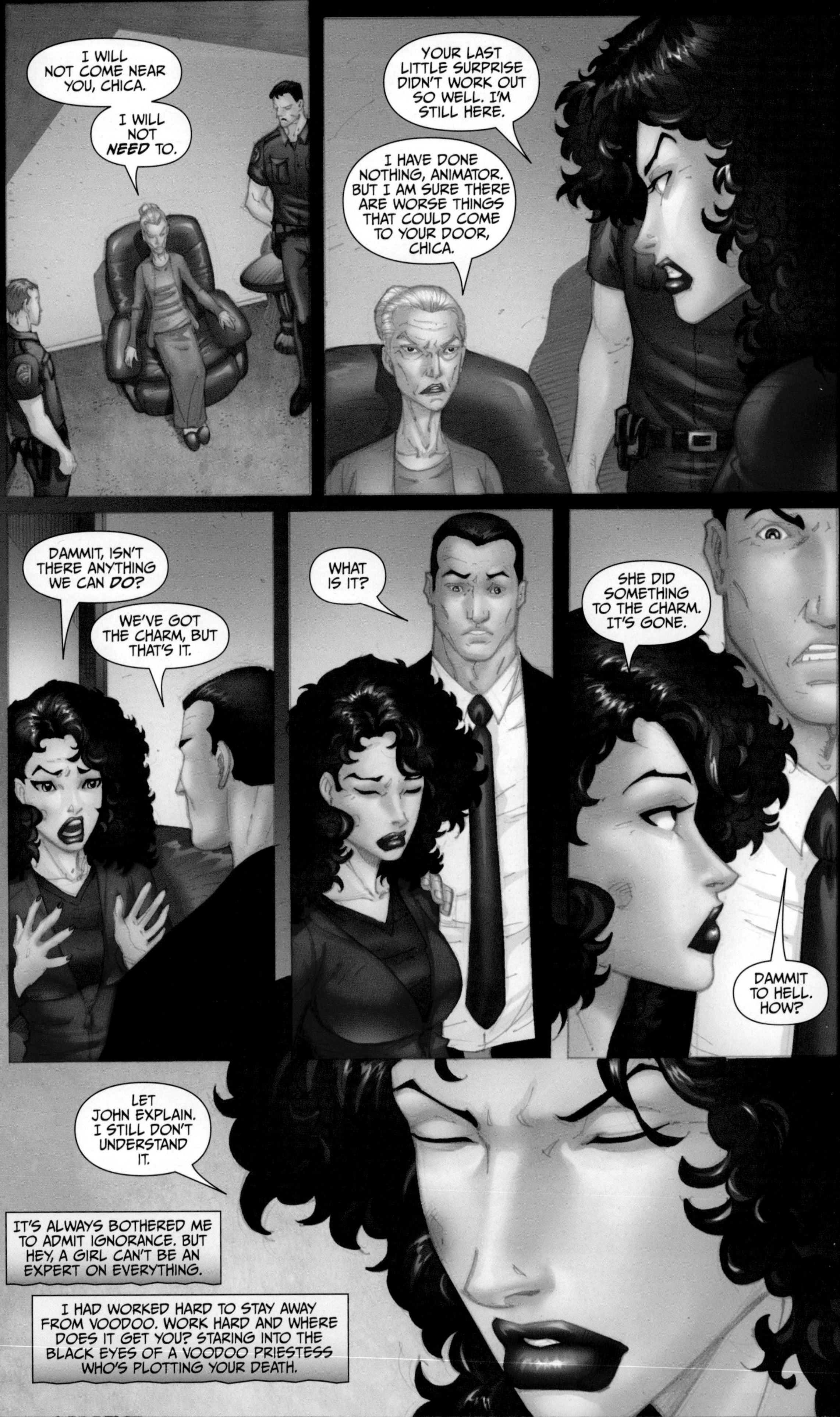
I WILL NOT COME NEAR YOU, CHICA.
I WILL NOT *NEED* TO.
YOUR LAST LITTLE SURPRISE DIDN'T WORK OUT SO WELL. I'M STILL HERE.
I HAVE DONE NOTHING, ANIMATOR. BUT I AM SURE THERE ARE WORSE THINGS THAT COULD COME TO YOUR DOOR, CHICA.
DAMMIT, ISN'T THERE ANYTHING WE CAN *DO*?
WE'VE GOT THE CHARM, BUT THAT'S IT.
WHAT IS IT?
SHE DID SOMETHING TO THE CHARM. IT'S GONE.
DAMMIT TO HELL. HOW?
LET JOHN EXPLAIN. I STILL DON'T UNDERSTAND IT.
IT'S ALWAYS BOTHERED ME TO ADMIT IGNORANCE. BUT HEY, A GIRL CAN'T BE AN EXPERT ON EVERYTHING.
I HAD WORKED HARD TO STAY AWAY FROM VOODOO. WORK HARD AND WHERE DOES IT GET YOU? STARING INTO THE BLACK EYES OF A VOODOO PRIESTESS WHO'S PLOTTING YOUR DEATH.

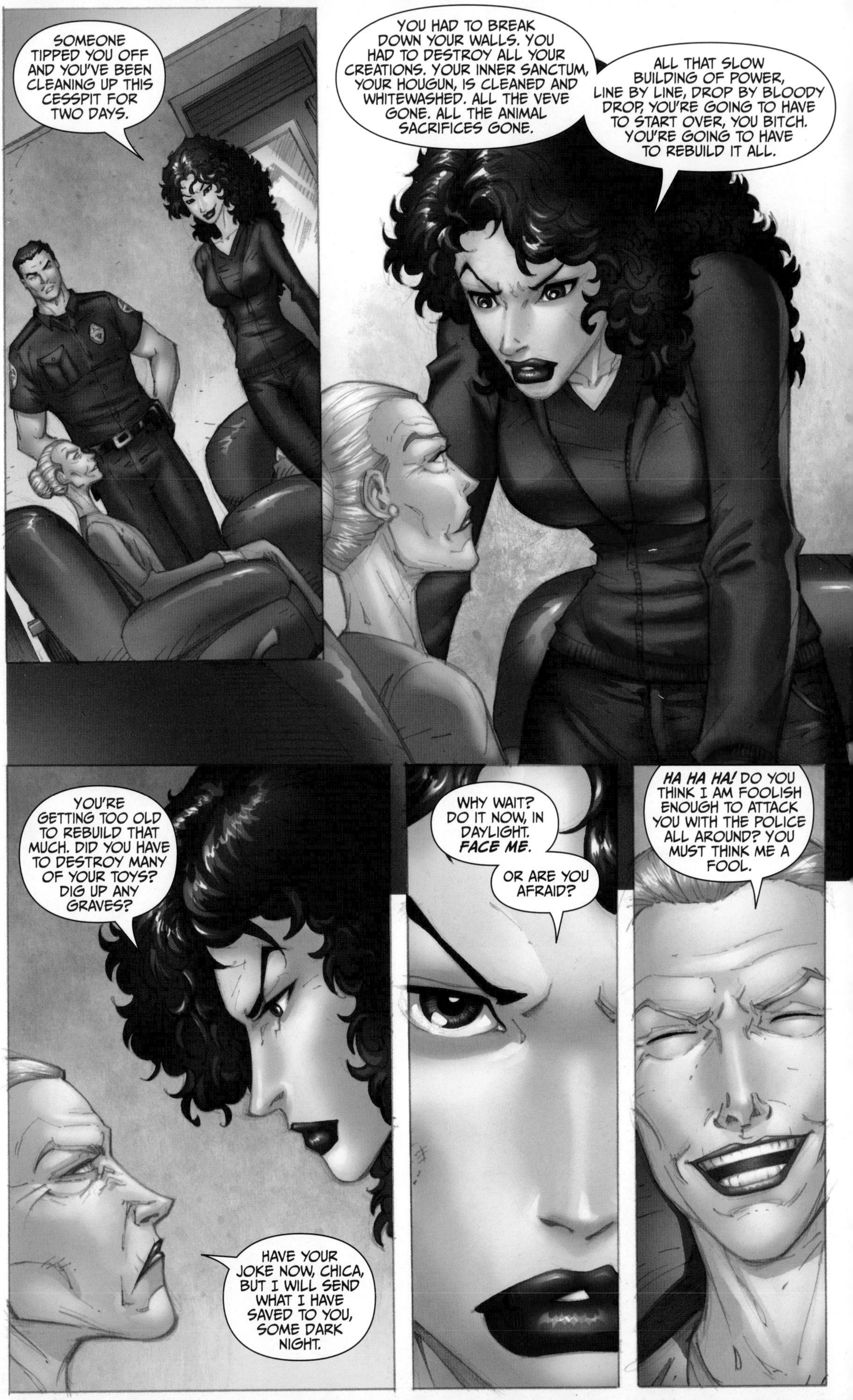
SOMEONE TIPPED YOU OFF AND YOU'VE BEEN CLEANING UP THIS CESSPIT FOR TWO DAYS.
YOU HAD TO BREAK DOWN YOUR WALLS. YOU HAD TO DESTROY ALL YOUR CREATIONS. YOUR INNER SANCTUM, YOUR HOUGUN, IS CLEANED AND WHITEWASHED. ALL THE VEVE GONE. ALL THE ANIMAL SACRIFICES GONE.
ALL THAT SLOW BUILDING OF POWER, LINE BY LINE, DROP BY BLOODY DROP, YOU'RE GOING TO HAVE TO START OVER, YOU BITCH. YOU'RE GOING TO HAVE TO REBUILD IT ALL.
YOU'RE GETTING TOO OLD TO REBUILD THAT MUCH. DID YOU HAVE TO DESTROY MANY OF YOUR TOYS? DIG UP ANY GRAVES?
HAVE YOUR JOKE NOW, CHICA, BUT I WILL SEND WHAT I HAVE SAVED TO YOU, SOME DARK NIGHT.
WHY WAIT? DO IT NOW, IN DAYLIGHT. ***FACE ME***.
OR ARE YOU AFRAID?
HA HA HA! DO YOU THINK I AM FOOLISH ENOUGH TO ATTACK YOU WITH THE POLICE ALL AROUND? YOU MUST THINK ME A FOOL.

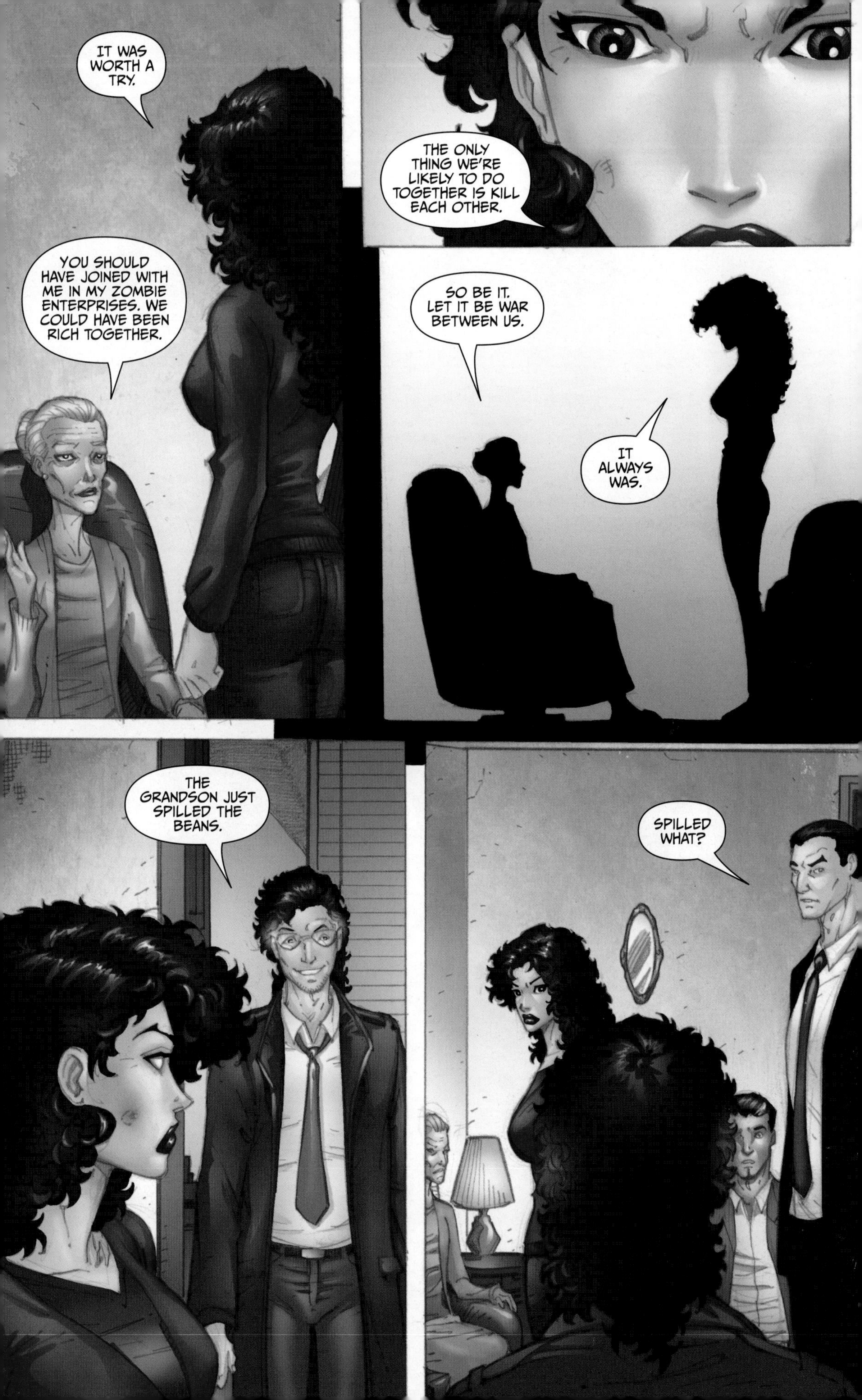
IT WAS WORTH A TRY.
YOU SHOULD HAVE JOINED WITH ME IN MY ZOMBIE ENTERPRISES. WE COULD HAVE BEEN RICH TOGETHER.
THE ONLY THING WE'RE LIKELY TO DO TOGETHER IS KILL EACH OTHER.
SO BE IT. LET IT BE WAR BETWEEN US.
IT ALWAYS WAS.
THE GRANDSON JUST SPILLED THE BEANS.
SPILLED WHAT?

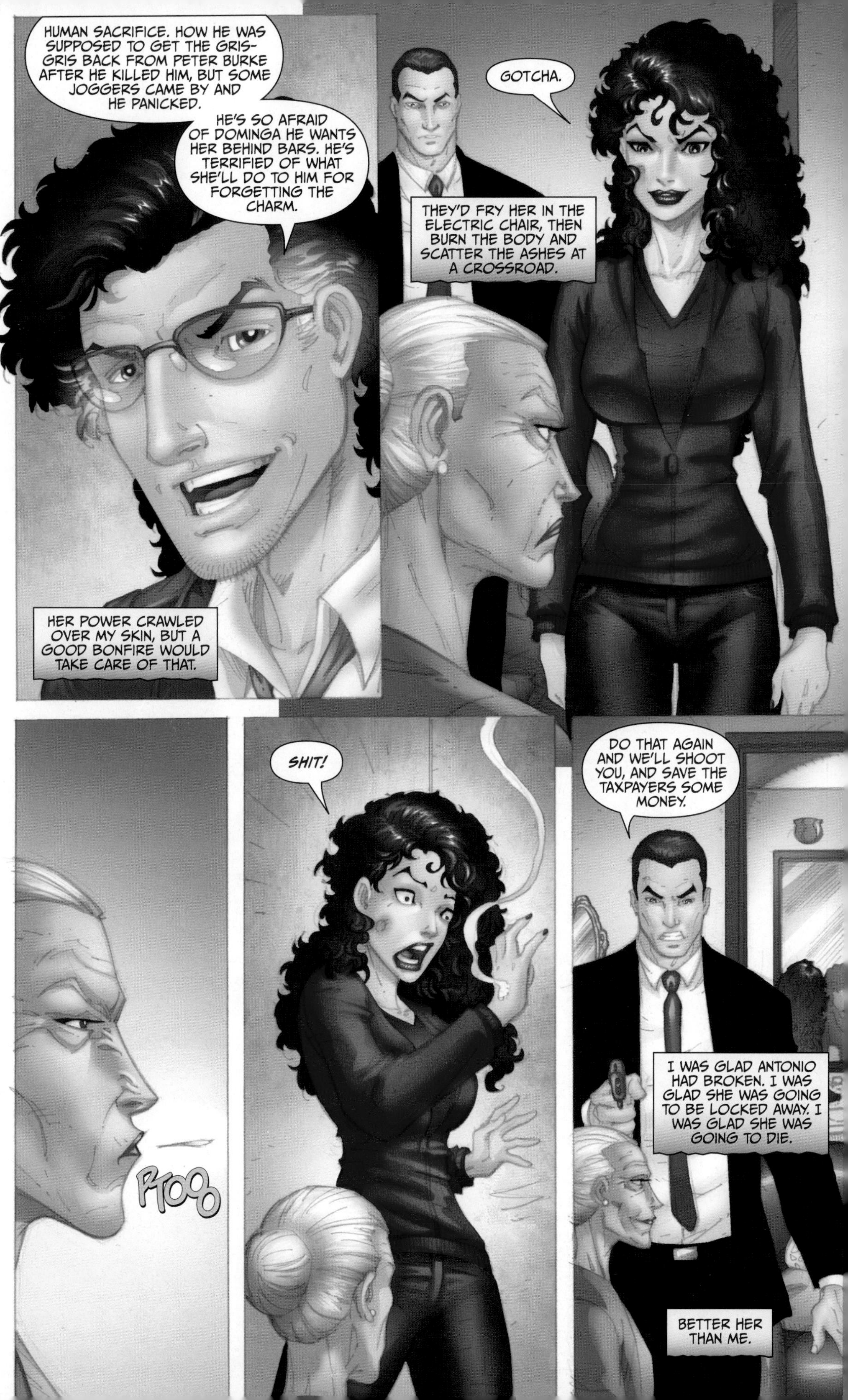
HUMAN SACRIFICE. HOW HE WAS SUPPOSED TO GET THE GRIS-GRIS BACK FROM PETER BURKE AFTER HE KILLED HIM, BUT SOME JOGGERS CAME BY AND HE PANICKED.
HE'S SO AFRAID OF DOMINGA HE WANTS HER BEHIND BARS. HE'S TERRIFIED OF WHAT SHE'LL DO TO HIM FOR FORGETTING THE CHARM.
HER POWER CRAWLED OVER MY SKIN, BUT A GOOD BONFIRE WOULD TAKE CARE OF THAT.
GOTCHA.
THEY'D FRY HER IN THE ELECTRIC CHAIR, THEN BURN THE BODY AND SCATTER THE ASHES AT A CROSSROAD.
PTOO
SHIT!
DO THAT AGAIN AND WE'LL SHOOT YOU, AND SAVE THE TAXPAYERS SOME MONEY.
I WAS GLAD ANTONIO HAD BROKEN. I WAS GLAD SHE WAS GOING TO BE LOCKED AWAY. I WAS GLAD SHE WAS GOING TO DIE.
BETTER HER THAN ME.

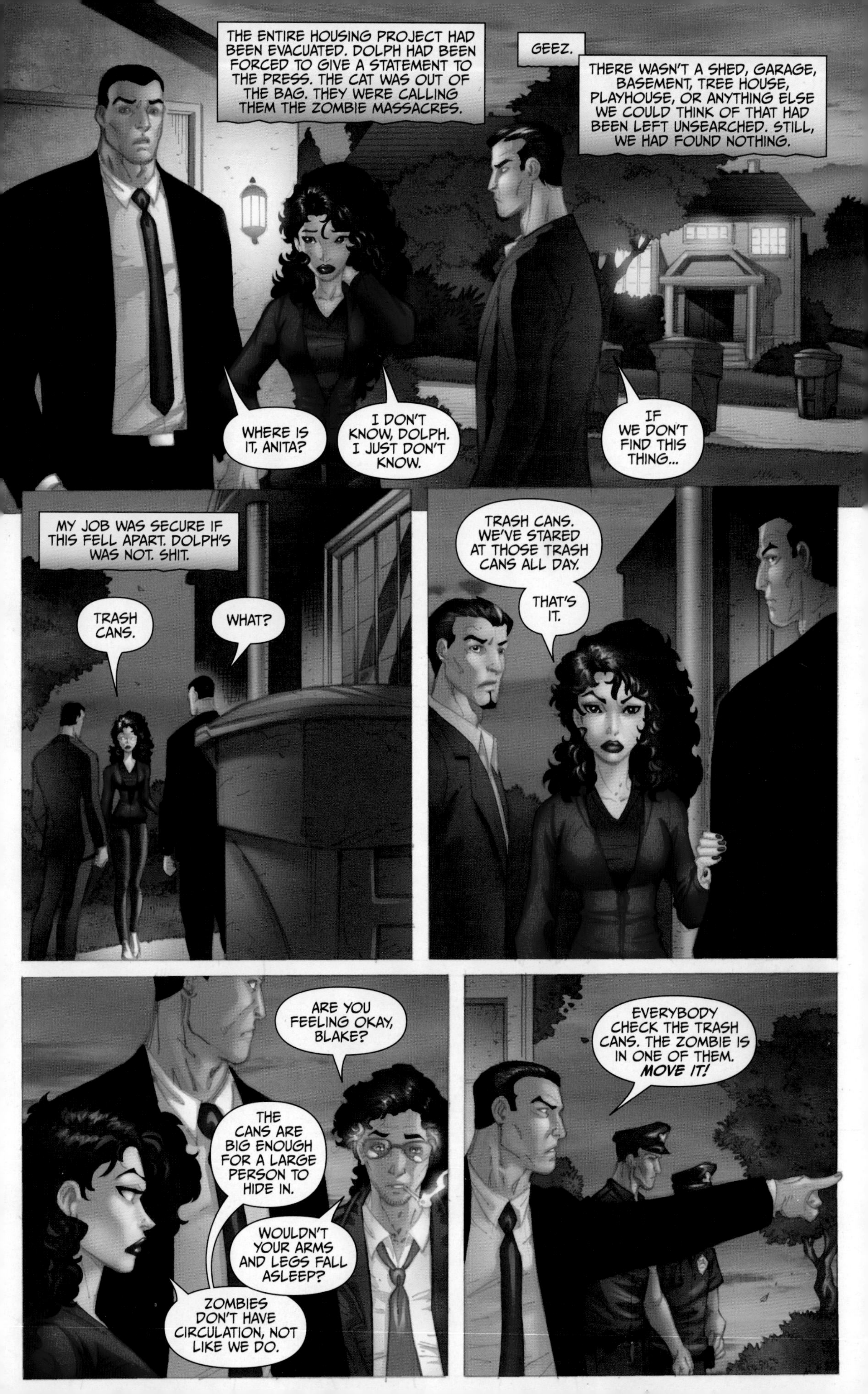
THE ENTIRE HOUSING PROJECT HAD BEEN EVACUATED. DOLPH HAD BEEN FORCED TO GIVE A STATEMENT TO THE PRESS. THE CAT WAS OUT OF THE BAG. THEY WERE CALLING THEM THE ZOMBIE MASSACRES.
GEEZ.
THERE WASN'T A SHED, GARAGE, BASEMENT, TREE HOUSE, PLAYHOUSE, OR ANYTHING ELSE WE COULD THINK OF THAT HAD BEEN LEFT UNSEARCHED. STILL, WE HAD FOUND NOTHING.
WHERE IS IT, ANITA?
I DON'T KNOW, DOLPH. I JUST DON'T KNOW.
IF WE DON'T FIND THIS THING...
MY JOB WAS SECURE IF THIS FELL APART. DOLPH'S WAS NOT. SHIT.
TRASH CANS.
WHAT?
TRASH CANS. WE'VE STARED AT THOSE TRASH CANS ALL DAY.
THAT'S IT.
ARE YOU FEELING OKAY, BLAKE?
THE CANS ARE BIG ENOUGH FOR A LARGE PERSON TO HIDE IN.
WOULDN'T YOUR ARMS AND LEGS FALL ASLEEP?
ZOMBIES DON'T HAVE CIRCULATION, NOT LIKE WE DO.
EVERYBODY CHECK THE TRASH CANS. THE ZOMBIE IS IN ONE OF THEM. *MOVE IT!*

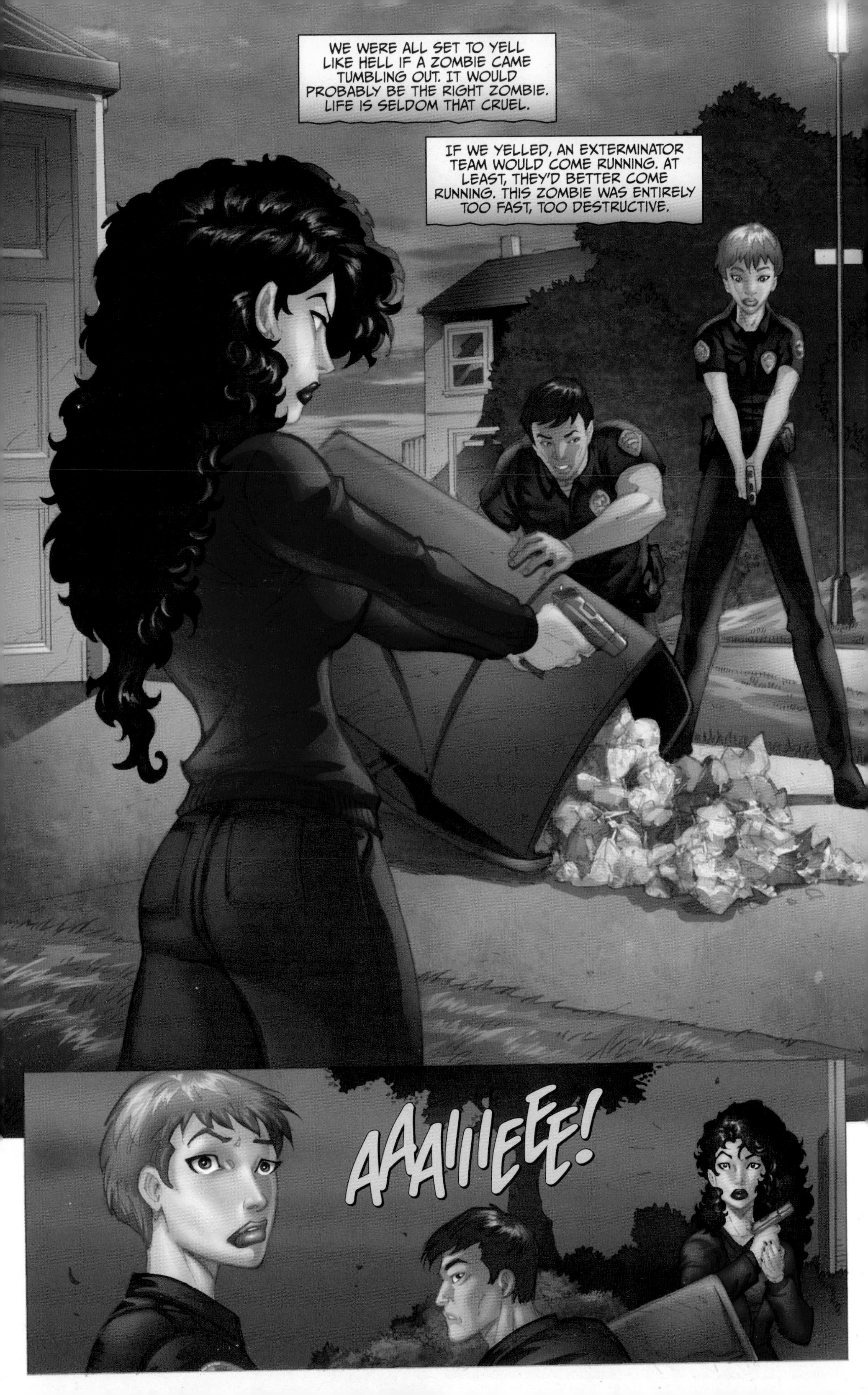
WE WERE ALL SET TO YELL LIKE HELL IF A ZOMBIE CAME TUMBLING OUT. IT WOULD PROBABLY BE THE RIGHT ZOMBIE. LIFE IS SELDOM THAT CRUEL.
IF WE YELLED, AN EXTERMINATOR TEAM WOULD COME RUNNING. AT LEAST, THEY'D BETTER COME RUNNING. THIS ZOMBIE WAS ENTIRELY TOO FAST, TOO DESTRUCTIVE.
AAAIIIEEE!

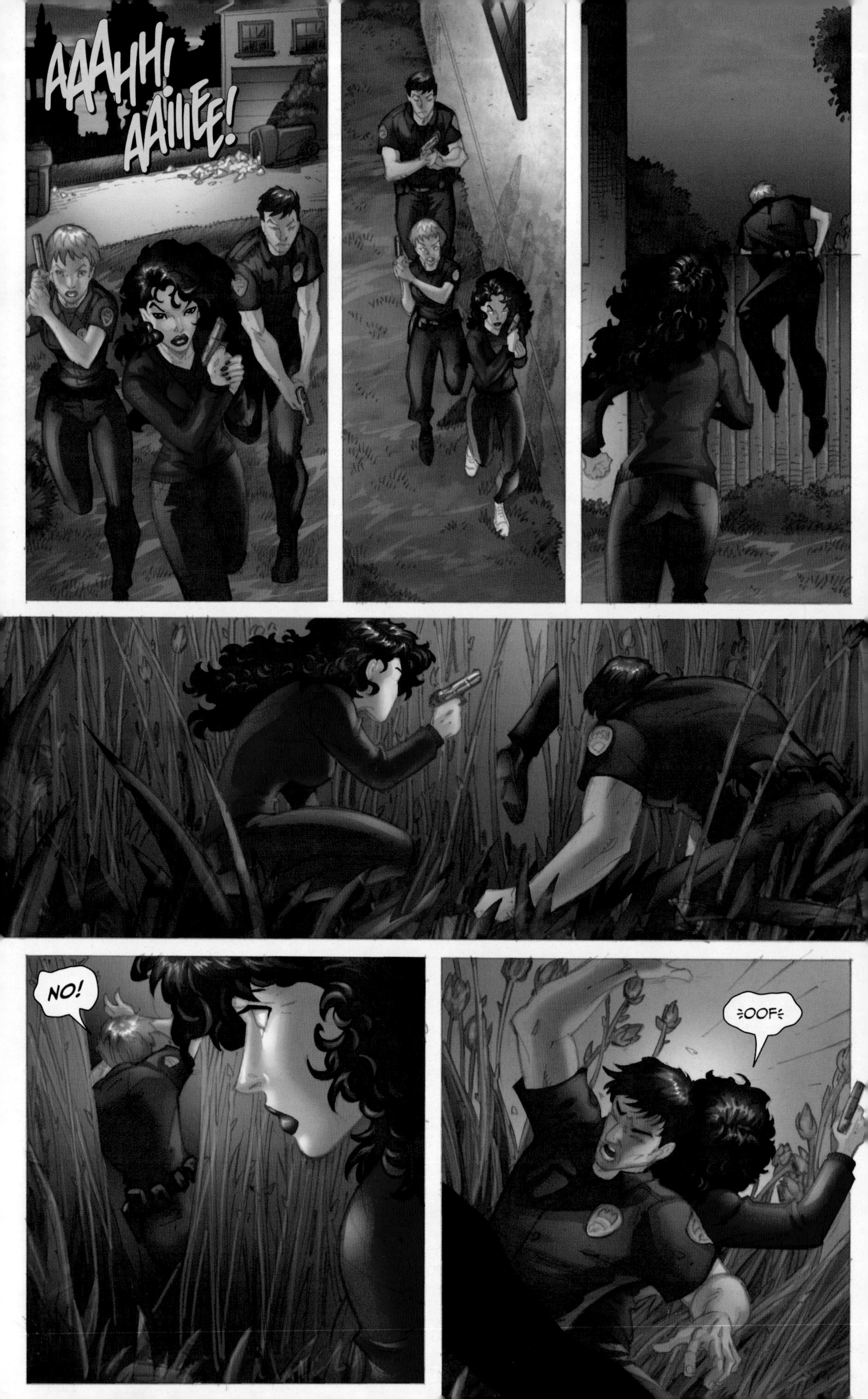
AAAHH! AAIIIEE!
NO!
OOF

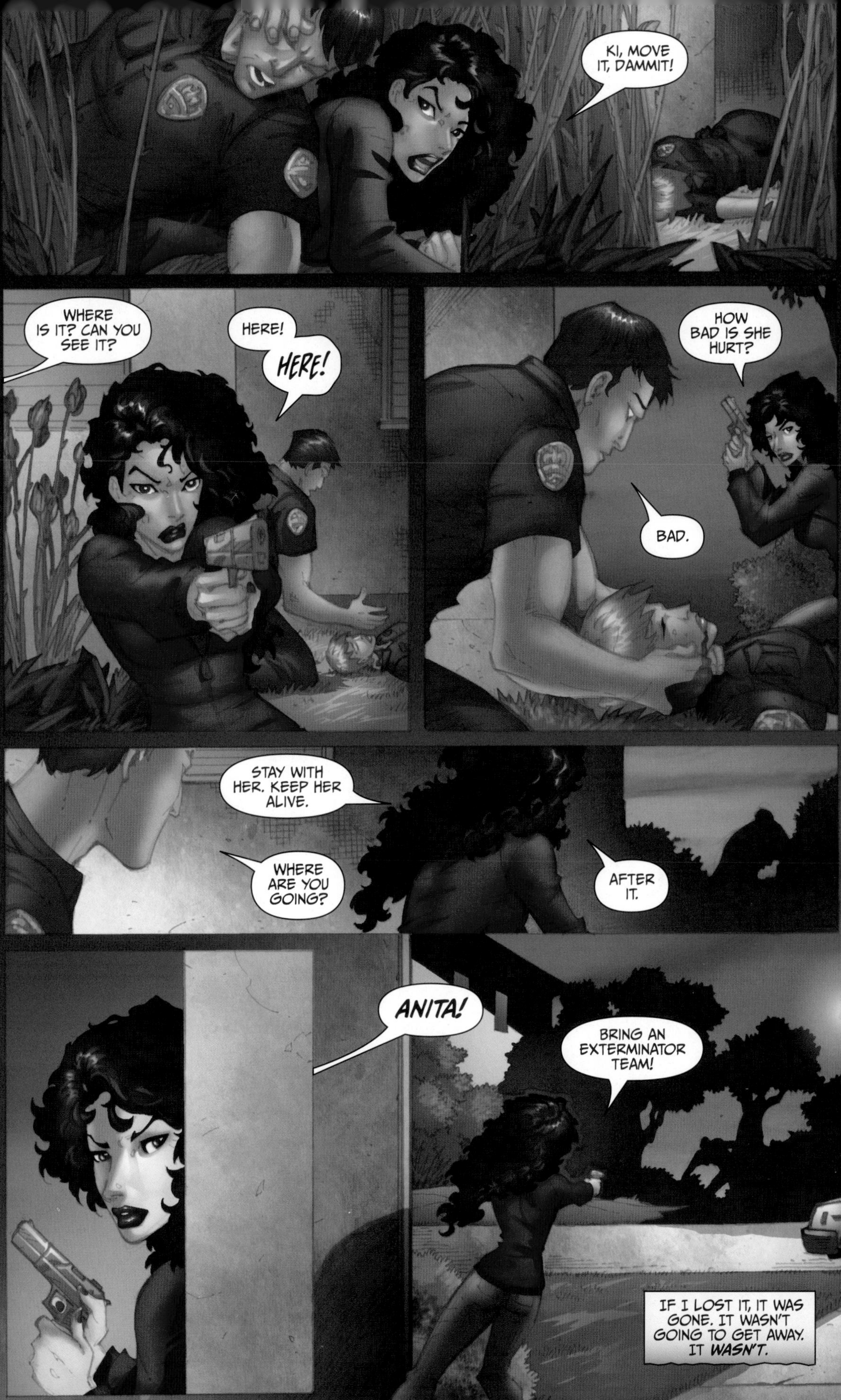
KI, MOVE IT, DAMMIT!
WHERE IS IT? CAN YOU SEE IT?
HERE!
HERE!
HOW BAD IS SHE HURT?
BAD.
STAY WITH HER. KEEP HER ALIVE.
WHERE ARE YOU GOING?
AFTER IT.
ANITA!
BRING AN EXTERMINATOR TEAM!
IF I LOST IT, IT WAS GONE. IT WASN'T GOING TO GET AWAY. IT *WASN'T*.

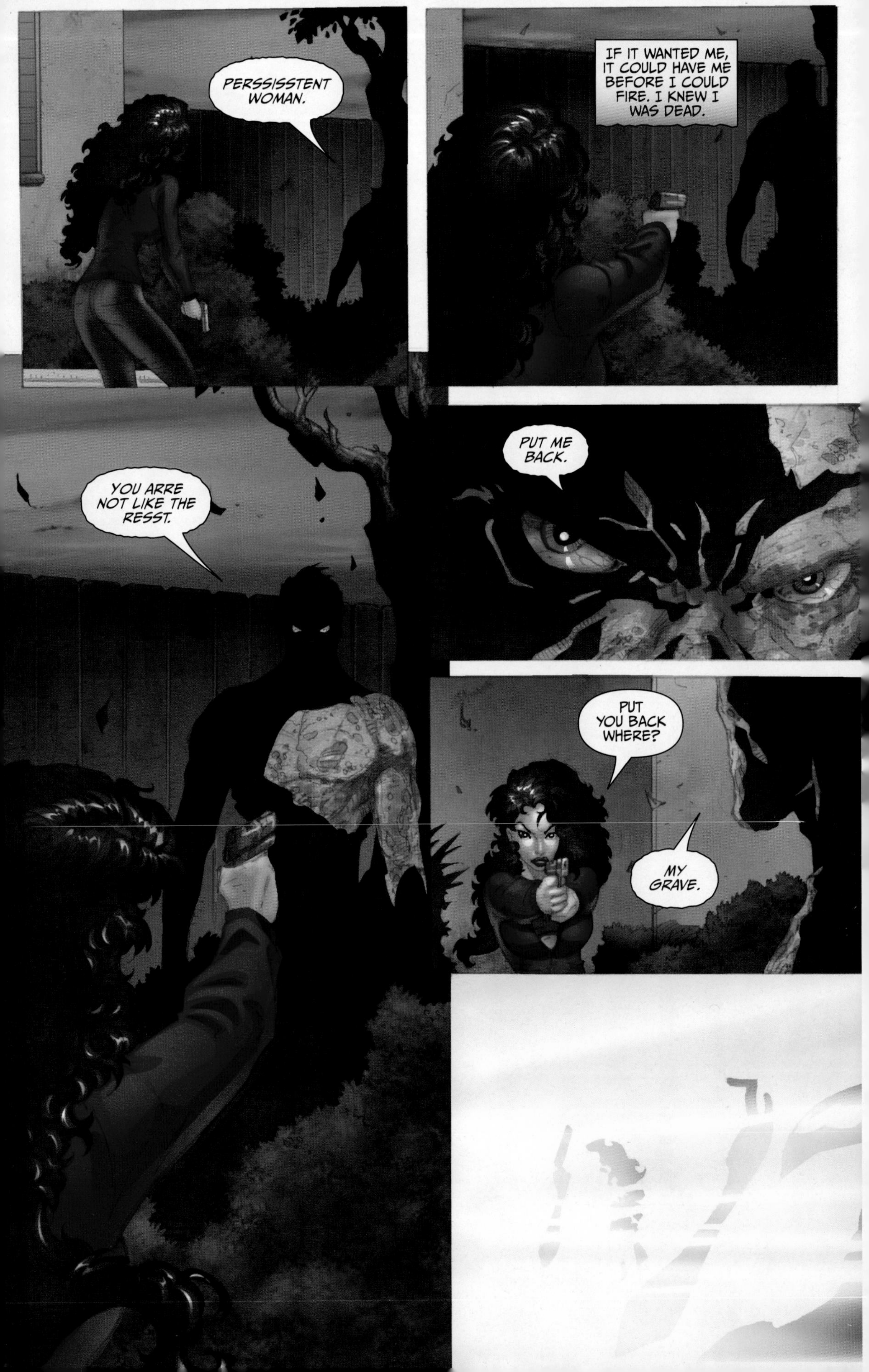
PERSSISSTENT WOMAN.
IF IT WANTED ME, IT COULD HAVE ME BEFORE I COULD FIRE. I KNEW I WAS DEAD.
YOU ARRE NOT LIKE THE RESST.
PUT ME BACK.
PUT YOU BACK WHERE?
MY GRAVE.

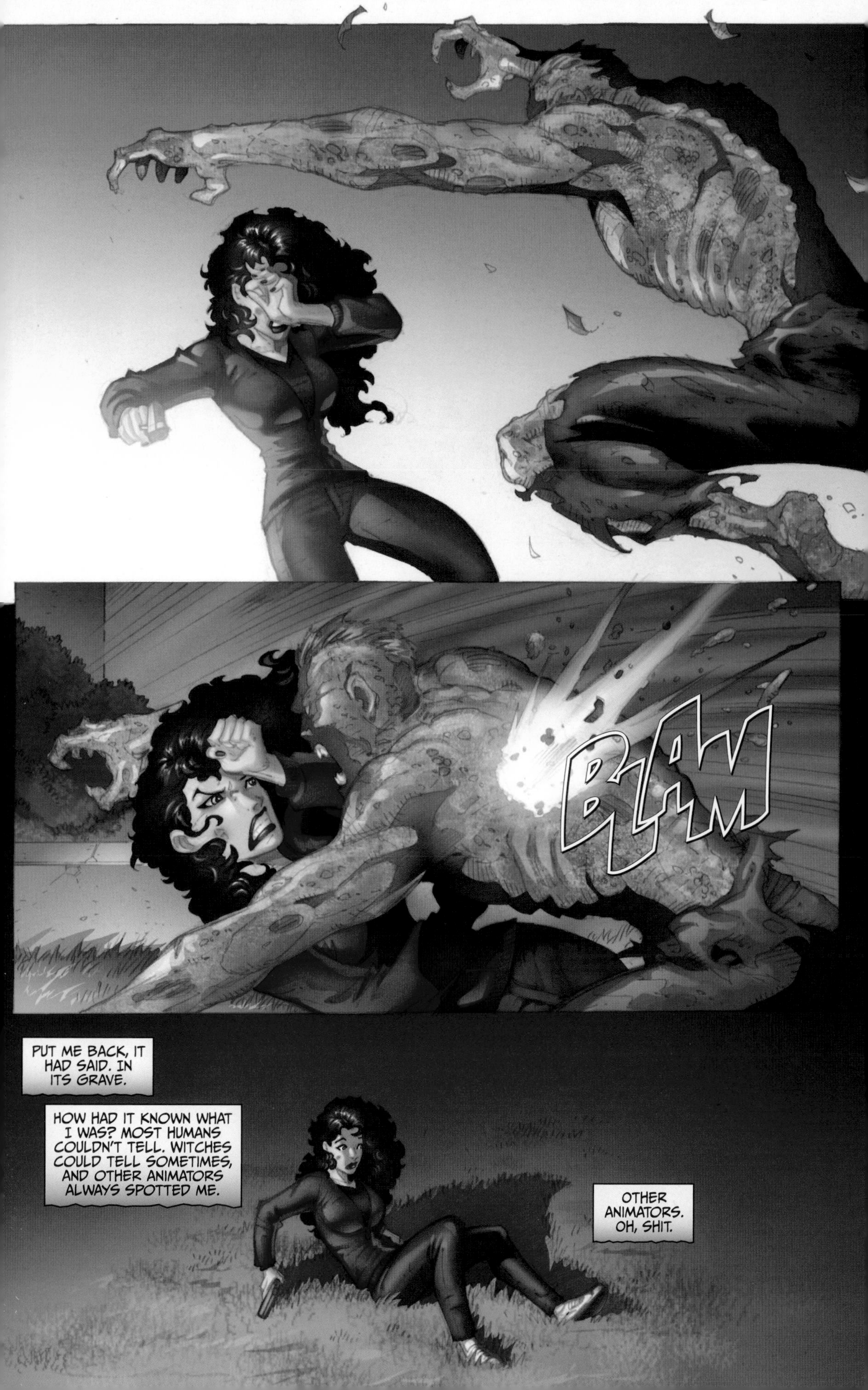
BLAM
PUT ME BACK, IT HAD SAID. IN ITS GRAVE.
HOW HAD IT KNOWN WHAT I WAS? MOST HUMANS COULDN'T TELL. WITCHES COULD TELL SOMETIMES, AND OTHER ANIMATORS ALWAYS SPOTTED ME.
OTHER ANIMATORS. OH, SHIT.

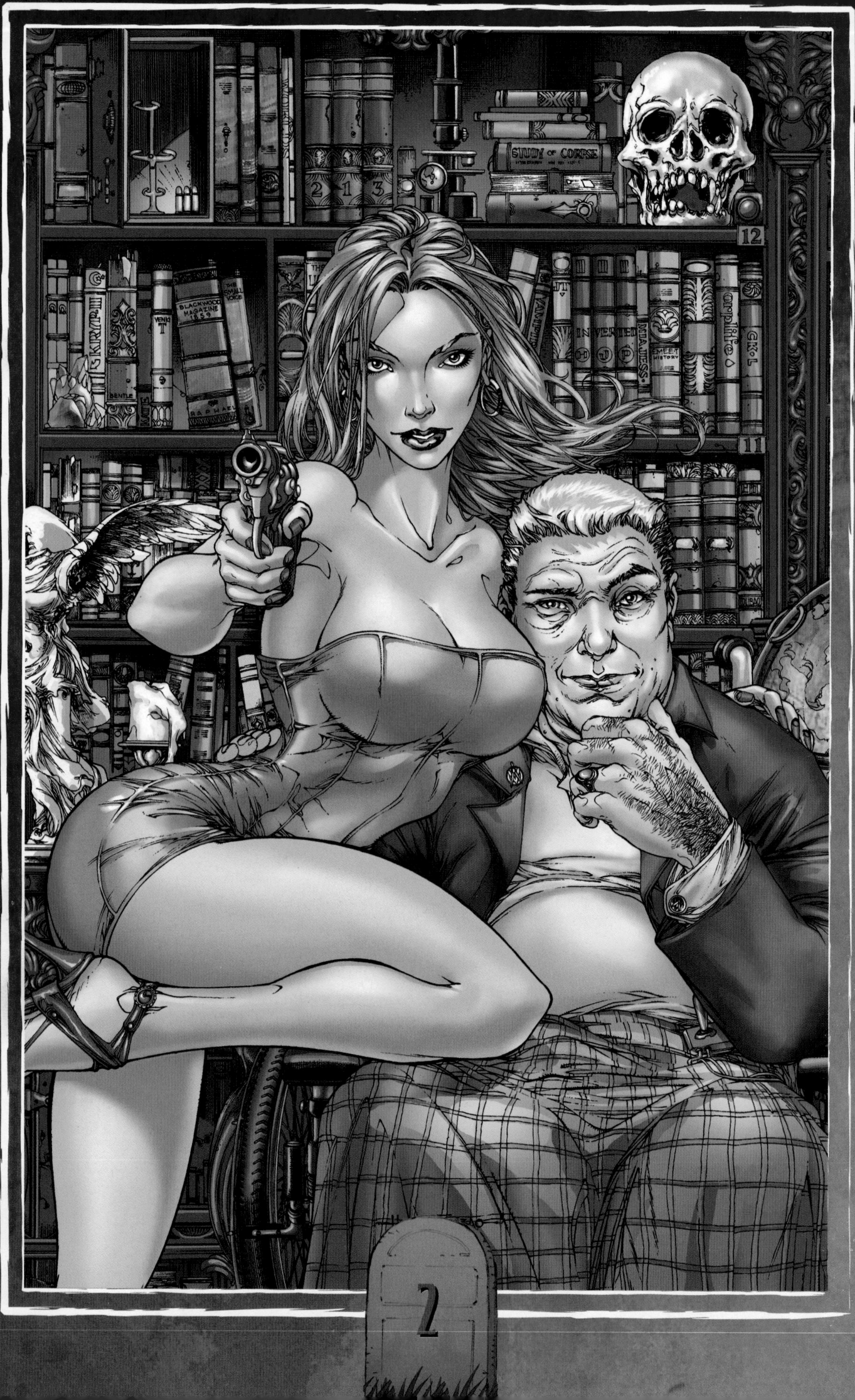
STUDY OF CORPSE
BLACKWOOD MAGAZINE 1859
INVERTED
12
11
2

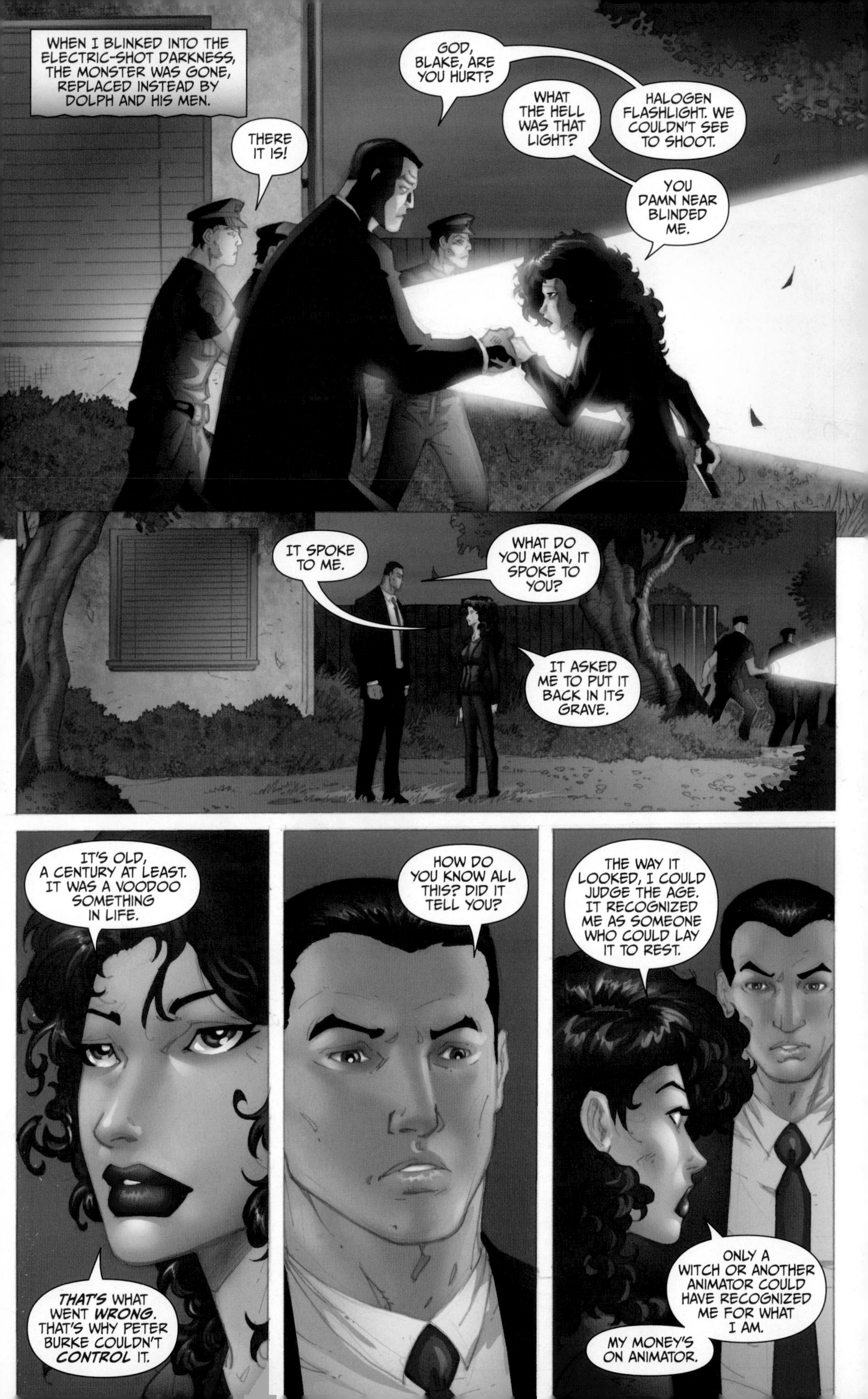
WHEN I BLINKED INTO THE ELECTRIC-SHOT DARKNESS, THE MONSTER WAS GONE, REPLACED INSTEAD BY DOLPH AND HIS MEN.
THERE IT IS!
GOD, BLAKE, ARE YOU HURT?
WHAT THE HELL WAS THAT LIGHT?
HALOGEN FLASHLIGHT. WE COULDN'T SEE TO SHOOT.
YOU DAMN NEAR BLINDED ME.
IT SPOKE TO ME.
WHAT DO YOU MEAN, IT SPOKE TO YOU?
IT ASKED ME TO PUT IT BACK IN ITS GRAVE.
IT'S OLD, A CENTURY AT LEAST. IT WAS A VOODOO SOMETHING IN LIFE.
THAT'S WHAT WENT **WRONG**. THAT'S WHY PETER BURKE COULDN'T ***CONTROL*** IT.
HOW DO YOU KNOW ALL THIS? DID IT TELL YOU?
THE WAY IT LOOKED, I COULD JUDGE THE AGE. IT RECOGNIZED ME AS SOMEONE WHO COULD LAY IT TO REST.
ONLY A WITCH OR ANOTHER ANIMATOR COULD HAVE RECOGNIZED ME FOR WHAT I AM.
MY MONEY'S ON ANIMATOR.

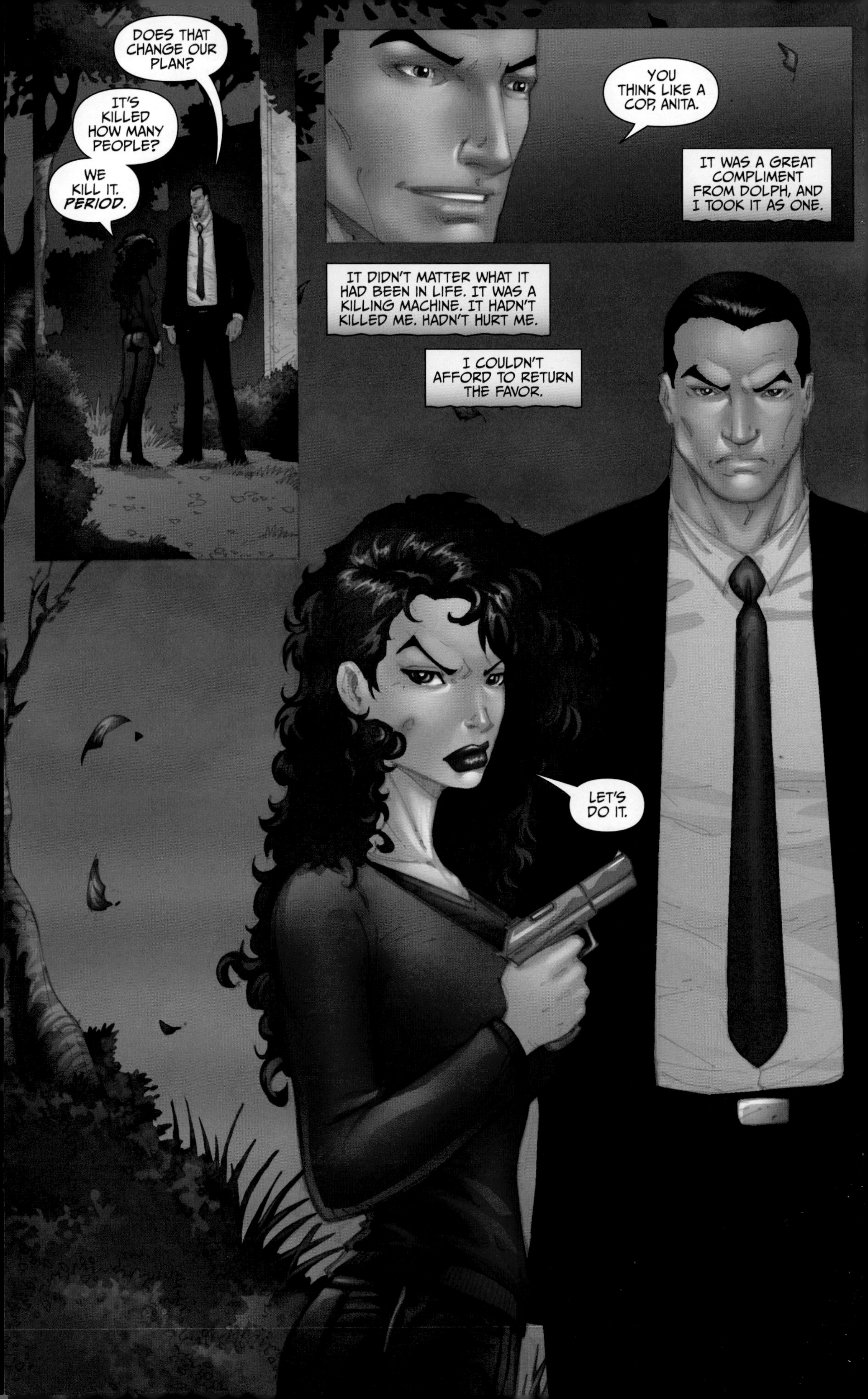
DOES THAT CHANGE OUR PLAN?
IT'S KILLED HOW MANY PEOPLE?
WE KILL IT. *PERIOD.*
YOU THINK LIKE A COP, ANITA.
IT WAS A GREAT COMPLIMENT FROM DOLPH, AND I TOOK IT AS ONE.
IT DIDN'T MATTER WHAT IT HAD BEEN IN LIFE. IT WAS A KILLING MACHINE. IT HADN'T KILLED ME. HADN'T HURT ME.
I COULDN'T AFFORD TO RETURN THE FAVOR.
LET'S DO IT.

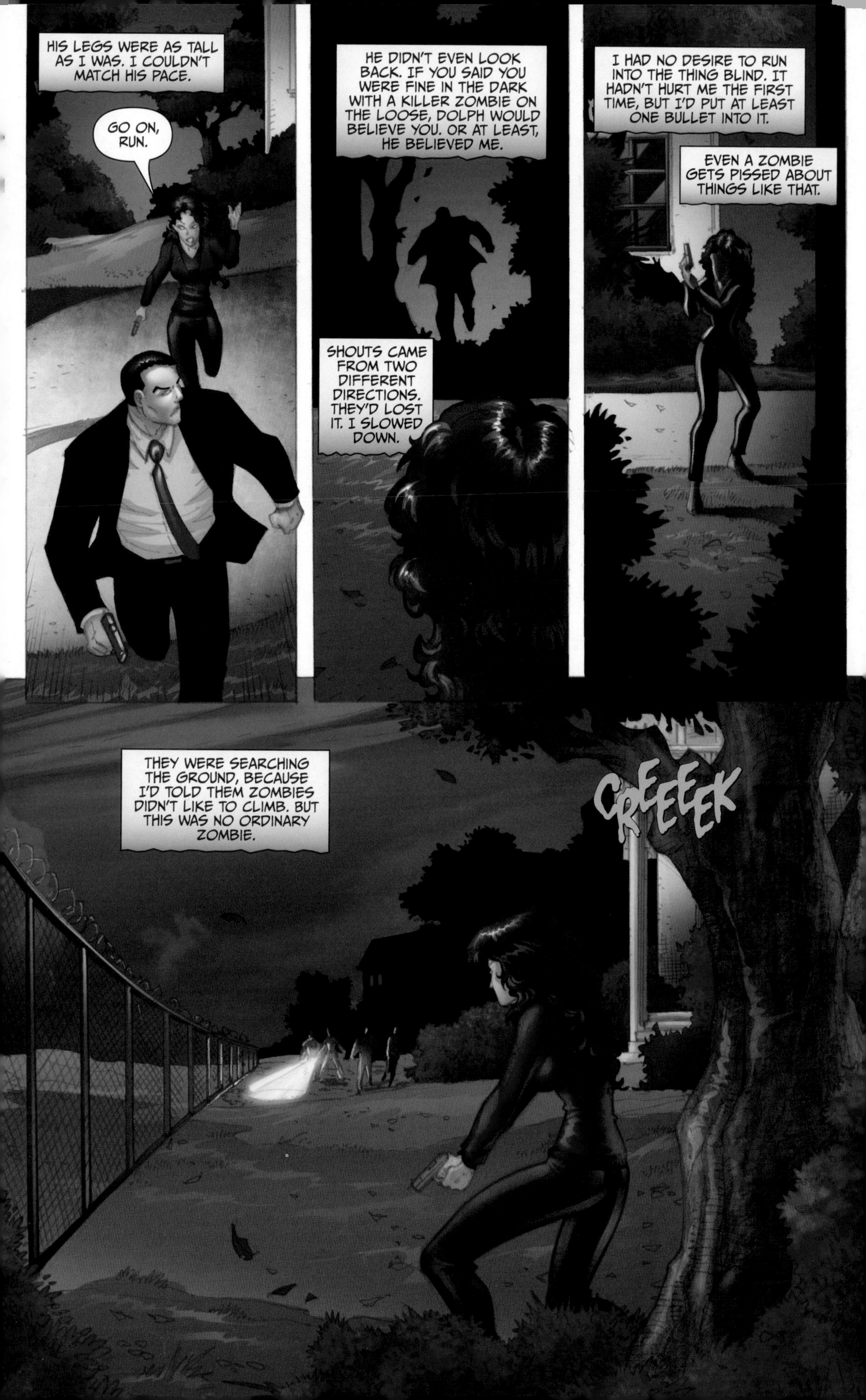
HIS LEGS WERE AS TALL AS I WAS. I COULDN'T MATCH HIS PACE.
GO ON, RUN.
HE DIDN'T EVEN LOOK BACK. IF YOU SAID YOU WERE FINE IN THE DARK WITH A KILLER ZOMBIE ON THE LOOSE, DOLPH WOULD BELIEVE YOU. OR AT LEAST, HE BELIEVED ME.
SHOUTS CAME FROM TWO DIFFERENT DIRECTIONS. THEY'D LOST IT. I SLOWED DOWN.
I HAD NO DESIRE TO RUN INTO THE THING BLIND. IT HADN'T HURT ME THE FIRST TIME, BUT I'D PUT AT LEAST ONE BULLET INTO IT.
EVEN A ZOMBIE GETS PISSED ABOUT THINGS LIKE THAT.
THEY WERE SEARCHING THE GROUND, BECAUSE I'D TOLD THEM ZOMBIES DIDN'T LIKE TO CLIMB. BUT THIS WAS NO ORDINARY ZOMBIE.
CREEEEK

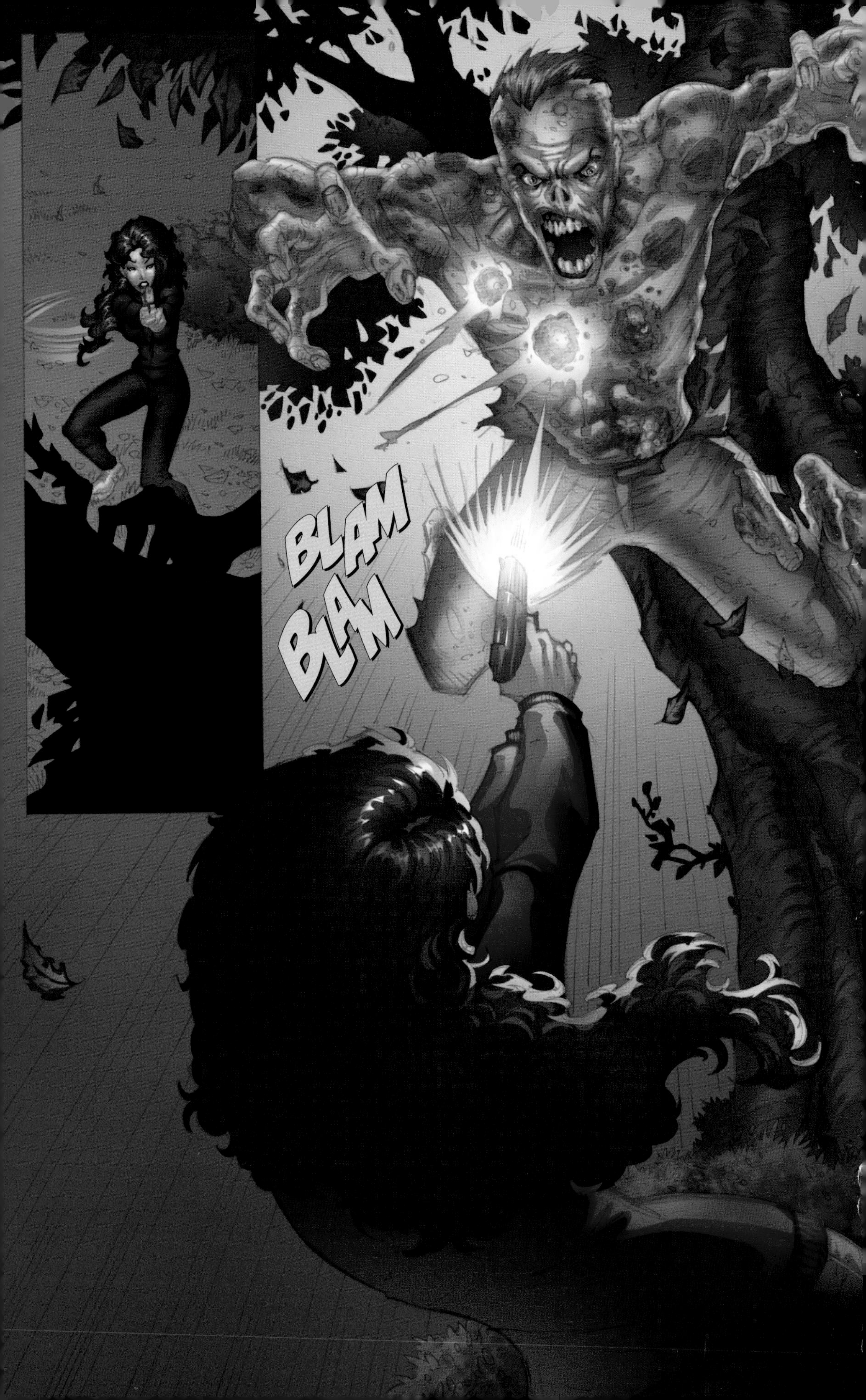
BLAM
BLAM

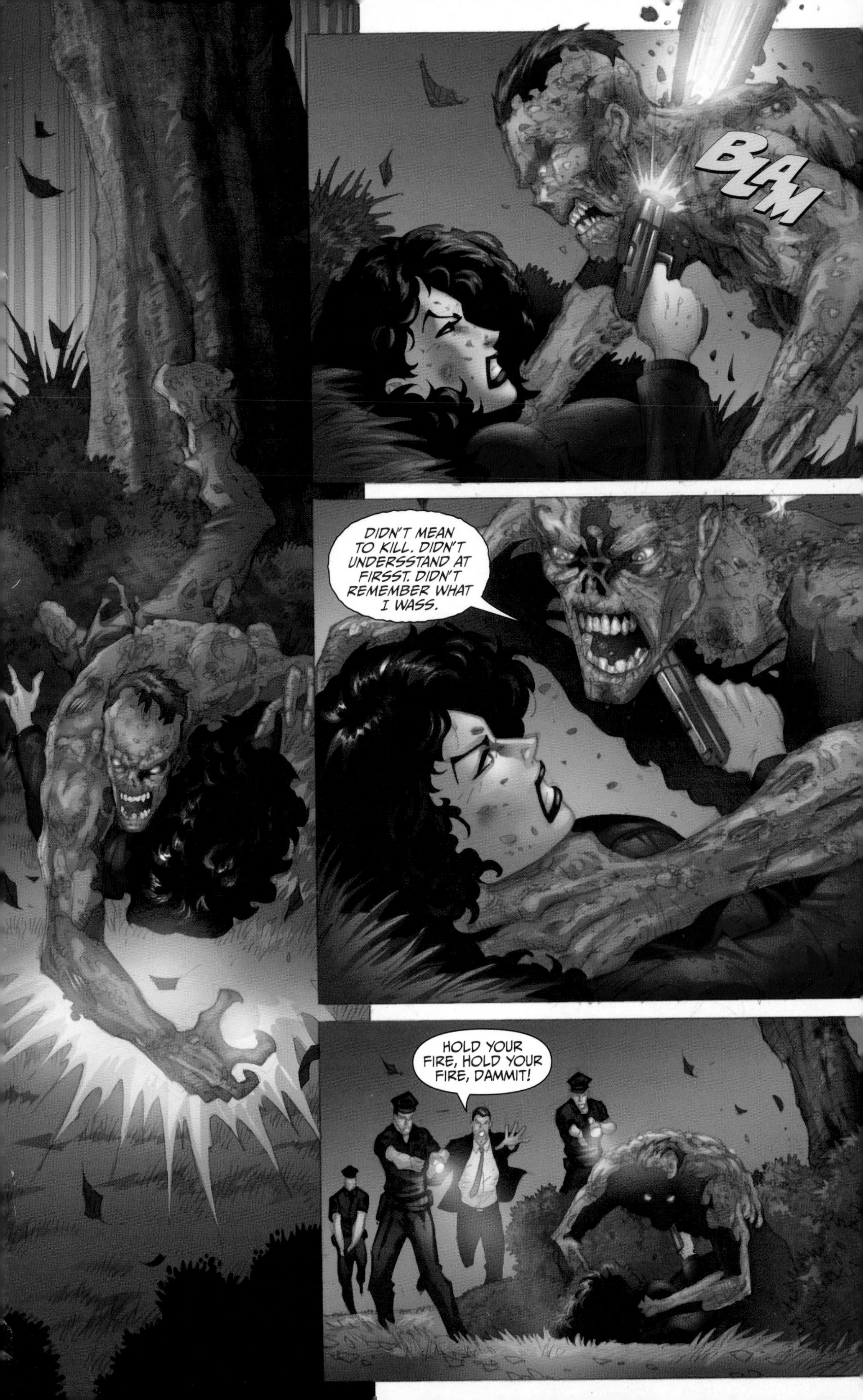
BLAM
DIDN'T MEAN TO KILL. DIDN'T UNDERSSTAND AT FIRSST. DIDN'T REMEMBER WHAT I WASS.
HOLD YOUR FIRE, HOLD YOUR FIRE, DAMMIT!

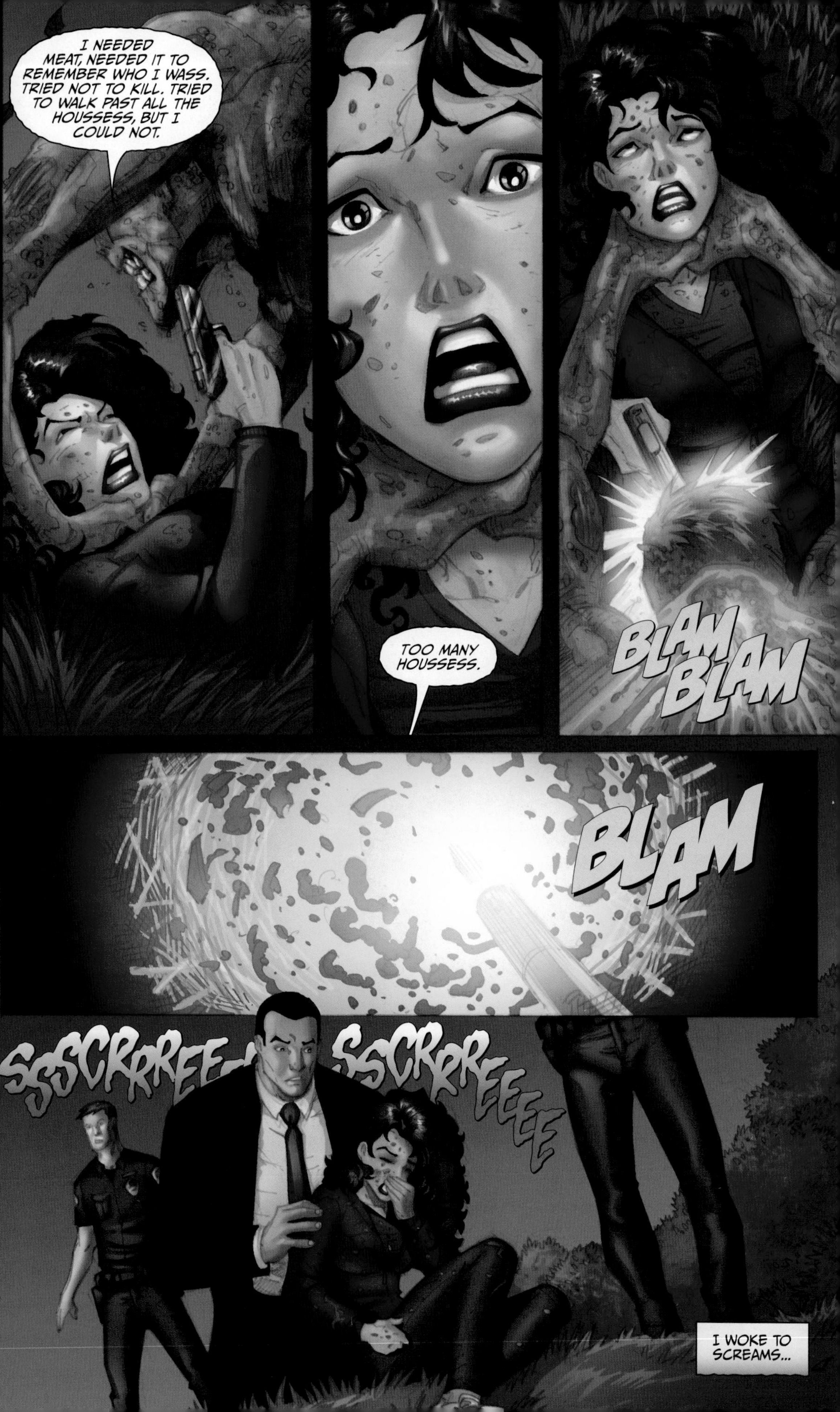
I NEEDED MEAT, NEEDED IT TO REMEMBER WHO I WASS. TRIED NOT TO KILL. TRIED TO WALK PAST ALL THE HOUSSESS, BUT I COULD NOT.
TOO MANY HOUSSESS.
BLAM BLAM
BLAM
SSSCRRREE-- SSCRRREEEE
I WOKE TO SCREAMS...

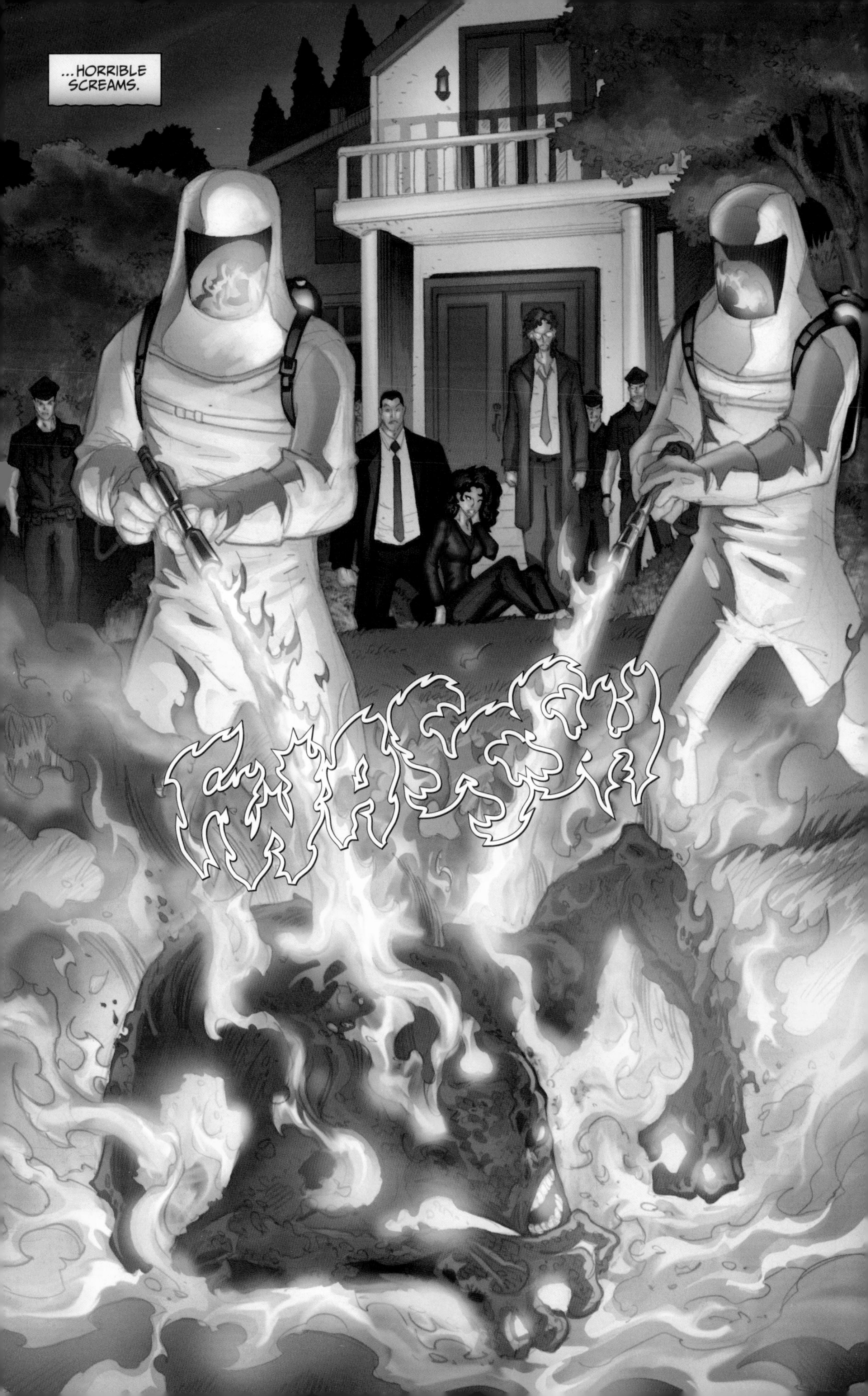
...HORRIBLE SCREAMS.
FWASSH

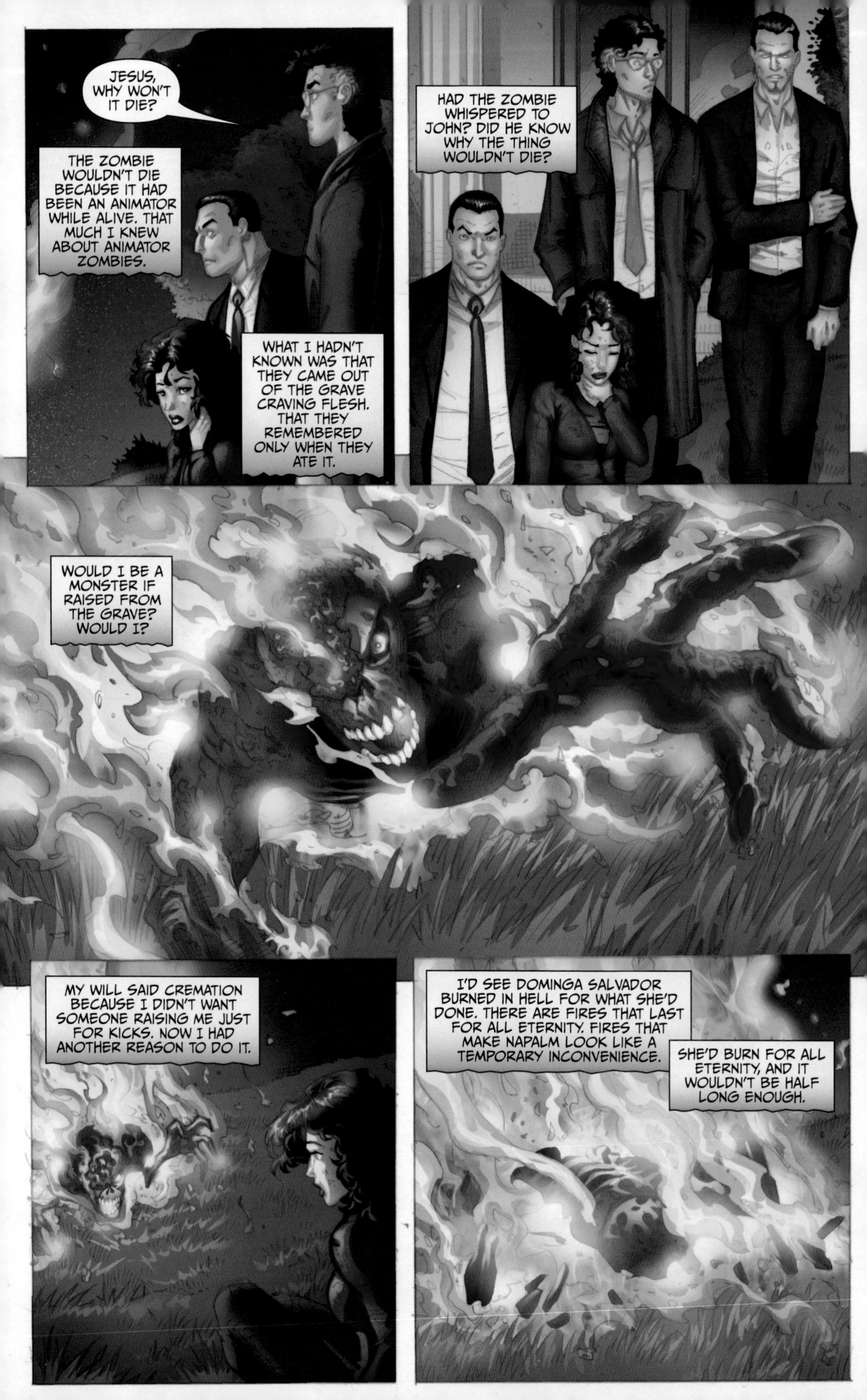
JESUS, WHY WON'T IT DIE?
THE ZOMBIE WOULDN'T DIE BECAUSE IT HAD BEEN AN ANIMATOR WHILE ALIVE. THAT MUCH I KNEW ABOUT ANIMATOR ZOMBIES.
WHAT I HADN'T KNOWN WAS THAT THEY CAME OUT OF THE GRAVE CRAVING FLESH. THAT THEY REMEMBERED ONLY WHEN THEY ATE IT.
HAD THE ZOMBIE WHISPERED TO JOHN? DID HE KNOW WHY THE THING WOULDN'T DIE?
WOULD I BE A MONSTER IF RAISED FROM THE GRAVE? WOULD I?
MY WILL SAID CREMATION BECAUSE I DIDN'T WANT SOMEONE RAISING ME JUST FOR KICKS. NOW I HAD ANOTHER REASON TO DO IT.
I'D SEE DOMINGA SALVADOR BURNED IN HELL FOR WHAT SHE'D DONE. THERE ARE FIRES THAT LAST FOR ALL ETERNITY. FIRES THAT MAKE NAPALM LOOK LIKE A TEMPORARY INCONVENIENCE.
SHE'D BURN FOR ALL ETERNITY, AND IT WOULDN'T BE HALF LONG ENOUGH.

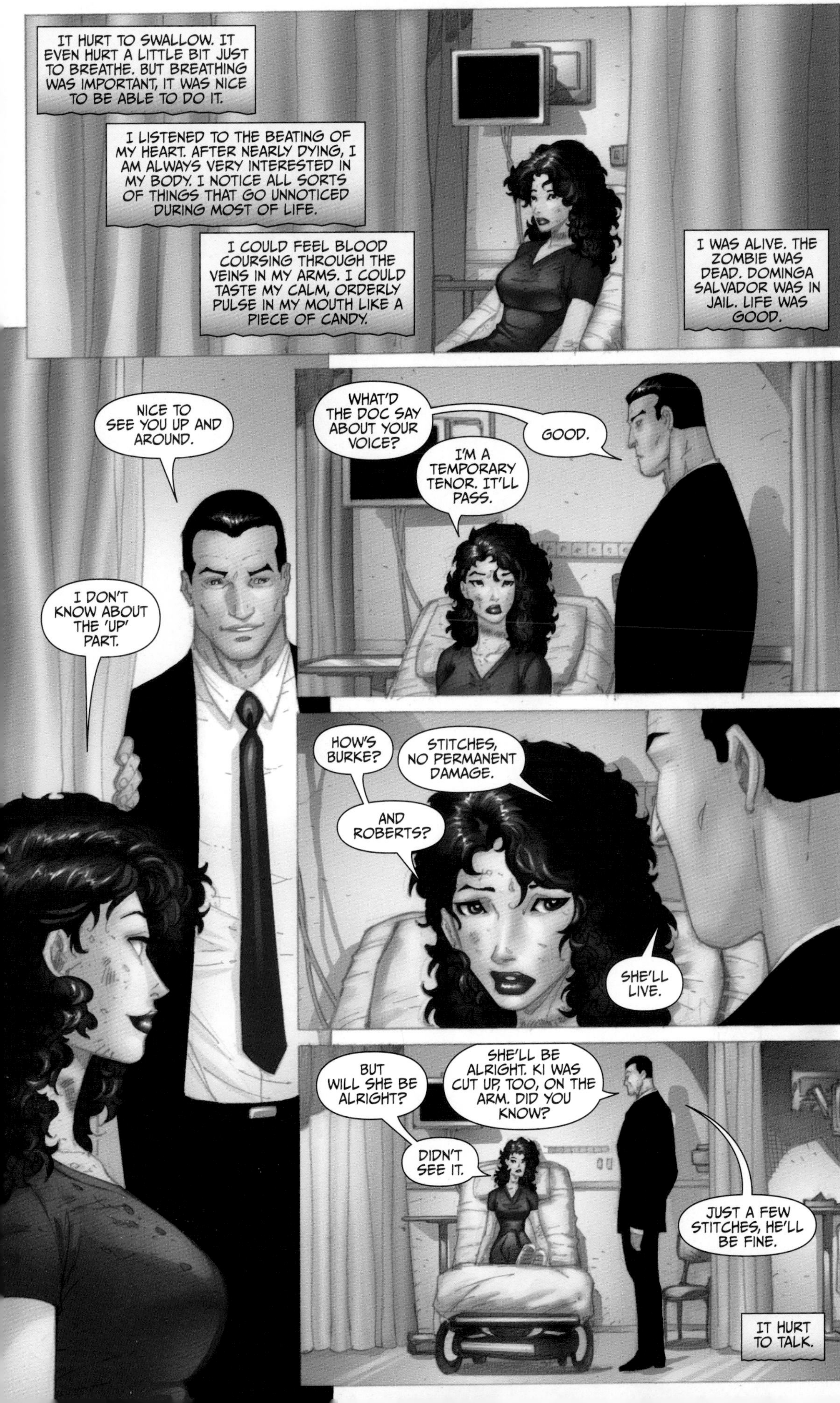
IT HURT TO SWALLOW. IT EVEN HURT A LITTLE BIT JUST TO BREATHE. BUT BREATHING WAS IMPORTANT, IT WAS NICE TO BE ABLE TO DO IT.
I LISTENED TO THE BEATING OF MY HEART. AFTER NEARLY DYING, I AM ALWAYS VERY INTERESTED IN MY BODY. I NOTICE ALL SORTS OF THINGS THAT GO UNNOTICED DURING MOST OF LIFE.
I COULD FEEL BLOOD COURSING THROUGH THE VEINS IN MY ARMS. I COULD TASTE MY CALM, ORDERLY PULSE IN MY MOUTH LIKE A PIECE OF CANDY.
I WAS ALIVE. THE ZOMBIE WAS DEAD. DOMINGA SALVADOR WAS IN JAIL. LIFE WAS GOOD.
NICE TO SEE YOU UP AND AROUND.
I DON'T KNOW ABOUT THE 'UP' PART.
WHAT'D THE DOC SAY ABOUT YOUR VOICE?
I'M A TEMPORARY TENOR. IT'LL PASS.
GOOD.
HOW'S BURKE?
STITCHES, NO PERMANENT DAMAGE.
AND ROBERTS?
SHE'LL LIVE.
BUT WILL SHE BE ALRIGHT?
SHE'LL BE ALRIGHT. KI WAS CUT UP, TOO, ON THE ARM. DID YOU KNOW?
DIDN'T SEE IT.
JUST A FEW STITCHES, HE'LL BE FINE.
IT HURT TO TALK.

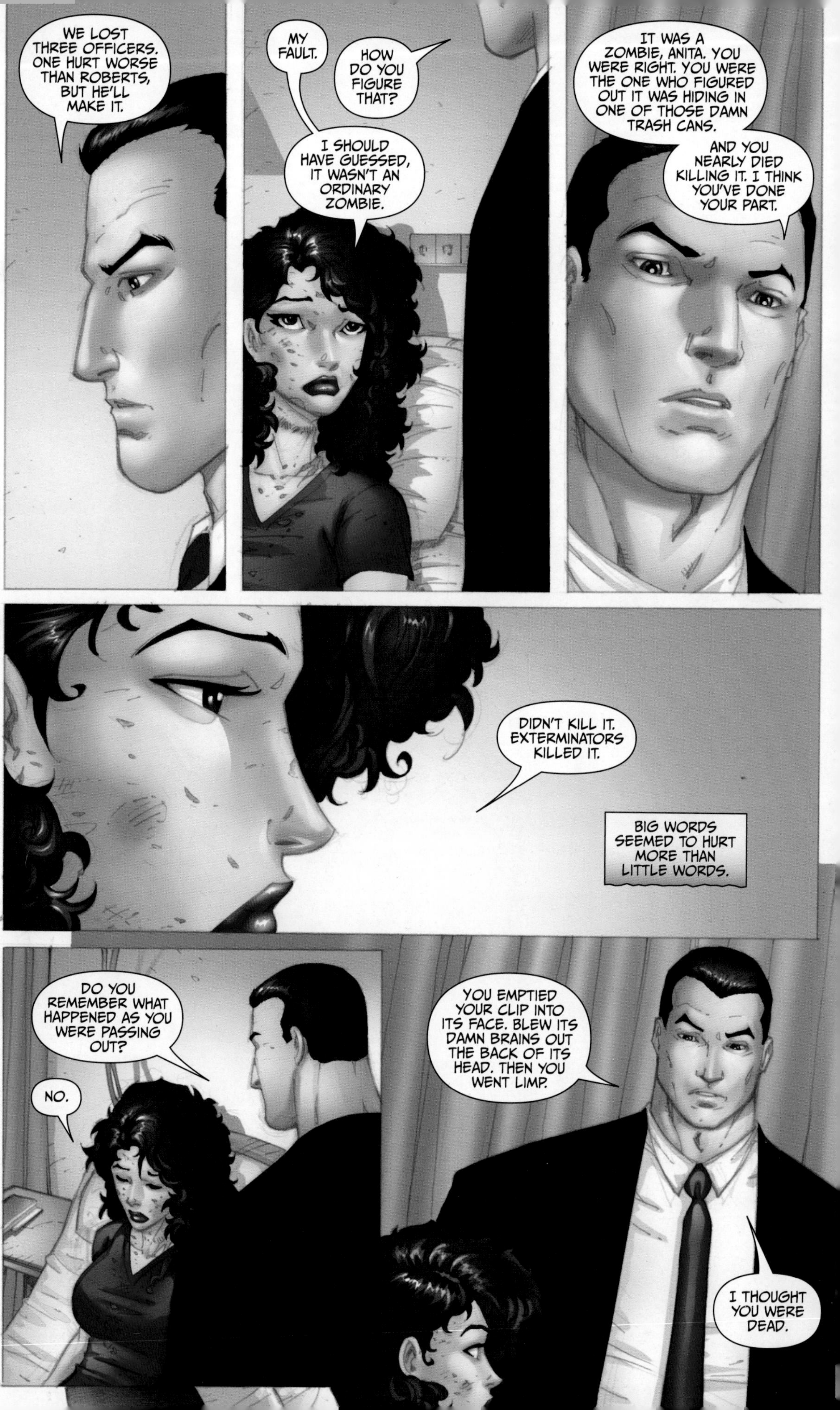
WE LOST THREE OFFICERS. ONE HURT WORSE THAN ROBERTS, BUT HE'LL MAKE IT.
MY FAULT.
HOW DO YOU FIGURE THAT?
I SHOULD HAVE GUESSED, IT WASN'T AN ORDINARY ZOMBIE.
IT WAS A ZOMBIE, ANITA. YOU WERE RIGHT. YOU WERE THE ONE WHO FIGURED OUT IT WAS HIDING IN ONE OF THOSE DAMN TRASH CANS.
AND YOU NEARLY DIED KILLING IT. I THINK YOU'VE DONE YOUR PART.
DIDN'T KILL IT. EXTERMINATORS KILLED IT.
BIG WORDS SEEMED TO HURT MORE THAN LITTLE WORDS.
DO YOU REMEMBER WHAT HAPPENED AS YOU WERE PASSING OUT?
NO.
YOU EMPTIED YOUR CLIP INTO ITS FACE. BLEW ITS DAMN BRAINS OUT THE BACK OF ITS HEAD. THEN YOU WENT LIMP.
I THOUGHT YOU WERE DEAD.

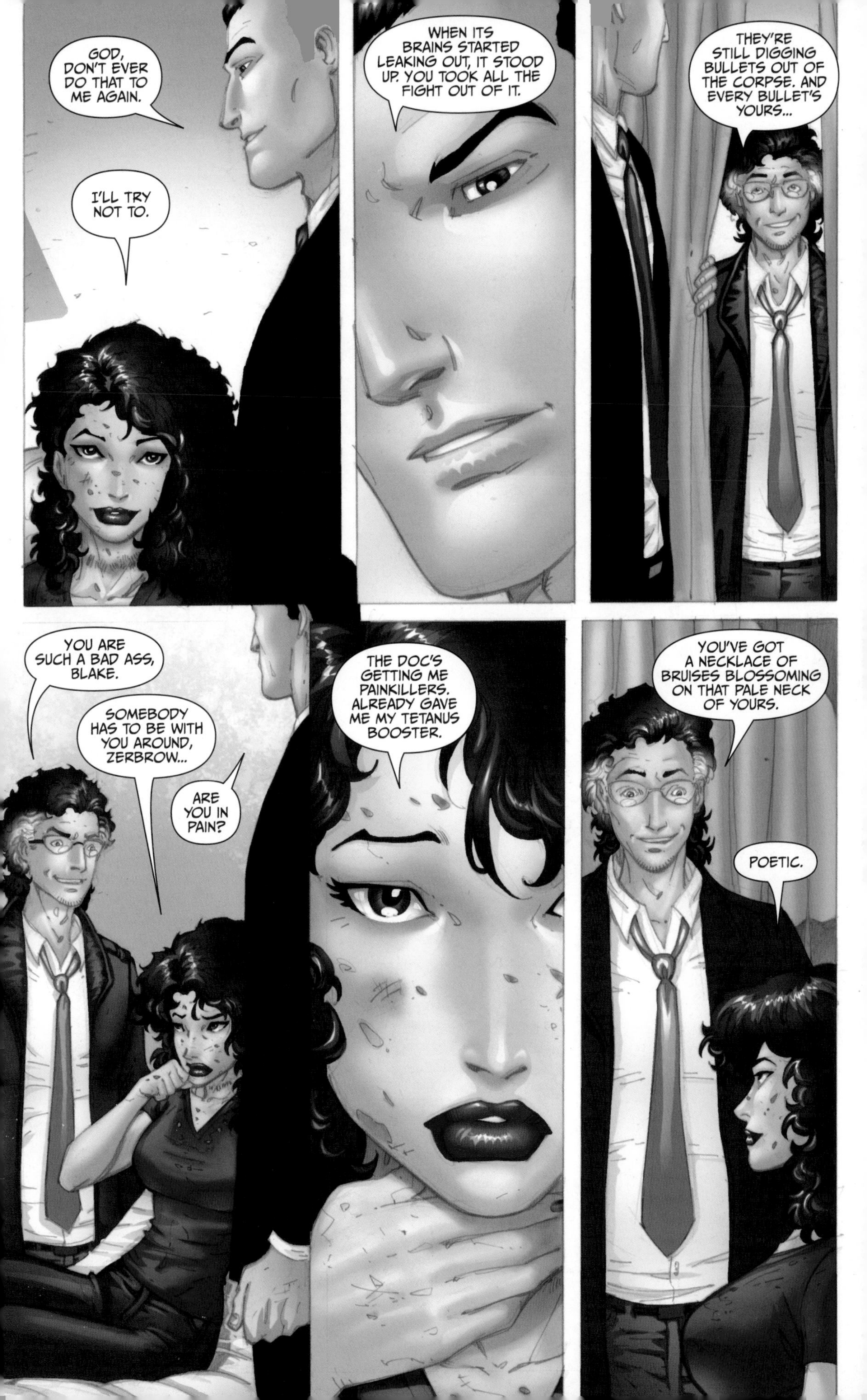
GOD, DON'T EVER DO THAT TO ME AGAIN.
I'LL TRY NOT TO.
WHEN ITS BRAINS STARTED LEAKING OUT, IT STOOD UP. YOU TOOK ALL THE FIGHT OUT OF IT.
THEY'RE STILL DIGGING BULLETS OUT OF THE CORPSE. AND EVERY BULLET'S YOURS...
YOU ARE SUCH A BAD ASS, BLAKE.
SOMEBODY HAS TO BE WITH YOU AROUND, ZERBROW...
ARE YOU IN PAIN?
THE DOC'S GETTING ME PAINKILLERS. ALREADY GAVE ME MY TETANUS BOOSTER.
YOU'VE GOT A NECKLACE OF BRUISES BLOSSOMING ON THAT PALE NECK OF YOURS.
POETIC.

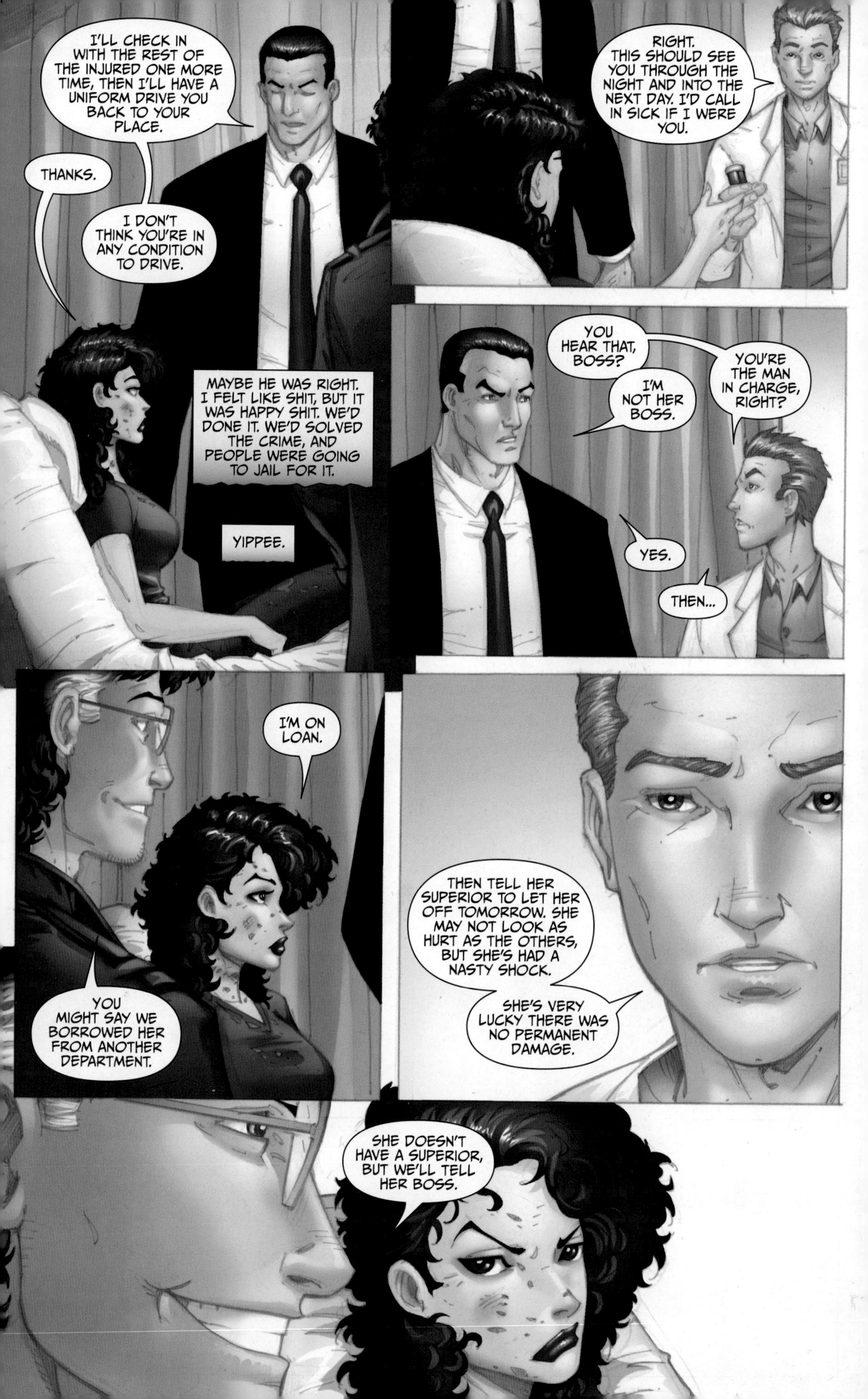
I'LL CHECK IN WITH THE REST OF THE INJURED ONE MORE TIME, THEN I'LL HAVE A UNIFORM DRIVE YOU BACK TO YOUR PLACE.
THANKS.
I DON'T THINK YOU'RE IN ANY CONDITION TO DRIVE.
MAYBE HE WAS RIGHT. I FELT LIKE SHIT, BUT IT WAS HAPPY SHIT. WE'D DONE IT. WE'D SOLVED THE CRIME, AND PEOPLE WERE GOING TO JAIL FOR IT.
YIPPEE.
RIGHT. THIS SHOULD SEE YOU THROUGH THE NIGHT AND INTO THE NEXT DAY. I'D CALL IN SICK IF I WERE YOU.
YOU HEAR THAT, BOSS?
I'M NOT HER BOSS.
YOU'RE THE MAN IN CHARGE, RIGHT?
YES.
THEN...
I'M ON LOAN.
YOU MIGHT SAY WE BORROWED HER FROM ANOTHER DEPARTMENT.
THEN TELL HER SUPERIOR TO LET HER OFF TOMORROW. SHE MAY NOT LOOK AS HURT AS THE OTHERS, BUT SHE'S HAD A NASTY SHOCK.
SHE'S VERY LUCKY THERE WAS NO PERMANENT DAMAGE.
SHE DOESN'T HAVE A SUPERIOR, BUT WE'LL TELL HER BOSS.

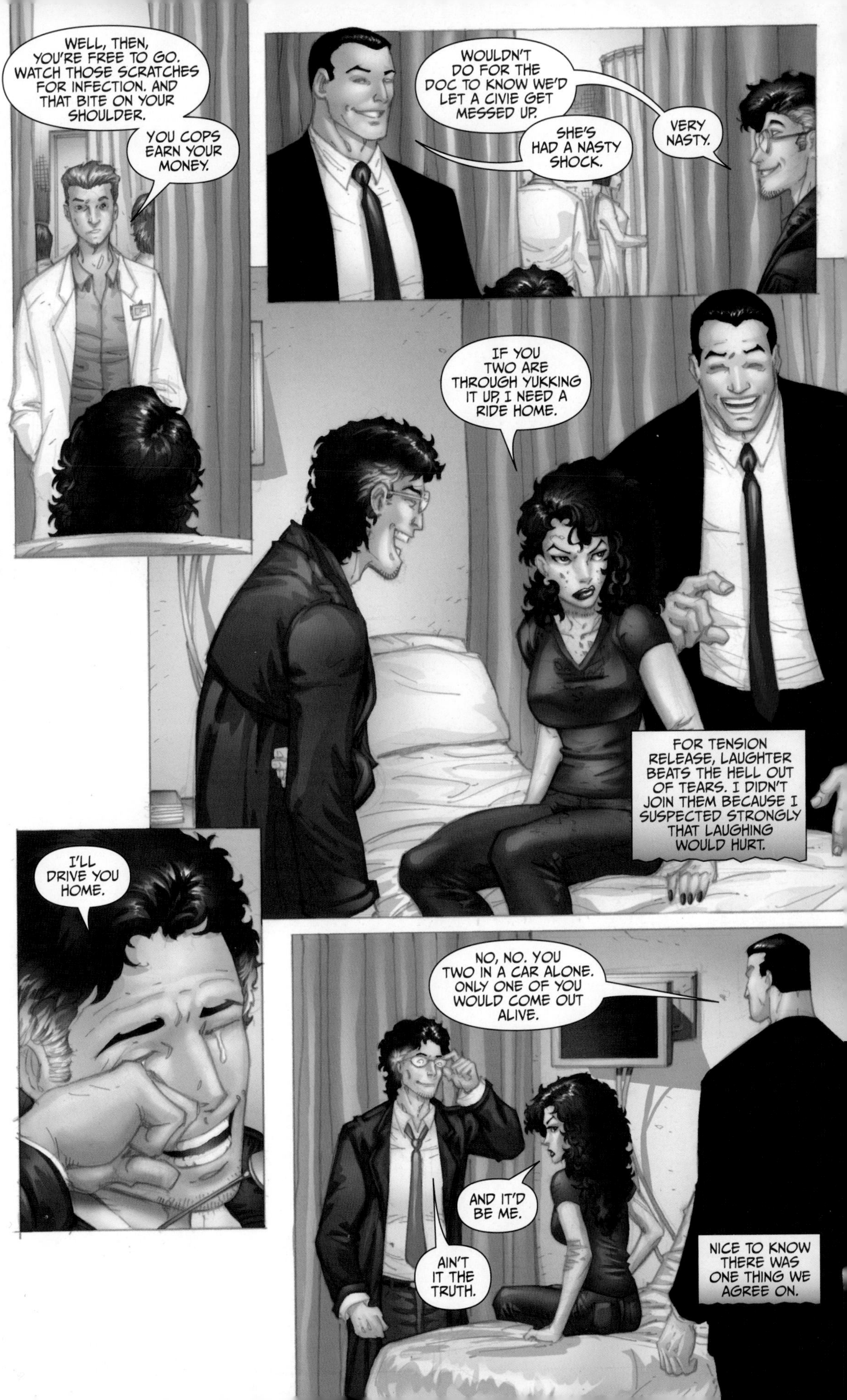
WELL, THEN, YOU'RE FREE TO GO. WATCH THOSE SCRATCHES FOR INFECTION. AND THAT BITE ON YOUR SHOULDER.
YOU COPS EARN YOUR MONEY.
WOULDN'T DO FOR THE DOC TO KNOW WE'D LET A CIVIE GET MESSED UP.
SHE'S HAD A NASTY SHOCK.
VERY NASTY.
IF YOU TWO ARE THROUGH YUKKING IT UP, I NEED A RIDE HOME.
FOR TENSION RELEASE, LAUGHTER BEATS THE HELL OUT OF TEARS. I DIDN'T JOIN THEM BECAUSE I SUSPECTED STRONGLY THAT LAUGHING WOULD HURT.
I'LL DRIVE YOU HOME.
NO, NO. YOU TWO IN A CAR ALONE. ONLY ONE OF YOU WOULD COME OUT ALIVE.
AND IT'D BE ME.
AIN'T IT THE TRUTH.
NICE TO KNOW THERE WAS ONE THING WE AGREE ON.

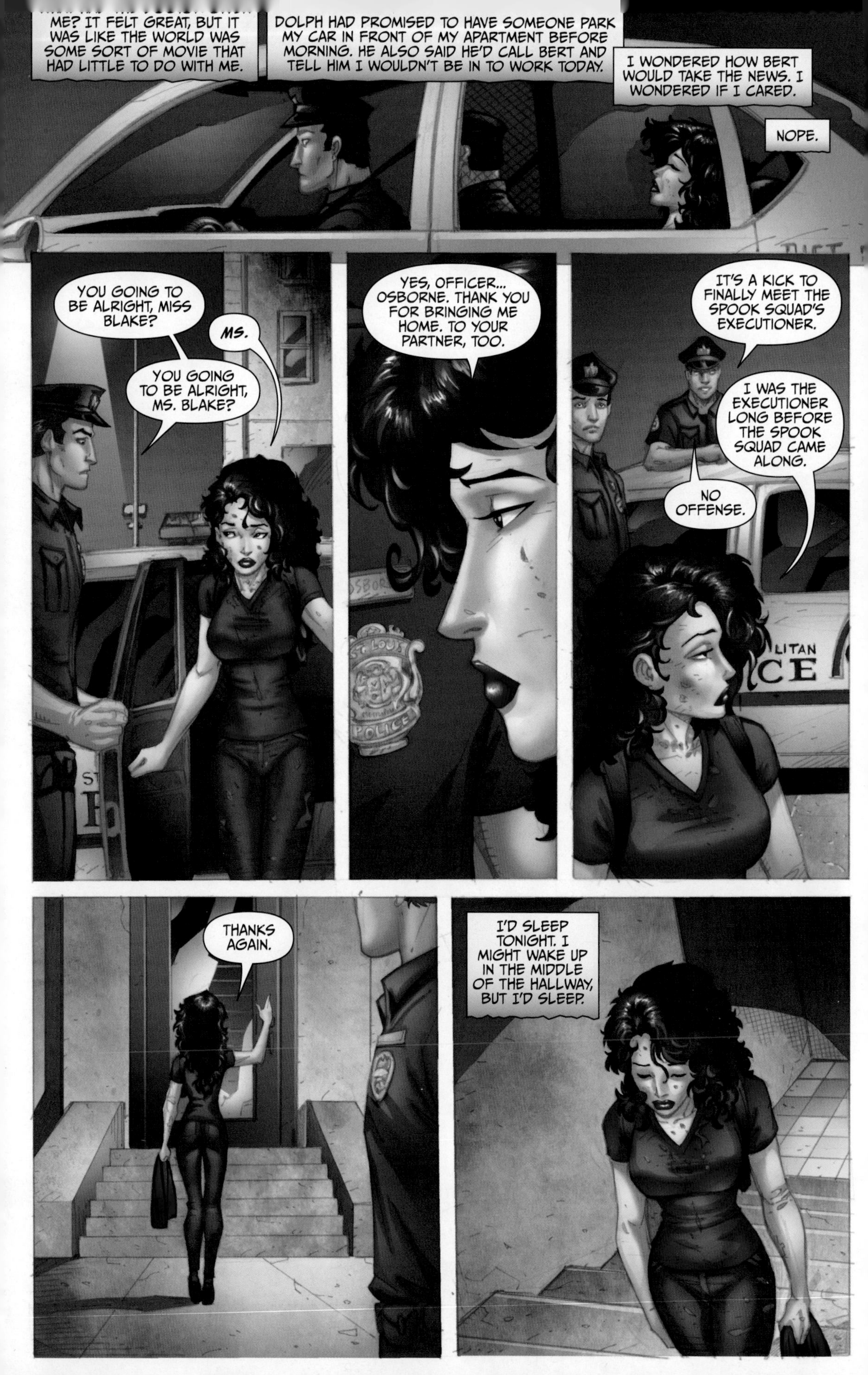
ME? IT FELT GREAT, BUT IT WAS LIKE THE WORLD WAS SOME SORT OF MOVIE THAT HAD LITTLE TO DO WITH ME.
DOLPH HAD PROMISED TO HAVE SOMEONE PARK MY CAR IN FRONT OF MY APARTMENT BEFORE MORNING. HE ALSO SAID HE'D CALL BERT AND TELL HIM I WOULDN'T BE IN TO WORK TODAY.
I WONDERED HOW BERT WOULD TAKE THE NEWS. I WONDERED IF I CARED.
NOPE.
YOU GOING TO BE ALRIGHT, MISS BLAKE?
MS.
YOU GOING TO BE ALRIGHT, MS. BLAKE?
YES, OFFICER... OSBORNE. THANK YOU FOR BRINGING ME HOME. TO YOUR PARTNER, TOO.
IT'S A KICK TO FINALLY MEET THE SPOOK SQUAD'S EXECUTIONER.
I WAS THE EXECUTIONER LONG BEFORE THE SPOOK SQUAD CAME ALONG.
NO OFFENSE.
THANKS AGAIN.
I'D SLEEP TONIGHT. I MIGHT WAKE UP IN THE MIDDLE OF THE HALLWAY, BUT I'D SLEEP.

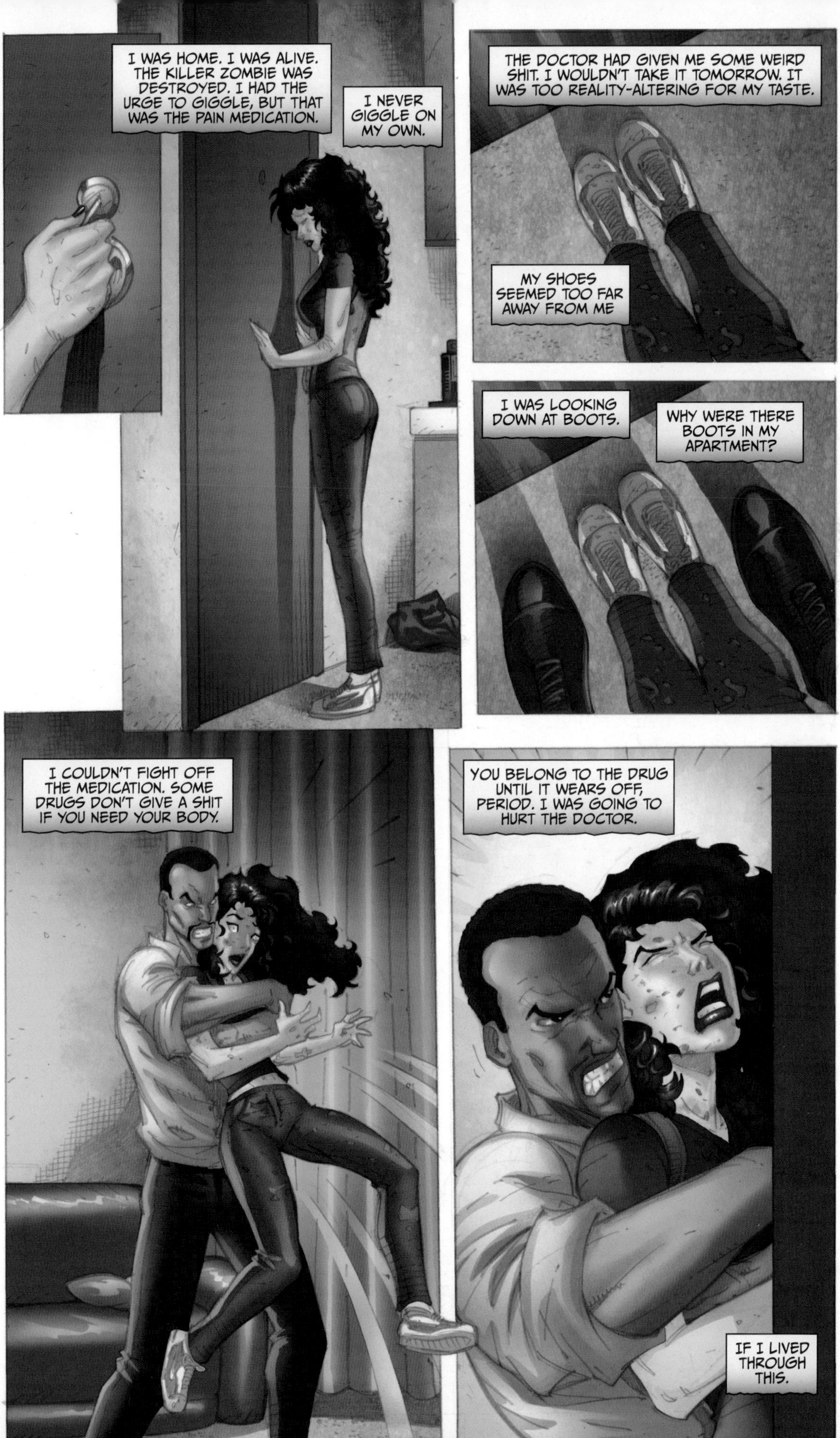
I WAS HOME. I WAS ALIVE. THE KILLER ZOMBIE WAS DESTROYED. I HAD THE URGE TO GIGGLE, BUT THAT WAS THE PAIN MEDICATION.
I NEVER GIGGLE ON MY OWN.
THE DOCTOR HAD GIVEN ME SOME WEIRD SHIT. I WOULDN'T TAKE IT TOMORROW. IT WAS TOO REALITY-ALTERING FOR MY TASTE.
MY SHOES SEEMED TOO FAR AWAY FROM ME
I WAS LOOKING DOWN AT BOOTS.
WHY WERE THERE BOOTS IN MY APARTMENT?
I COULDN'T FIGHT OFF THE MEDICATION. SOME DRUGS DON'T GIVE A SHIT IF YOU NEED YOUR BODY.
YOU BELONG TO THE DRUG UNTIL IT WEARS OFF, PERIOD. I WAS GOING TO HURT THE DOCTOR.
IF I LIVED THROUGH THIS.

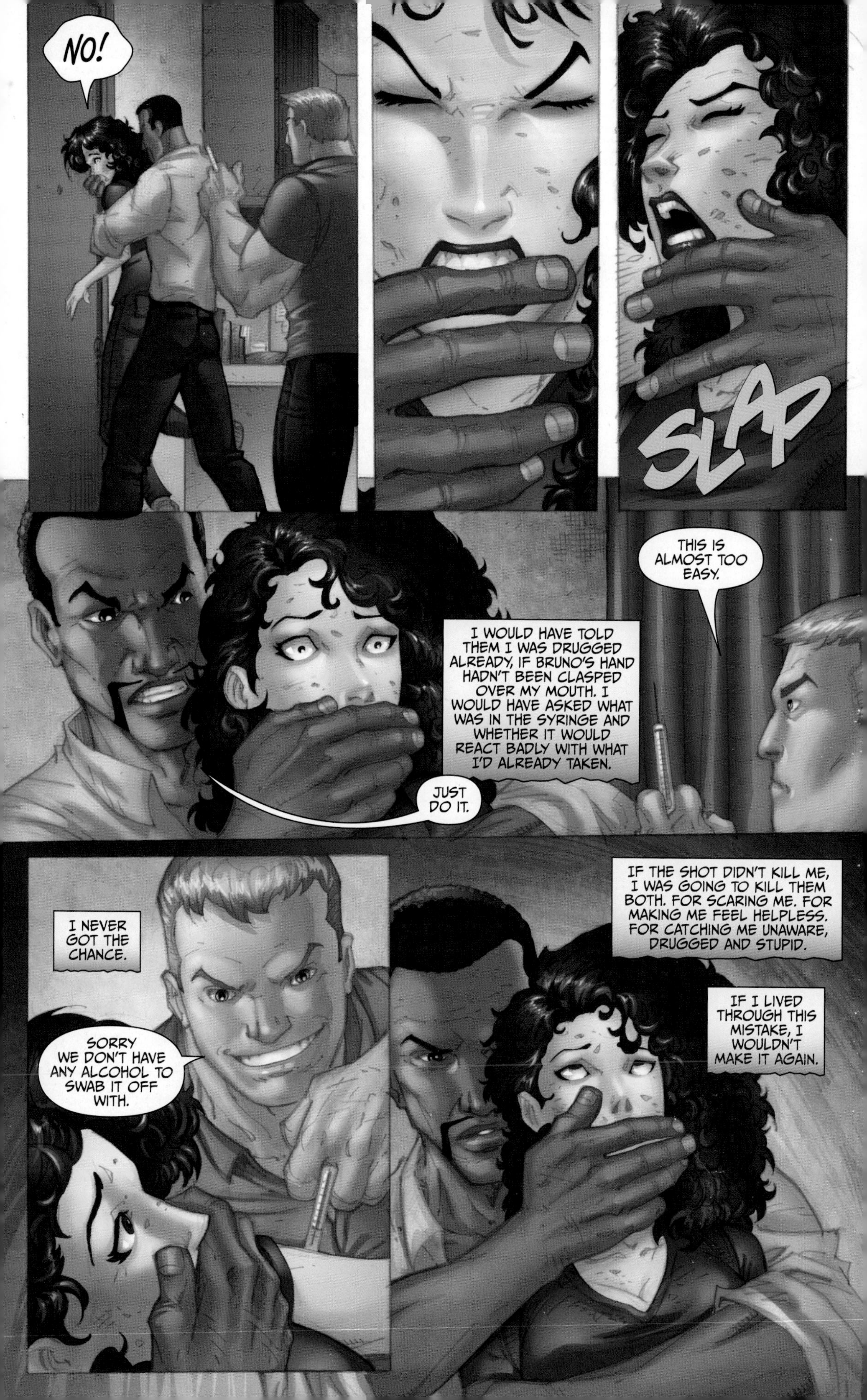
NO!
SLAP
THIS IS ALMOST TOO EASY.
I WOULD HAVE TOLD THEM I WAS DRUGGED ALREADY, IF BRUNO'S HAND HADN'T BEEN CLASPED OVER MY MOUTH. I WOULD HAVE ASKED WHAT WAS IN THE SYRINGE AND WHETHER IT WOULD REACT BADLY WITH WHAT I'D ALREADY TAKEN.
JUST DO IT.
I NEVER GOT THE CHANCE.
SORRY WE DON'T HAVE ANY ALCOHOL TO SWAB IT OFF WITH.
IF THE SHOT DIDN'T KILL ME, I WAS GOING TO KILL THEM BOTH. FOR SCARING ME. FOR MAKING ME FEEL HELPLESS. FOR CATCHING ME UNAWARE, DRUGGED AND STUPID.
IF I LIVED THROUGH THIS MISTAKE, I WOULDN'T MAKE IT AGAIN.

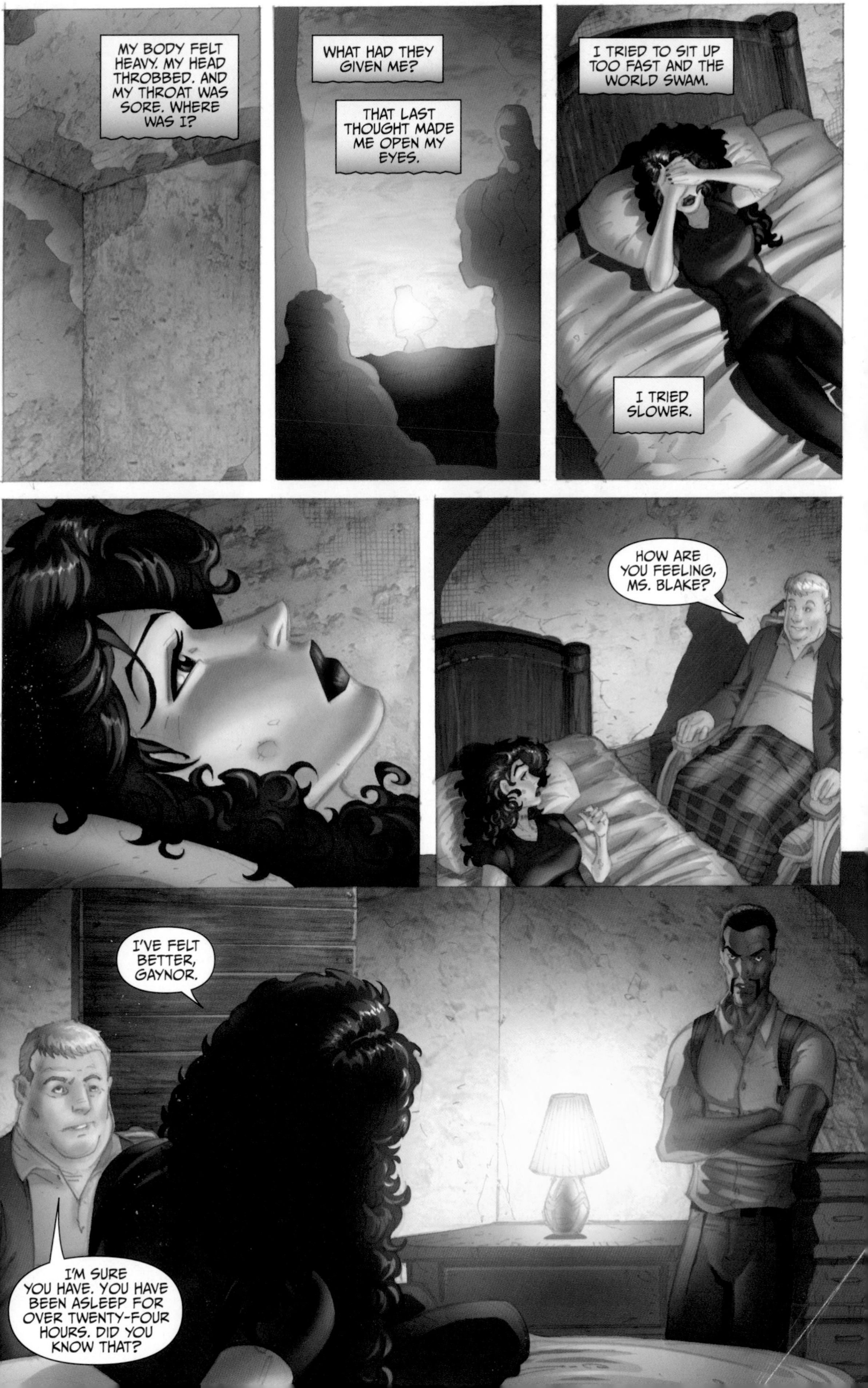

MY BODY FELT HEAVY. MY HEAD THROBBED. AND MY THROAT WAS SORE. WHERE WAS I?
WHAT HAD THEY GIVEN ME?
THAT LAST THOUGHT MADE ME OPEN MY EYES.
I TRIED TO SIT UP TOO FAST AND THE WORLD SWAM.
I TRIED SLOWER.
HOW ARE YOU FEELING, MS. BLAKE?
I'VE FELT BETTER, GAYNOR.
I'M SURE YOU HAVE. YOU HAVE BEEN ASLEEP FOR OVER TWENTY-FOUR HOURS. DID YOU KNOW THAT?

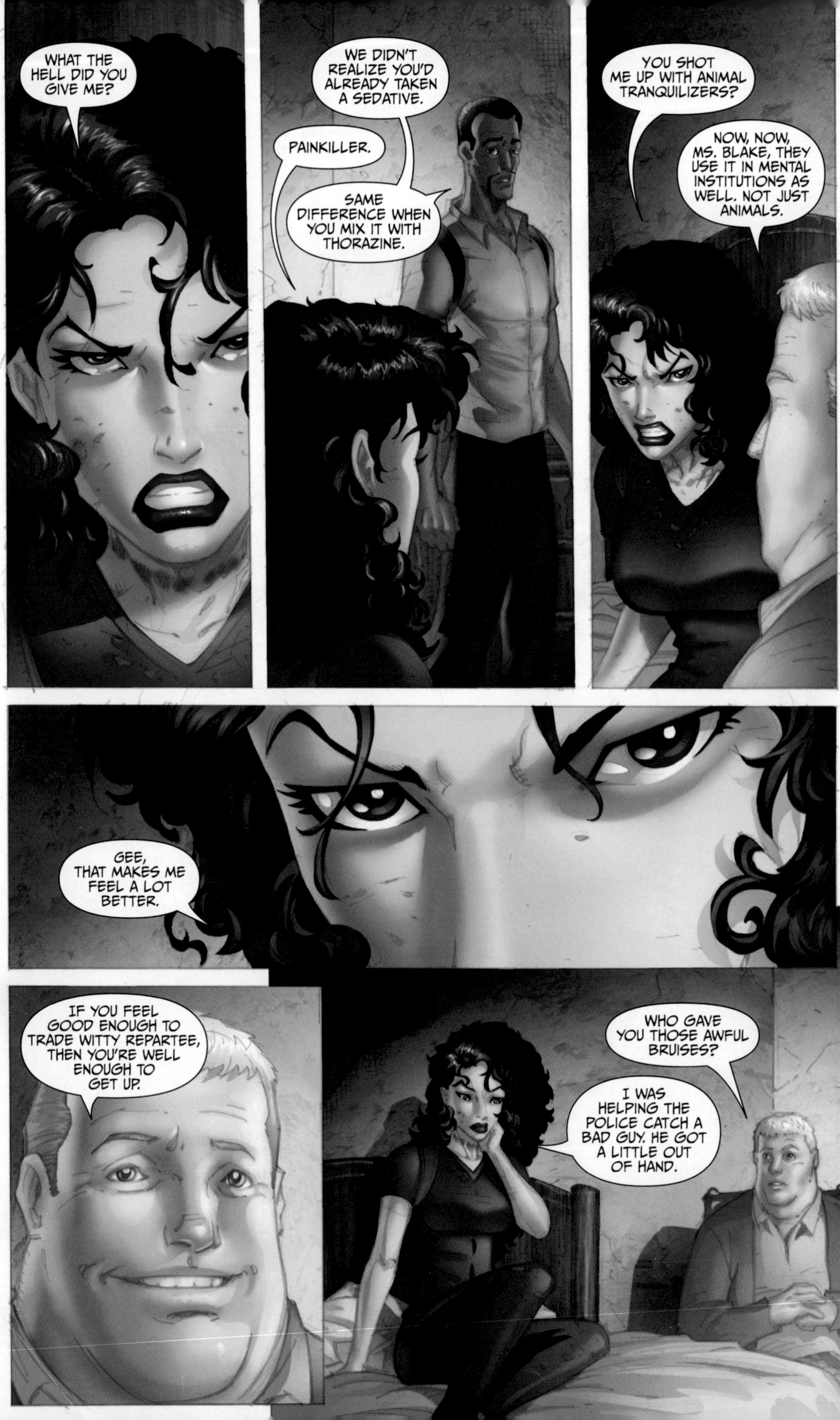
WHAT THE HELL DID YOU GIVE ME?
WE DIDN'T REALIZE YOU'D ALREADY TAKEN A SEDATIVE.
PAINKILLER.
SAME DIFFERENCE WHEN YOU MIX IT WITH THORAZINE.
YOU SHOT ME UP WITH ANIMAL TRANQUILIZERS?
NOW, NOW, MS. BLAKE, THEY USE IT IN MENTAL INSTITUTIONS AS WELL. NOT JUST ANIMALS.
GEE, THAT MAKES ME FEEL A LOT BETTER.
IF YOU FEEL GOOD ENOUGH TO TRADE WITTY REPARTEE, THEN YOU'RE WELL ENOUGH TO GET UP.
WHO GAVE YOU THOSE AWFUL BRUISES?
I WAS HELPING THE POLICE CATCH A BAD GUY. HE GOT A LITTLE OUT OF HAND.

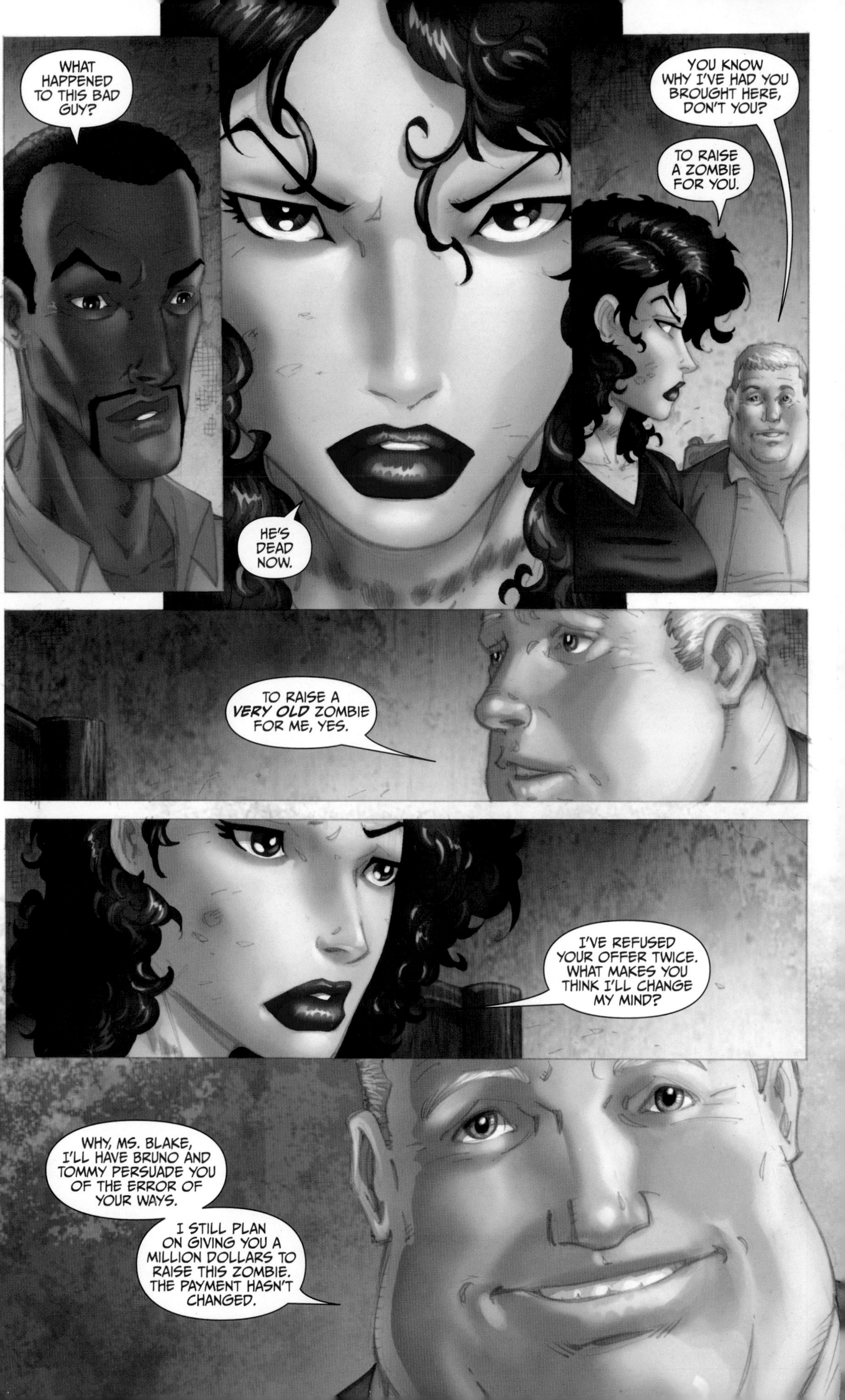
WHAT HAPPENED TO THIS BAD GUY?
HE'S DEAD NOW.
YOU KNOW WHY I'VE HAD YOU BROUGHT HERE, DON'T YOU?
TO RAISE A ZOMBIE FOR YOU.
TO RAISE A *VERY OLD* ZOMBIE FOR ME, YES.
I'VE REFUSED YOUR OFFER TWICE. WHAT MAKES YOU THINK I'LL CHANGE MY MIND?
WHY, MS. BLAKE, I'LL HAVE BRUNO AND TOMMY PERSUADE YOU OF THE ERROR OF YOUR WAYS.
I STILL PLAN ON GIVING YOU A MILLION DOLLARS TO RAISE THIS ZOMBIE. THE PAYMENT HASN'T CHANGED.

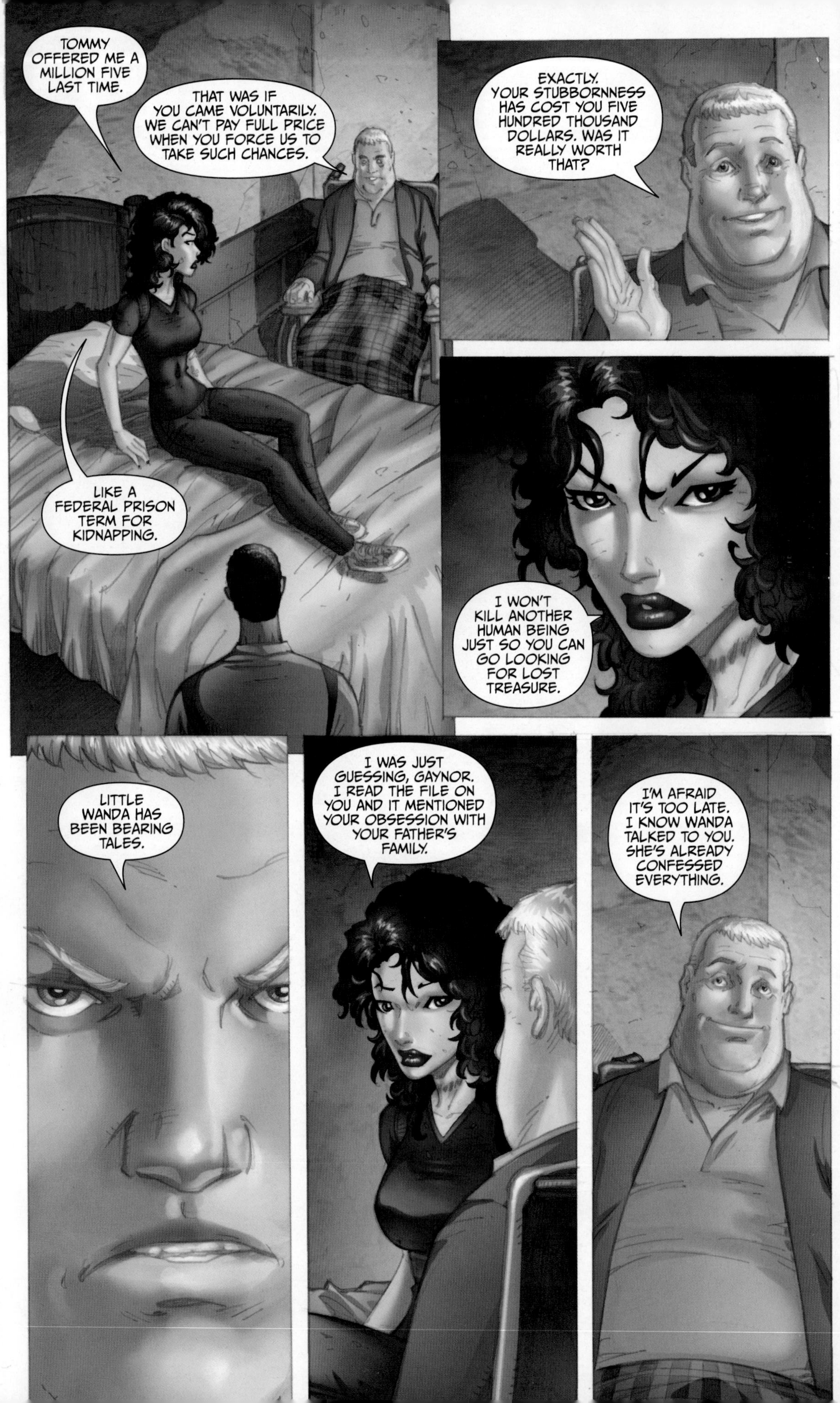
TOMMY OFFERED ME A MILLION FIVE LAST TIME.
THAT WAS IF YOU CAME VOLUNTARILY. WE CAN'T PAY FULL PRICE WHEN YOU FORCE US TO TAKE SUCH CHANCES.
LIKE A FEDERAL PRISON TERM FOR KIDNAPPING.
EXACTLY. YOUR STUBBORNNESS HAS COST YOU FIVE HUNDRED THOUSAND DOLLARS. WAS IT REALLY WORTH THAT?
I WON'T KILL ANOTHER HUMAN BEING JUST SO YOU CAN GO LOOKING FOR LOST TREASURE.
LITTLE WANDA HAS BEEN BEARING TALES.
I WAS JUST GUESSING, GAYNOR. I READ THE FILE ON YOU AND IT MENTIONED YOUR OBSESSION WITH YOUR FATHER'S FAMILY.
I'M AFRAID IT'S TOO LATE. I KNOW WANDA TALKED TO YOU. SHE'S ALREADY CONFESSED EVERYTHING.

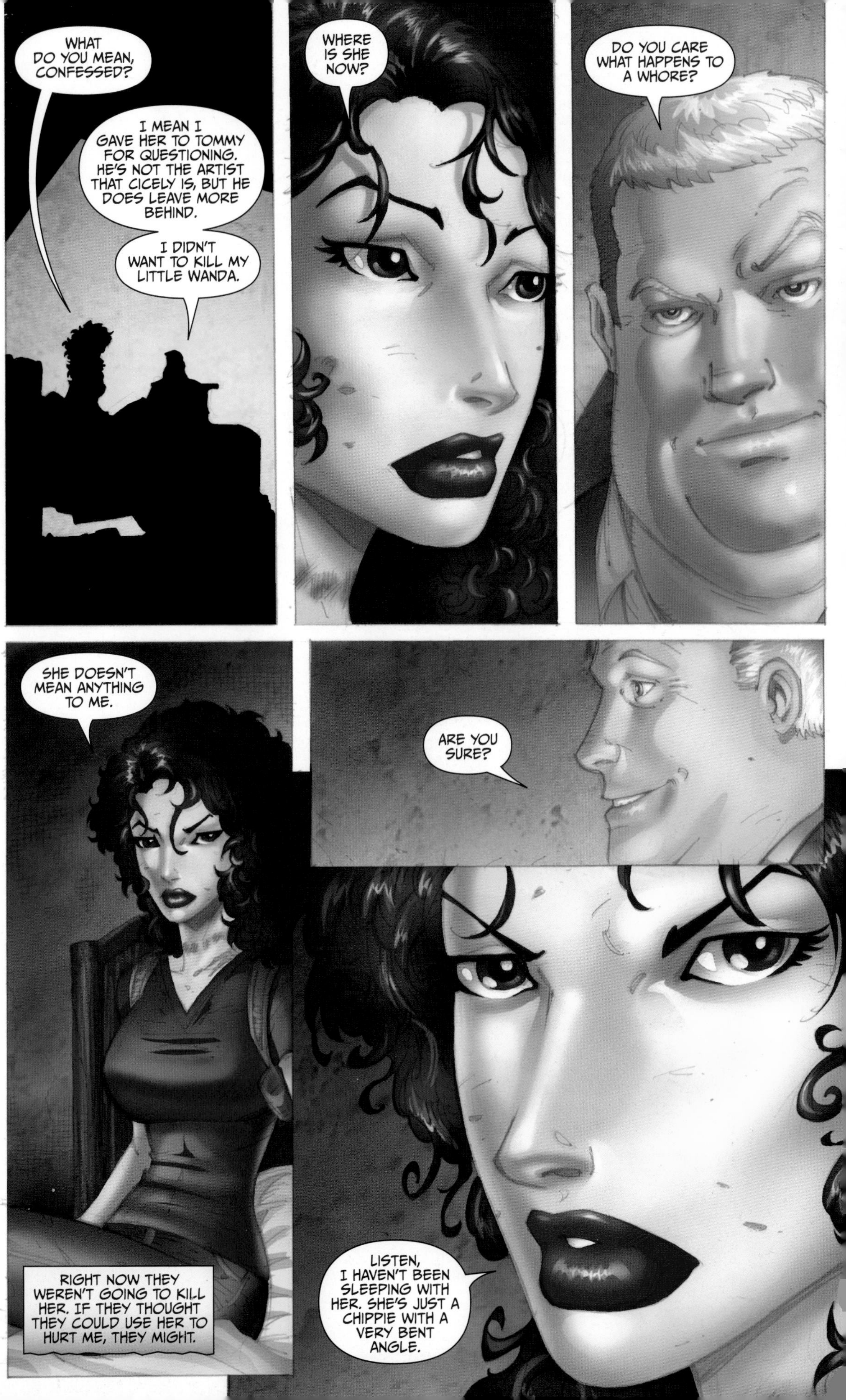
WHAT DO YOU MEAN, CONFESSED?
I MEAN I GAVE HER TO TOMMY FOR QUESTIONING. HE'S NOT THE ARTIST THAT CICELY IS, BUT HE DOES LEAVE MORE BEHIND.
I DIDN'T WANT TO KILL MY LITTLE WANDA.
WHERE IS SHE NOW?
DO YOU CARE WHAT HAPPENS TO A WHORE?
SHE DOESN'T MEAN ANYTHING TO ME.
RIGHT NOW THEY WEREN'T GOING TO KILL HER. IF THEY THOUGHT THEY COULD USE HER TO HURT ME, THEY MIGHT.
ARE YOU SURE?
LISTEN, I HAVEN'T BEEN SLEEPING WITH HER. SHE'S JUST A CHIPPIE WITH A VERY BENT ANGLE.

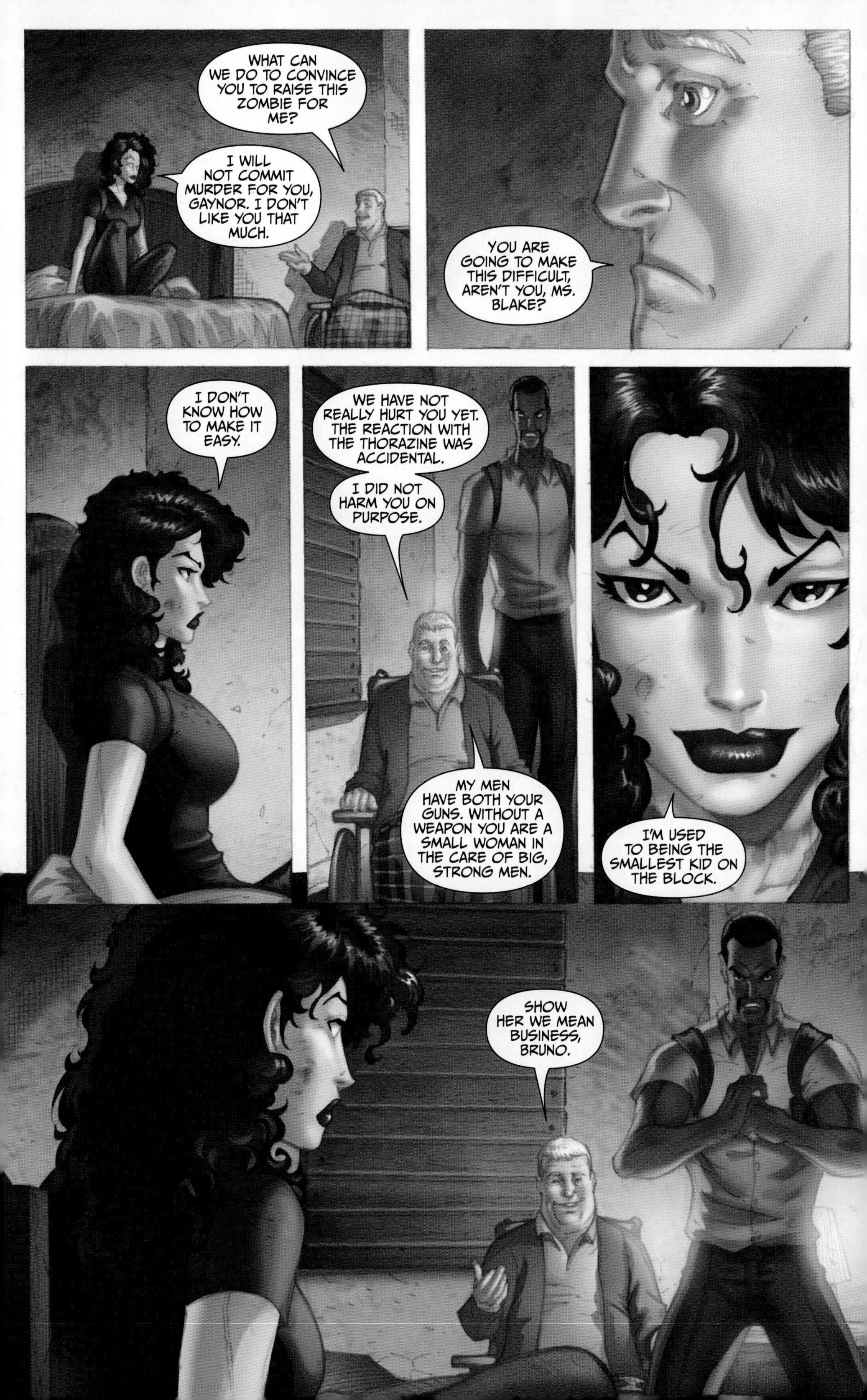
WHAT CAN WE DO TO CONVINCE YOU TO RAISE THIS ZOMBIE FOR ME?
I WILL NOT COMMIT MURDER FOR YOU, GAYNOR. I DON'T LIKE YOU THAT MUCH.
YOU ARE GOING TO MAKE THIS DIFFICULT, AREN'T YOU, MS. BLAKE?
I DON'T KNOW HOW TO MAKE IT EASY.
WE HAVE NOT REALLY HURT YOU YET. THE REACTION WITH THE THORAZINE WAS ACCIDENTAL.
I DID NOT HARM YOU ON PURPOSE.
MY MEN HAVE BOTH YOUR GUNS. WITHOUT A WEAPON YOU ARE A SMALL WOMAN IN THE CARE OF BIG, STRONG MEN.
I'M USED TO BEING THE SMALLEST KID ON THE BLOCK.
SHOW HER WE MEAN BUSINESS, BRUNO.

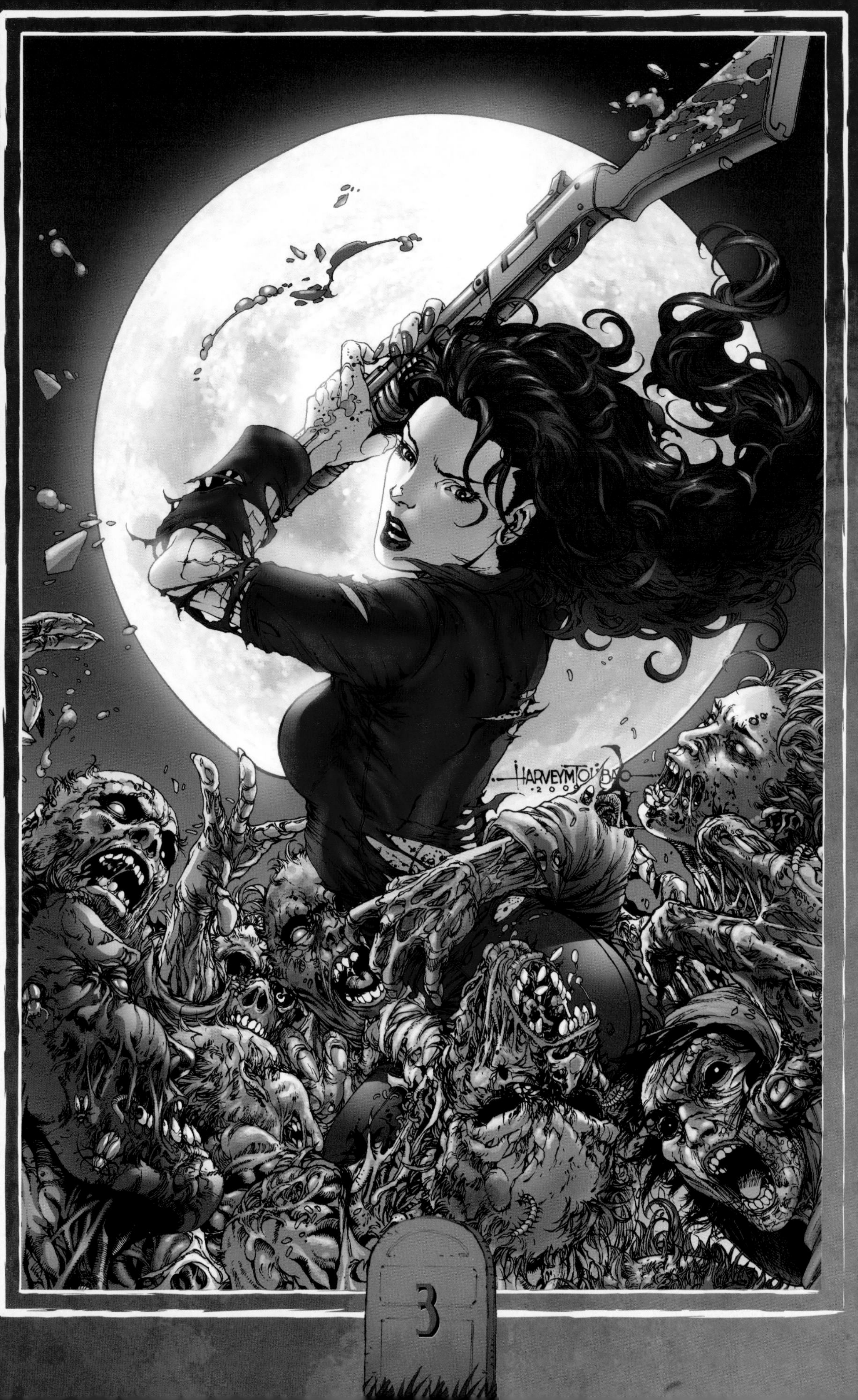
3

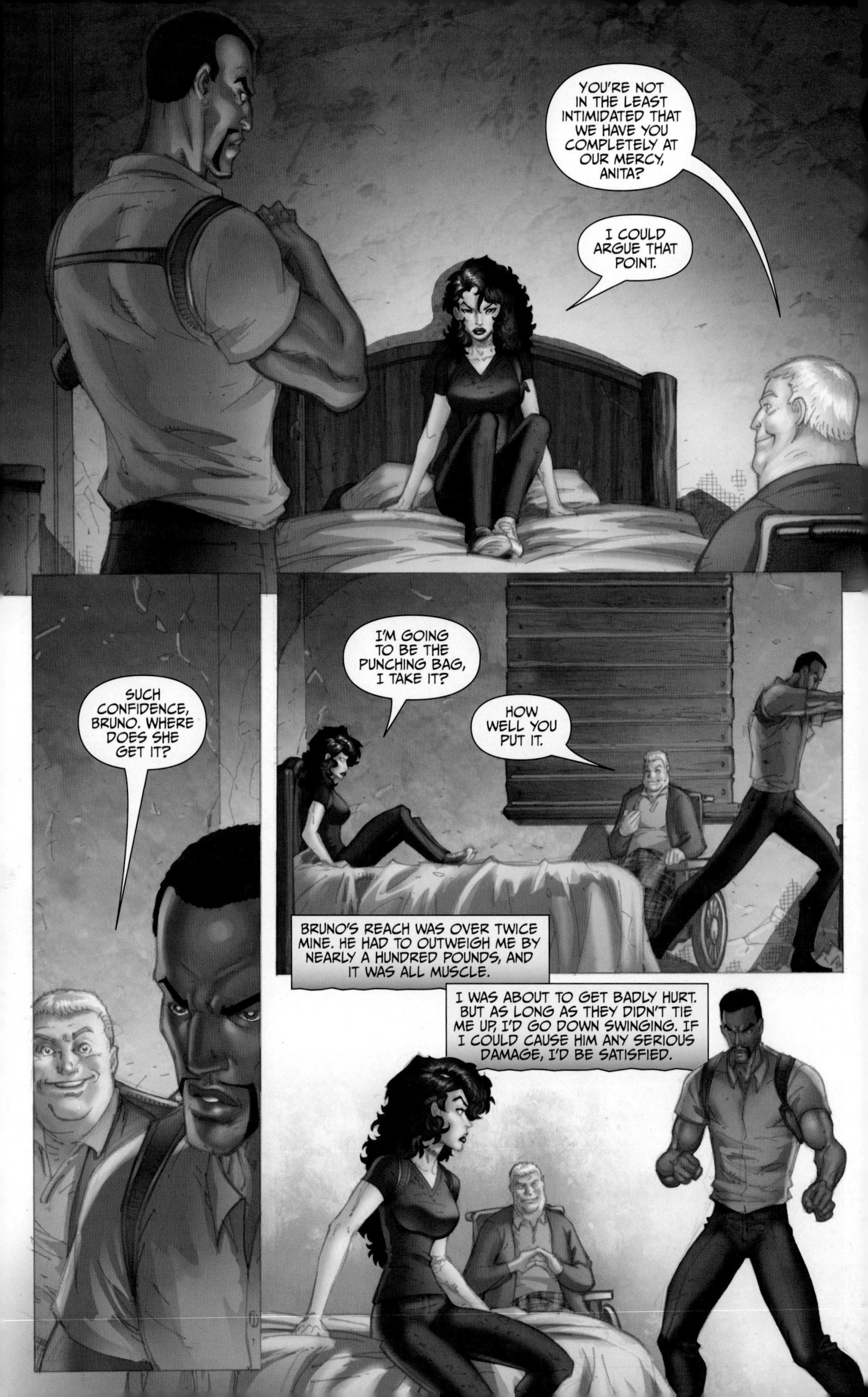
YOU'RE NOT IN THE LEAST INTIMIDATED THAT WE HAVE YOU COMPLETELY AT OUR MERCY, ANITA?
I COULD ARGUE THAT POINT.
SUCH CONFIDENCE, BRUNO. WHERE DOES SHE GET IT?
I'M GOING TO BE THE PUNCHING BAG, I TAKE IT?
HOW WELL YOU PUT IT.
BRUNO'S REACH WAS OVER TWICE MINE. HE HAD TO OUTWEIGH ME BY NEARLY A HUNDRED POUNDS, AND IT WAS ALL MUSCLE.
I WAS ABOUT TO GET BADLY HURT. BUT AS LONG AS THEY DIDN'T TIE ME UP, I'D GO DOWN SWINGING. IF I COULD CAUSE HIM ANY SERIOUS DAMAGE, I'D BE SATISFIED.

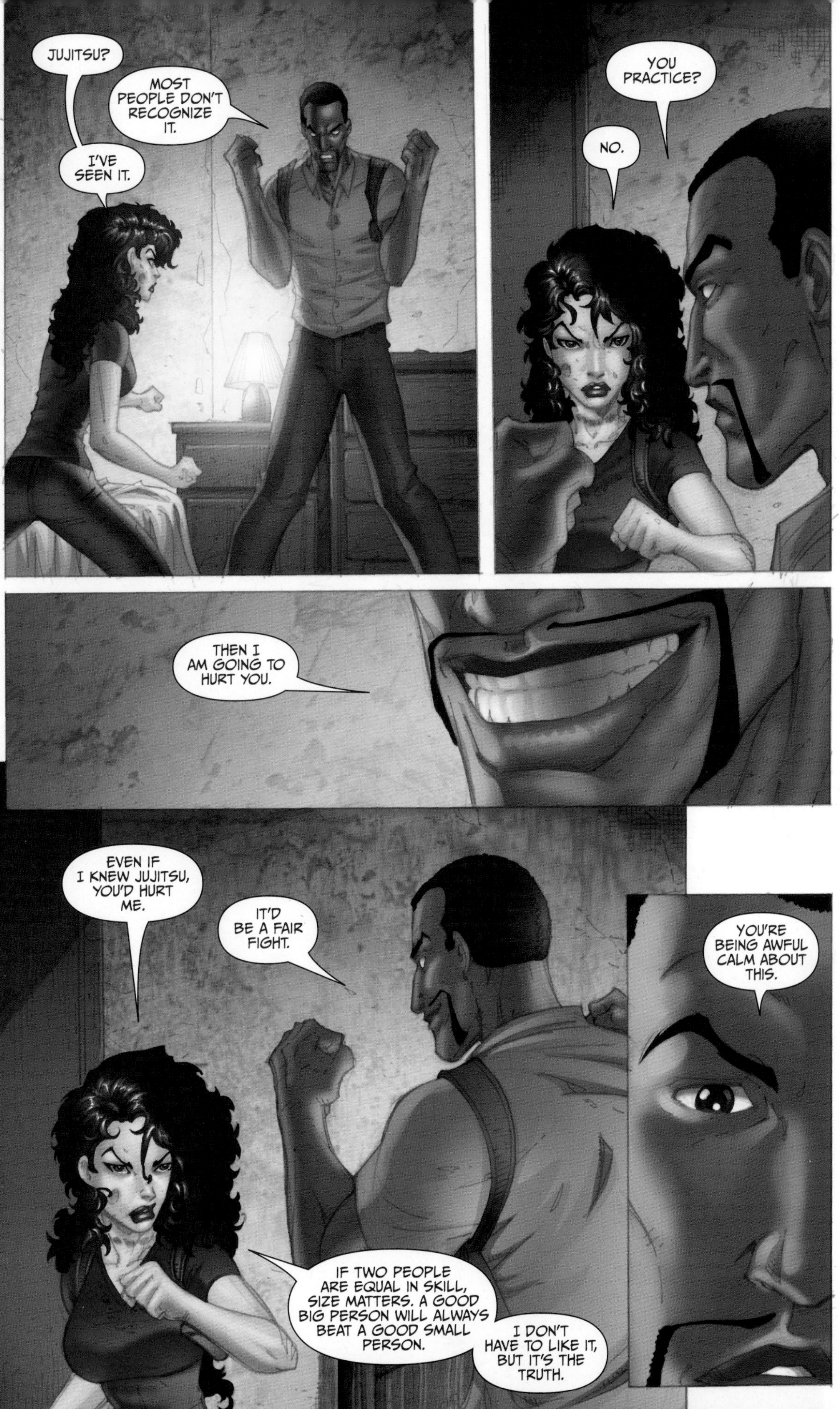
JUJITSU?
MOST PEOPLE DON'T RECOGNIZE IT.
I'VE SEEN IT.
YOU PRACTICE?
NO.
THEN I AM GOING TO HURT YOU.
EVEN IF I KNEW JUJITSU, YOU'D HURT ME.
IT'D BE A FAIR FIGHT.
IF TWO PEOPLE ARE EQUAL IN SKILL, SIZE MATTERS. A GOOD BIG PERSON WILL ALWAYS BEAT A GOOD SMALL PERSON.
I DON'T HAVE TO LIKE IT, BUT IT'S THE TRUTH.
YOU'RE BEING AWFUL CALM ABOUT THIS.

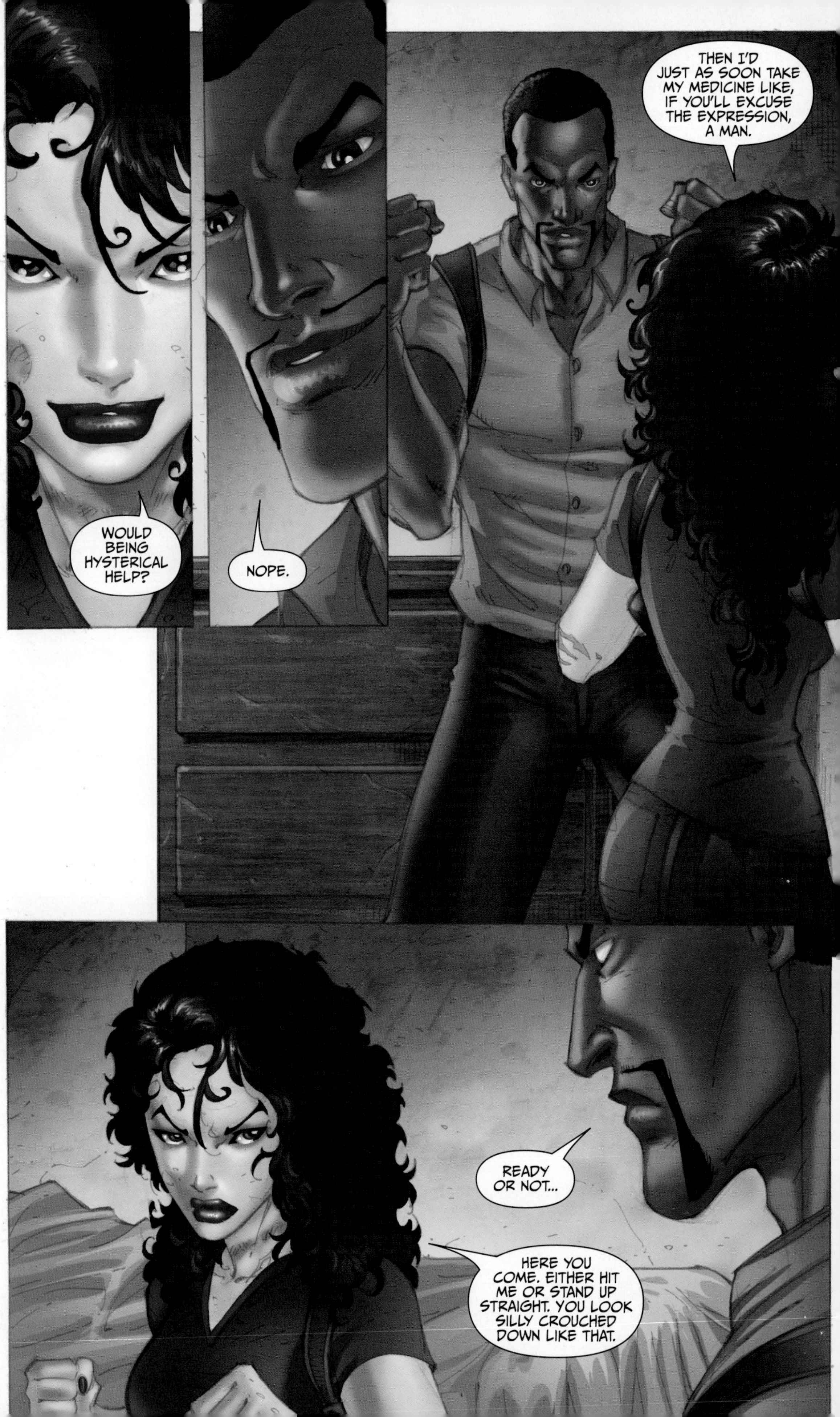
WOULD BEING HYSTERICAL HELP?
NOPE.
THEN I'D JUST AS SOON TAKE MY MEDICINE LIKE, IF YOU'LL EXCUSE THE EXPRESSION, A MAN.
READY OR NOT...
HERE YOU COME. EITHER HIT ME OR STAND UP STRAIGHT. YOU LOOK SILLY CROUCHED DOWN LIKE THAT.

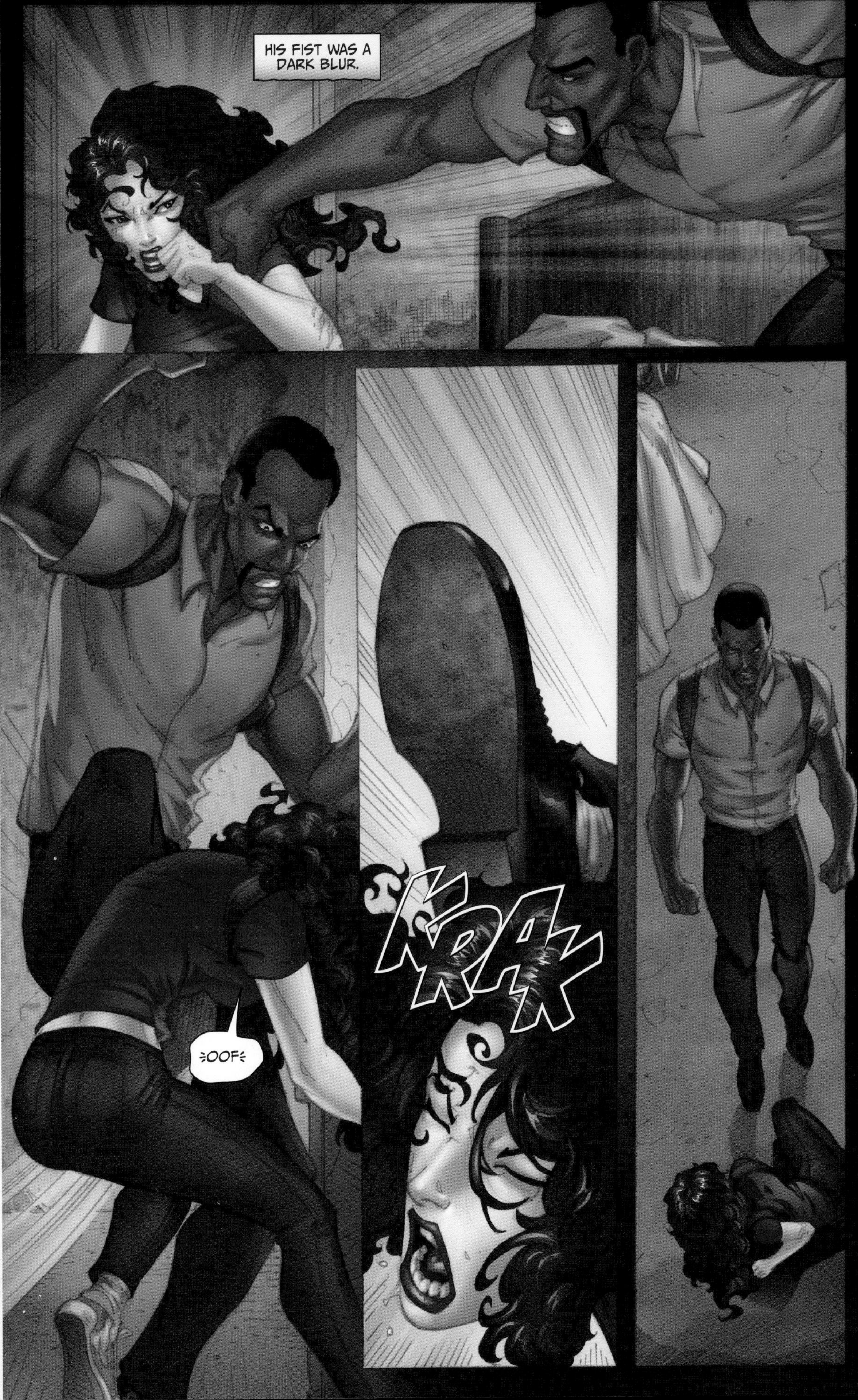
HIS FIST WAS A DARK BLUR.
OOF
KRAK

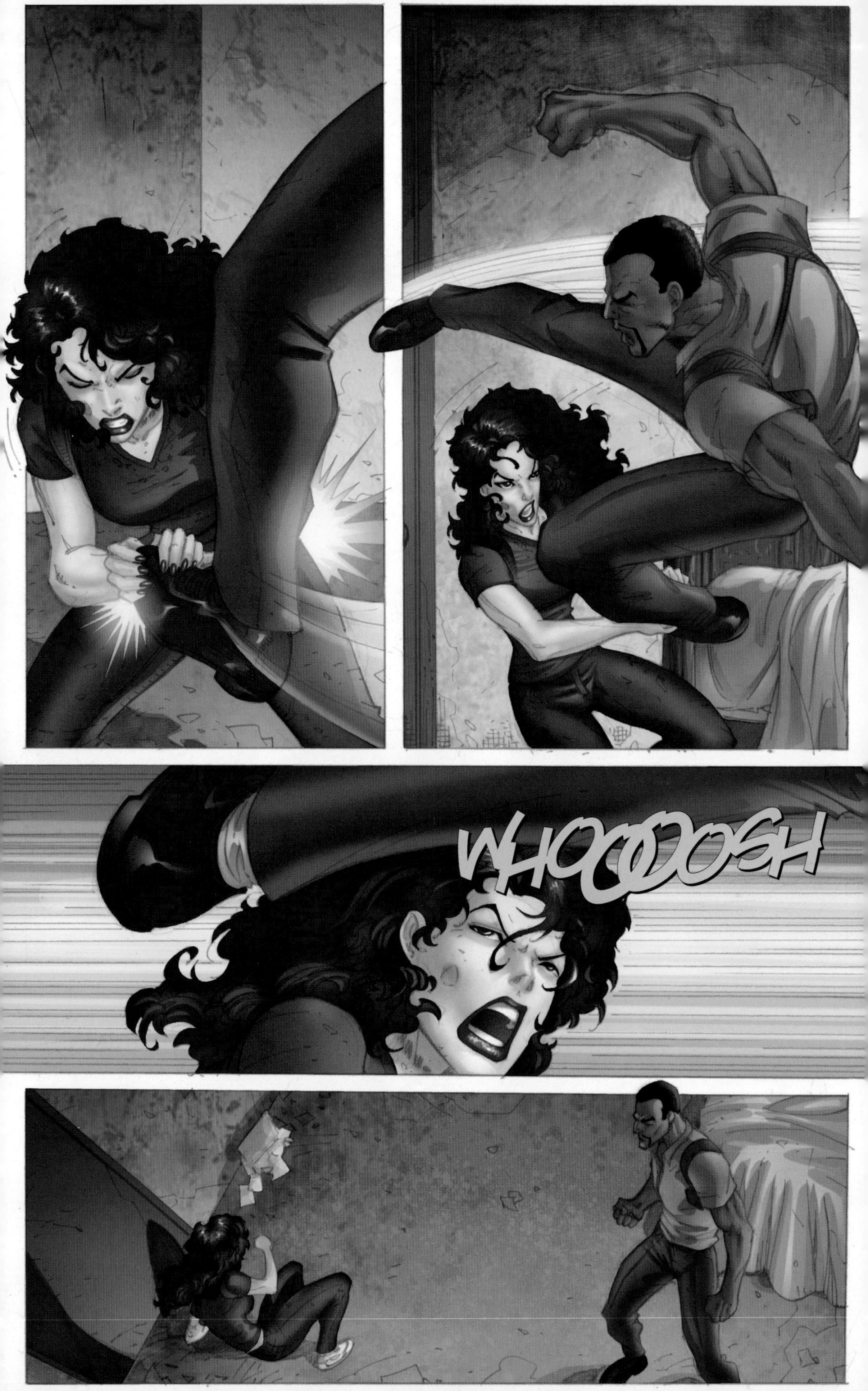
WHOOOOSH

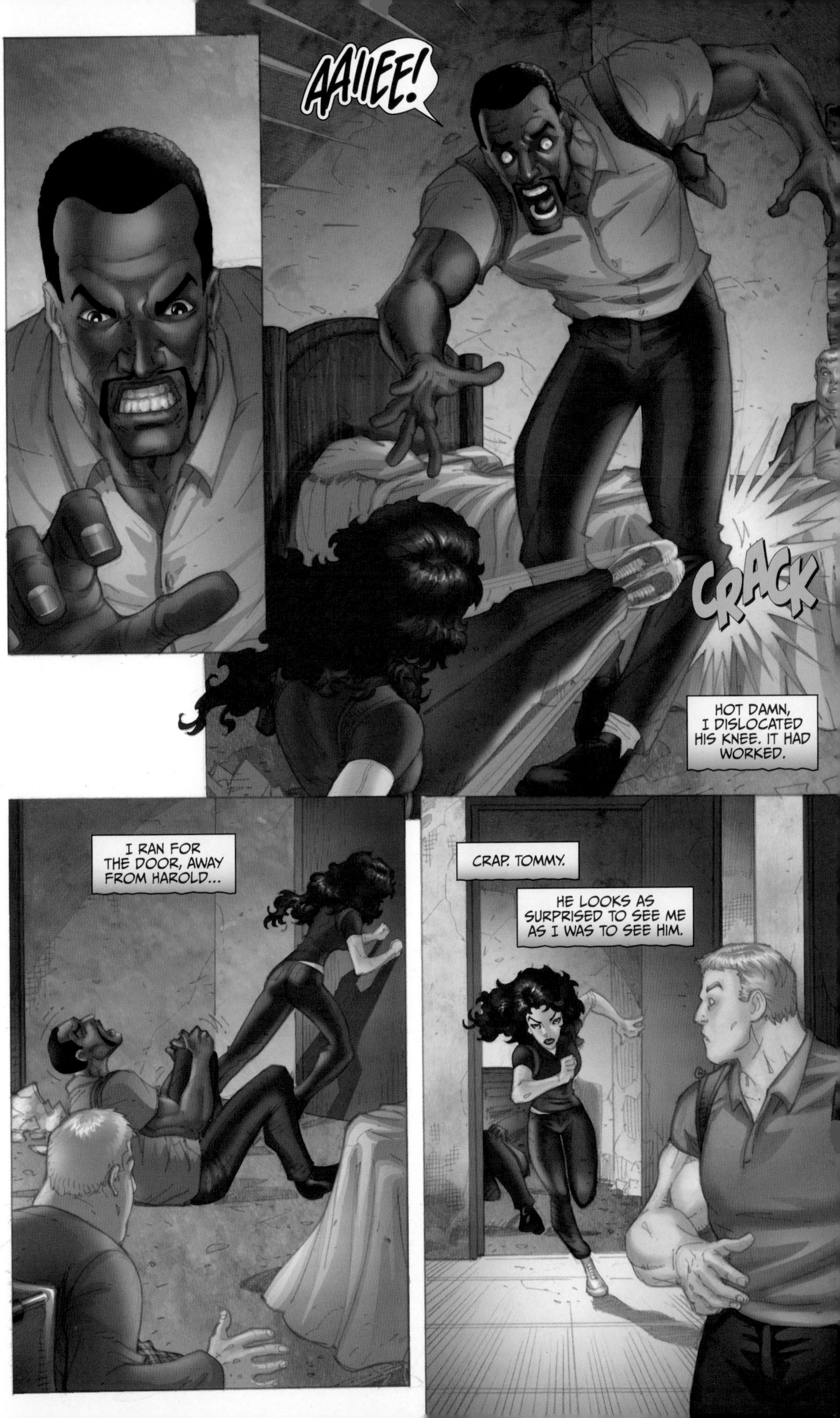
AAIIEE!
CRACK
HOT DAMN, I DISLOCATED HIS KNEE. IT HAD WORKED.
I RAN FOR THE DOOR, AWAY FROM HAROLD...
CRAP. TOMMY.
HE LOOKS AS SURPRISED TO SEE ME AS I WAS TO SEE HIM.

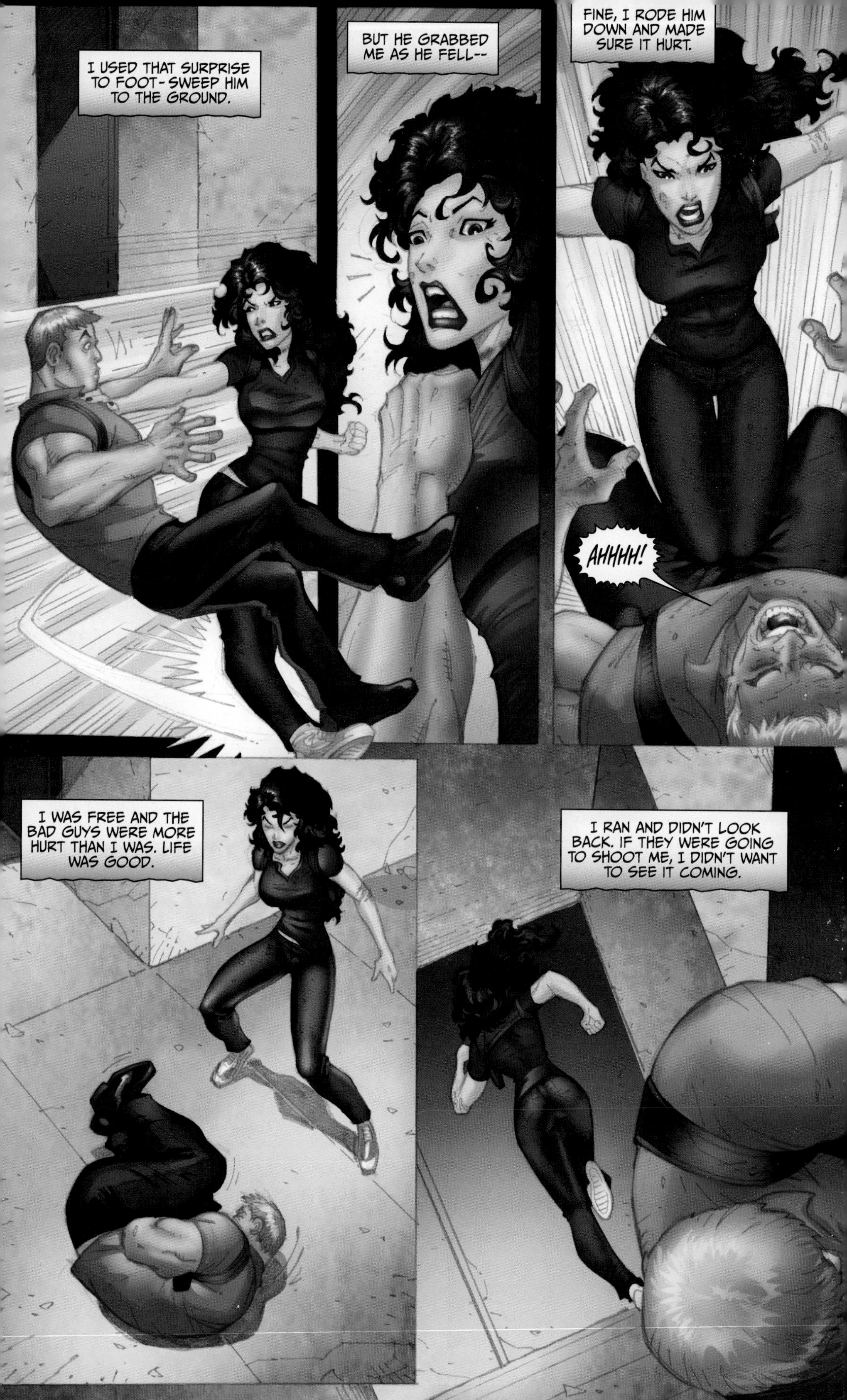
I USED THAT SURPRISE TO FOOT-SWEEP HIM TO THE GROUND.
BUT HE GRABBED ME AS HE FELL--
FINE, I RODE HIM DOWN AND MADE SURE IT HURT.
AHHHH!
I WAS FREE AND THE BAD GUYS WERE MORE HURT THAN I WAS. LIFE WAS GOOD.
I RAN AND DIDN'T LOOK BACK. IF THEY WERE GOING TO SHOOT ME, I DIDN'T WANT TO SEE IT COMING.

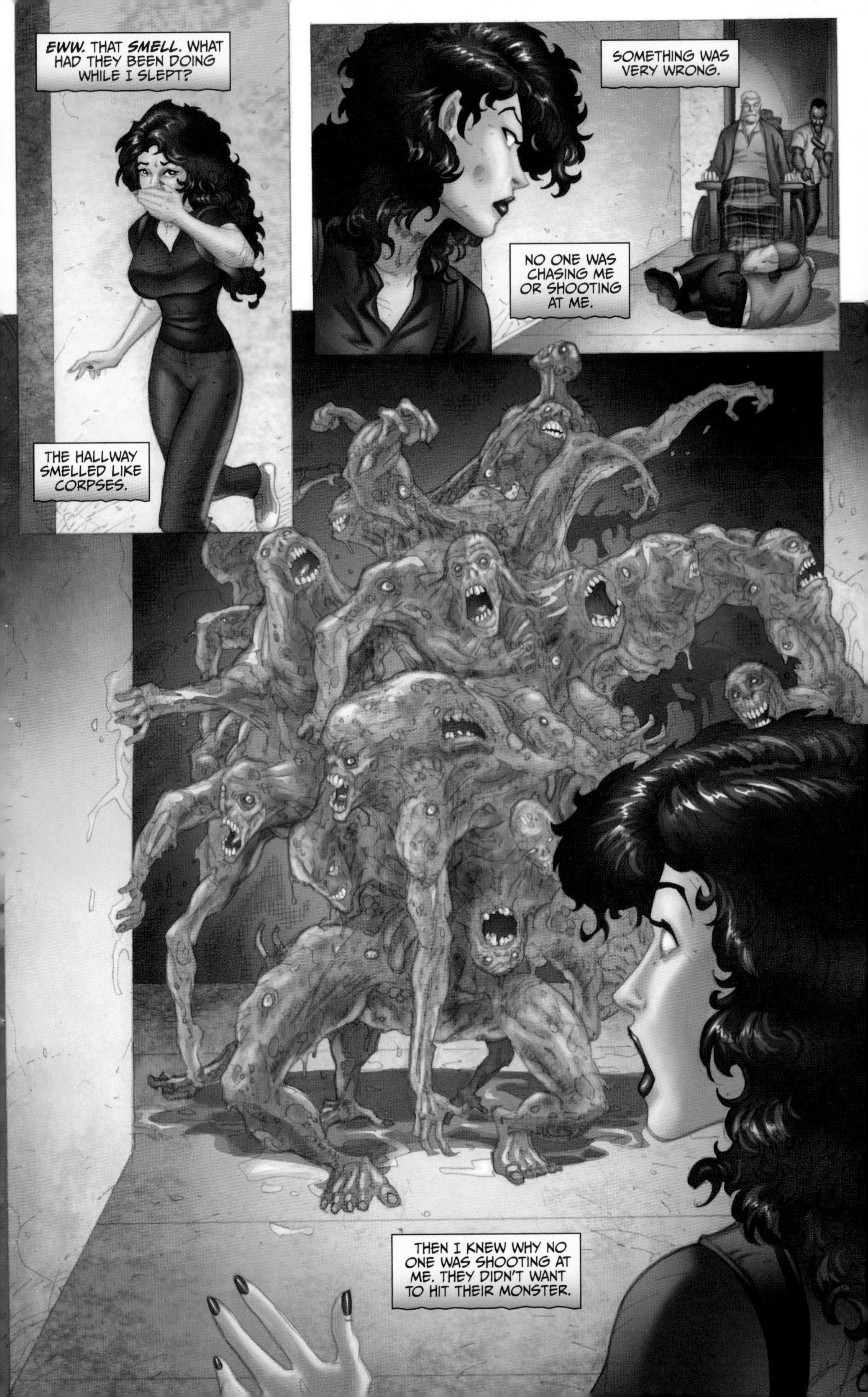
EWW. THAT SMELL. WHAT HAD THEY BEEN DOING WHILE I SLEPT?
THE HALLWAY SMELLED LIKE CORPSES.
SOMETHING WAS VERY WRONG.
NO ONE WAS CHASING ME OR SHOOTING AT ME.
THEN I KNEW WHY NO ONE WAS SHOOTING AT ME. THEY DIDN'T WANT TO HIT THEIR MONSTER.

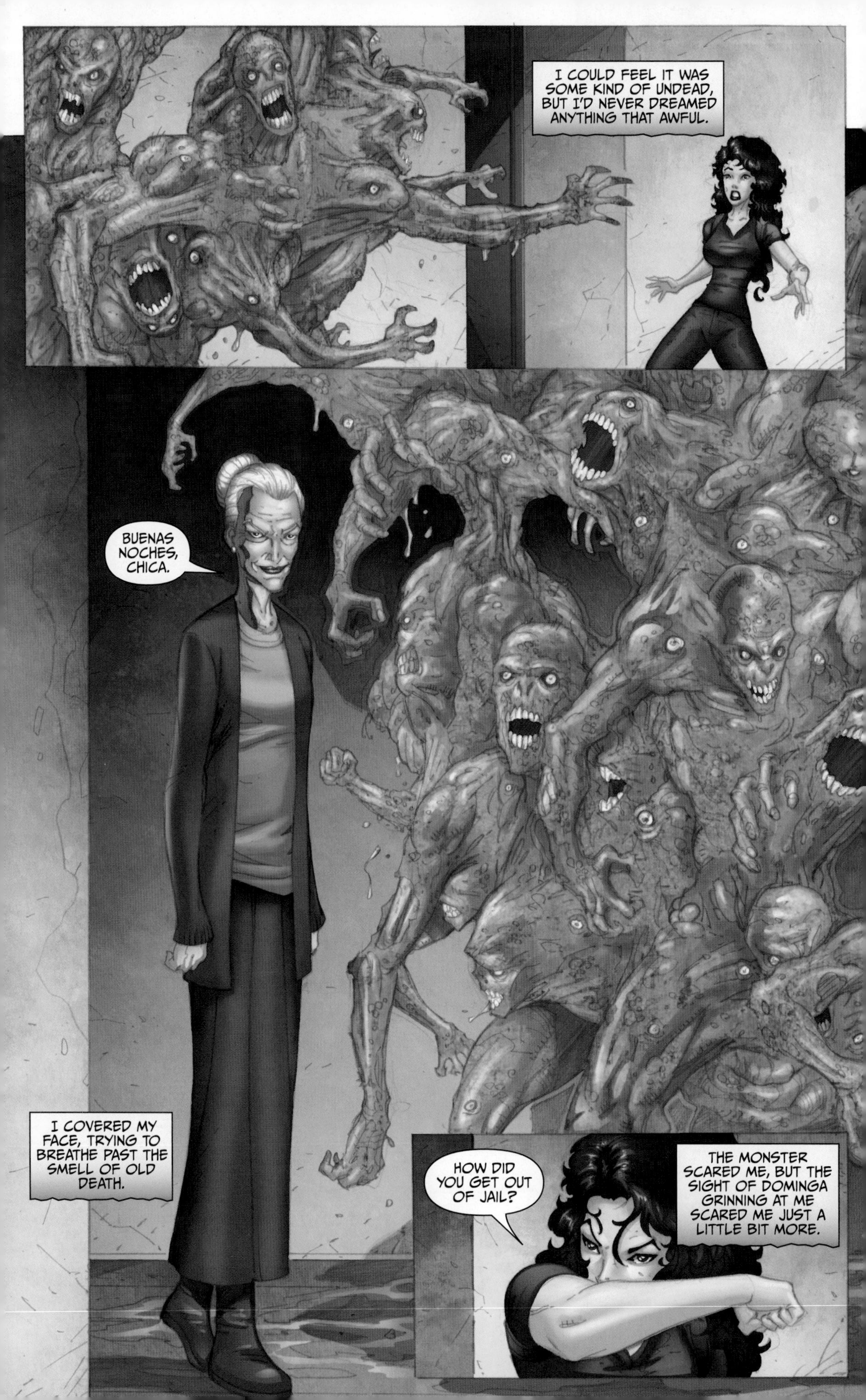
I COULD FEEL IT WAS SOME KIND OF UNDEAD, BUT I'D NEVER DREAMED ANYTHING THAT AWFUL.
BUENAS NOCHES, CHICA.
I COVERED MY FACE, TRYING TO BREATHE PAST THE SMELL OF OLD DEATH.
HOW DID YOU GET OUT OF JAIL?
THE MONSTER SCARED ME, BUT THE SIGHT OF DOMINGA GRINNING AT ME SCARED ME JUST A LITTLE BIT MORE.

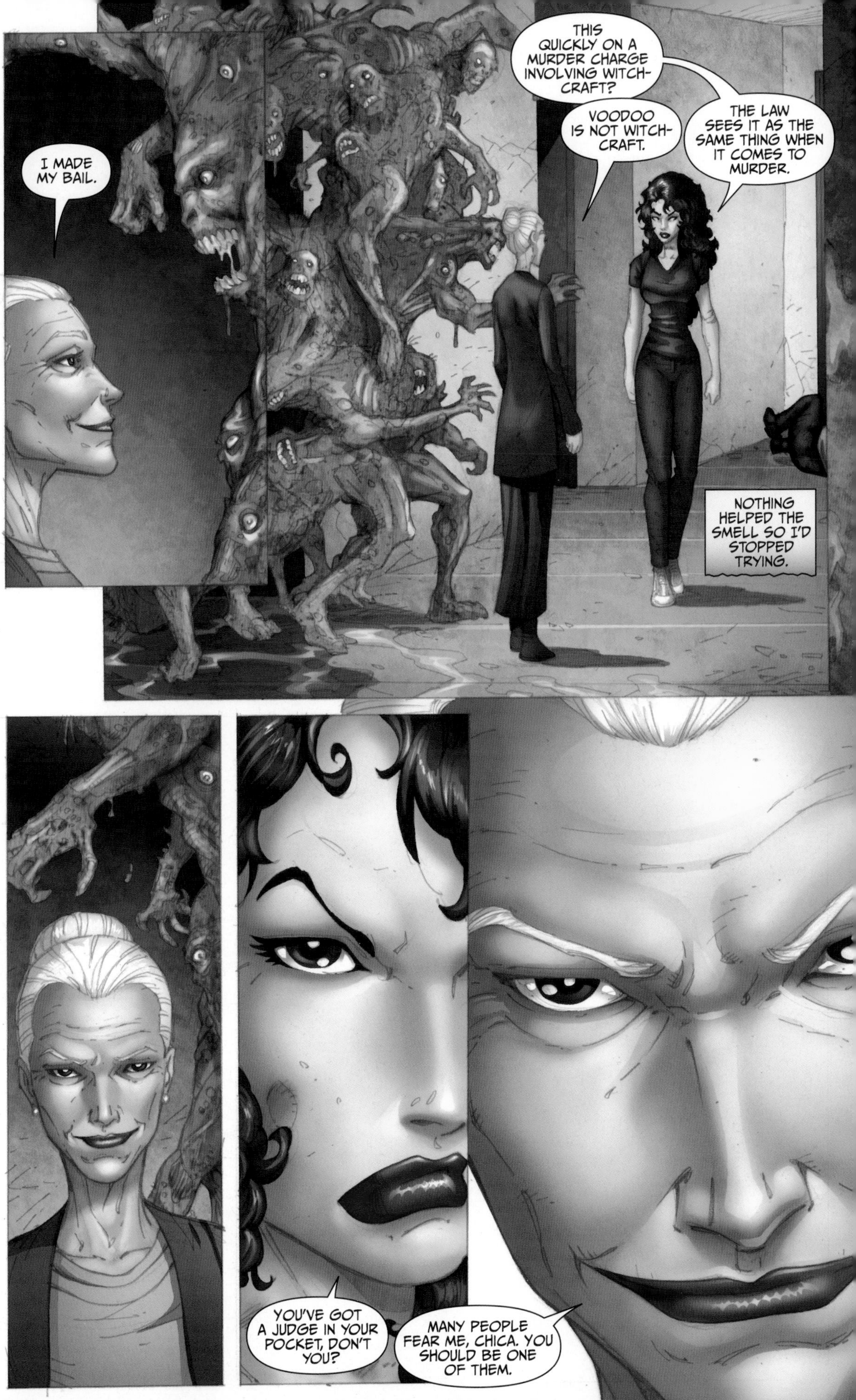
I MADE MY BAIL.
THIS QUICKLY ON A MURDER CHARGE INVOLVING WITCH-CRAFT?
VOODOO IS NOT WITCH-CRAFT.
THE LAW SEES IT AS THE SAME THING WHEN IT COMES TO MURDER.
NOTHING HELPED THE SMELL SO I'D STOPPED TRYING.
YOU'VE GOT A JUDGE IN YOUR POCKET, DON'T YOU?
MANY PEOPLE FEAR ME, CHICA. YOU SHOULD BE ONE OF THEM.

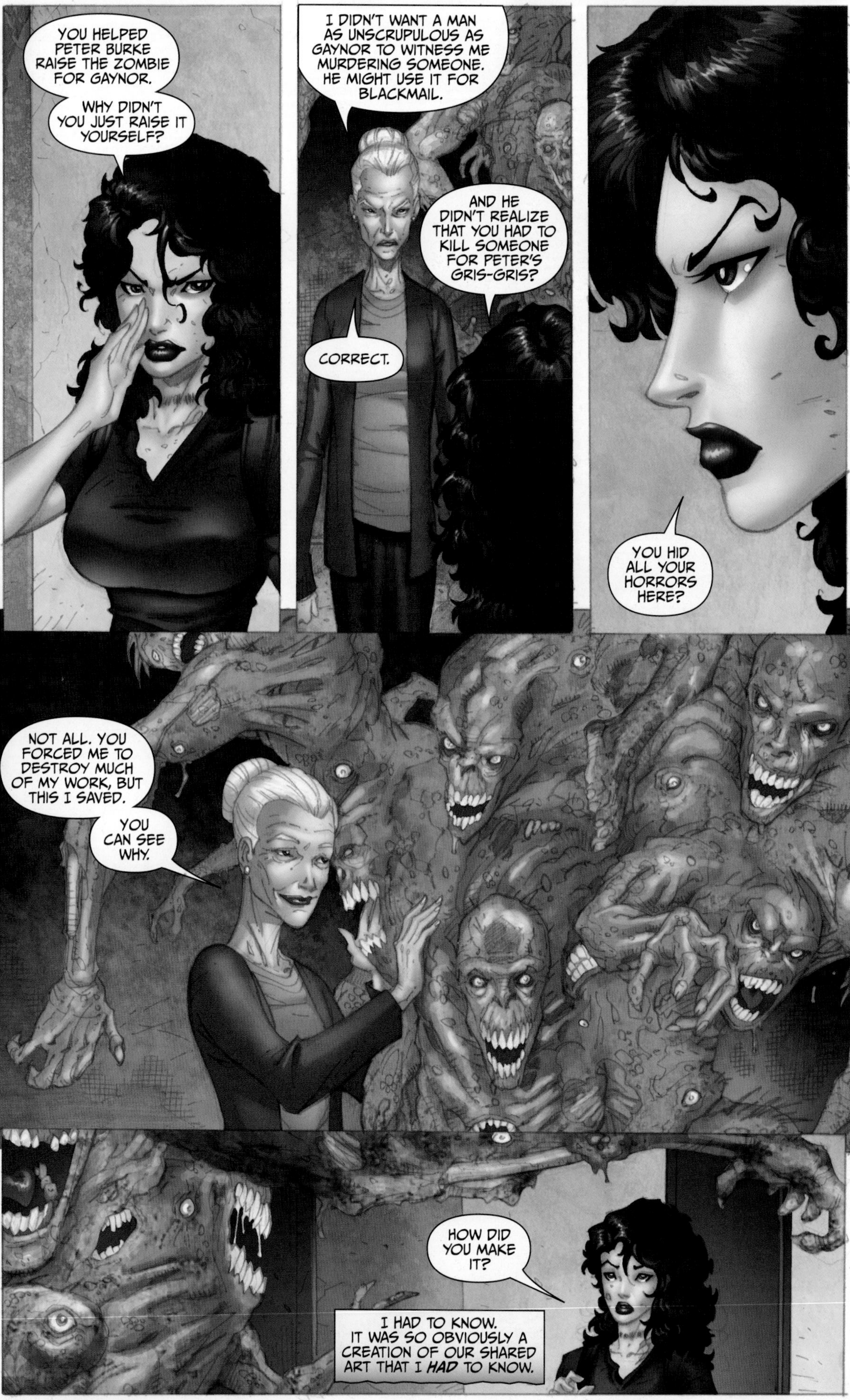

YOU HELPED PETER BURKE RAISE THE ZOMBIE FOR GAYNOR.
WHY DIDN'T YOU JUST RAISE IT YOURSELF?
I DIDN'T WANT A MAN AS UNSCRUPULOUS AS GAYNOR TO WITNESS ME MURDERING SOMEONE. HE MIGHT USE IT FOR BLACKMAIL.
AND HE DIDN'T REALIZE THAT YOU HAD TO KILL SOMEONE FOR PETER'S GRIS-GRIS?
CORRECT.
YOU HID ALL YOUR HORRORS HERE?
NOT ALL. YOU FORCED ME TO DESTROY MUCH OF MY WORK, BUT THIS I SAVED.
YOU CAN SEE WHY.
HOW DID YOU MAKE IT?
I HAD TO KNOW. IT WAS SO OBVIOUSLY A CREATION OF OUR SHARED ART THAT I *HAD* TO KNOW.

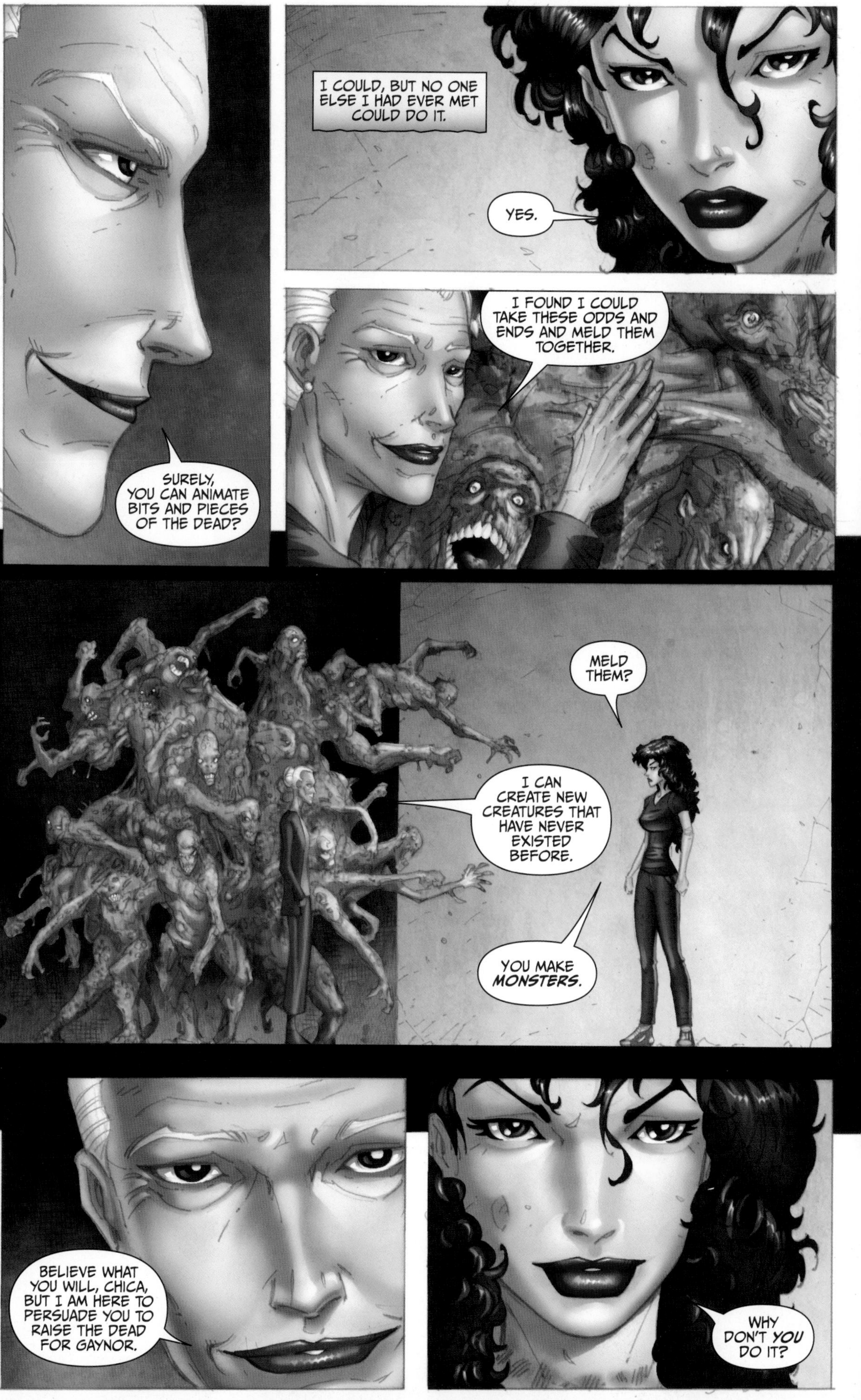
SURELY, YOU CAN ANIMATE BITS AND PIECES OF THE DEAD?
I COULD, BUT NO ONE ELSE I HAD EVER MET COULD DO IT.
YES.
I FOUND I COULD TAKE THESE ODDS AND ENDS AND MELD THEM TOGETHER.
MELD THEM?
I CAN CREATE NEW CREATURES THAT HAVE NEVER EXISTED BEFORE.
YOU MAKE *MONSTERS*.
BELIEVE WHAT YOU WILL, CHICA, BUT I AM HERE TO PERSUADE YOU TO RAISE THE DEAD FOR GAYNOR.
WHY DON'T *YOU* DO IT?

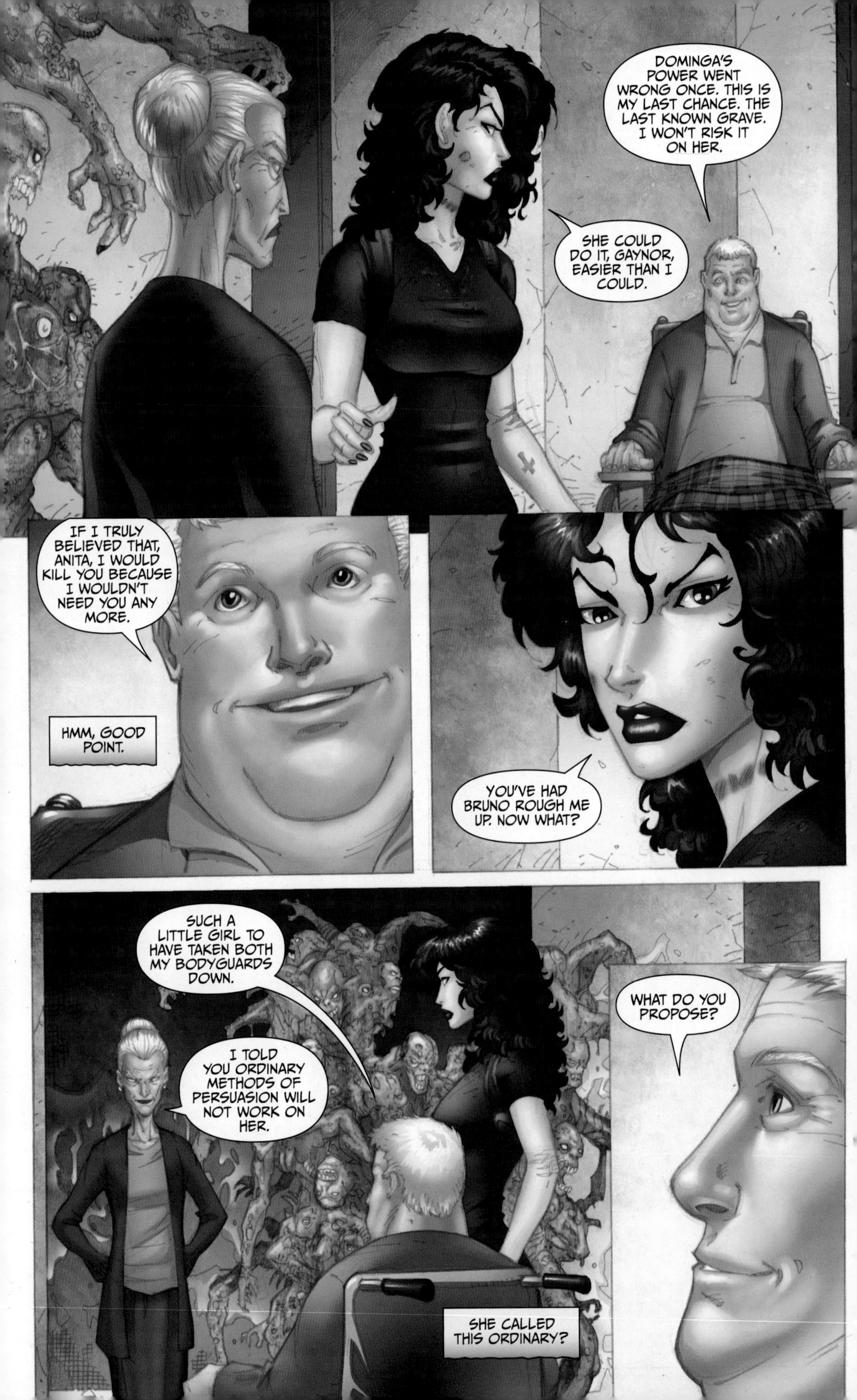
DOMINGA'S POWER WENT WRONG ONCE. THIS IS MY LAST CHANCE. THE LAST KNOWN GRAVE. I WON'T RISK IT ON HER.
SHE COULD DO IT, GAYNOR, EASIER THAN I COULD.
IF I TRULY BELIEVED THAT, ANITA, I WOULD KILL YOU BECAUSE I WOULDN'T NEED YOU ANY MORE.
HMM, GOOD POINT.
YOU'VE HAD BRUNO ROUGH ME UP. NOW WHAT?
SUCH A LITTLE GIRL TO HAVE TAKEN BOTH MY BODYGUARDS DOWN.
I TOLD YOU ORDINARY METHODS OF PERSUASION WILL NOT WORK ON HER.
WHAT DO YOU PROPOSE?
SHE CALLED THIS ORDINARY?

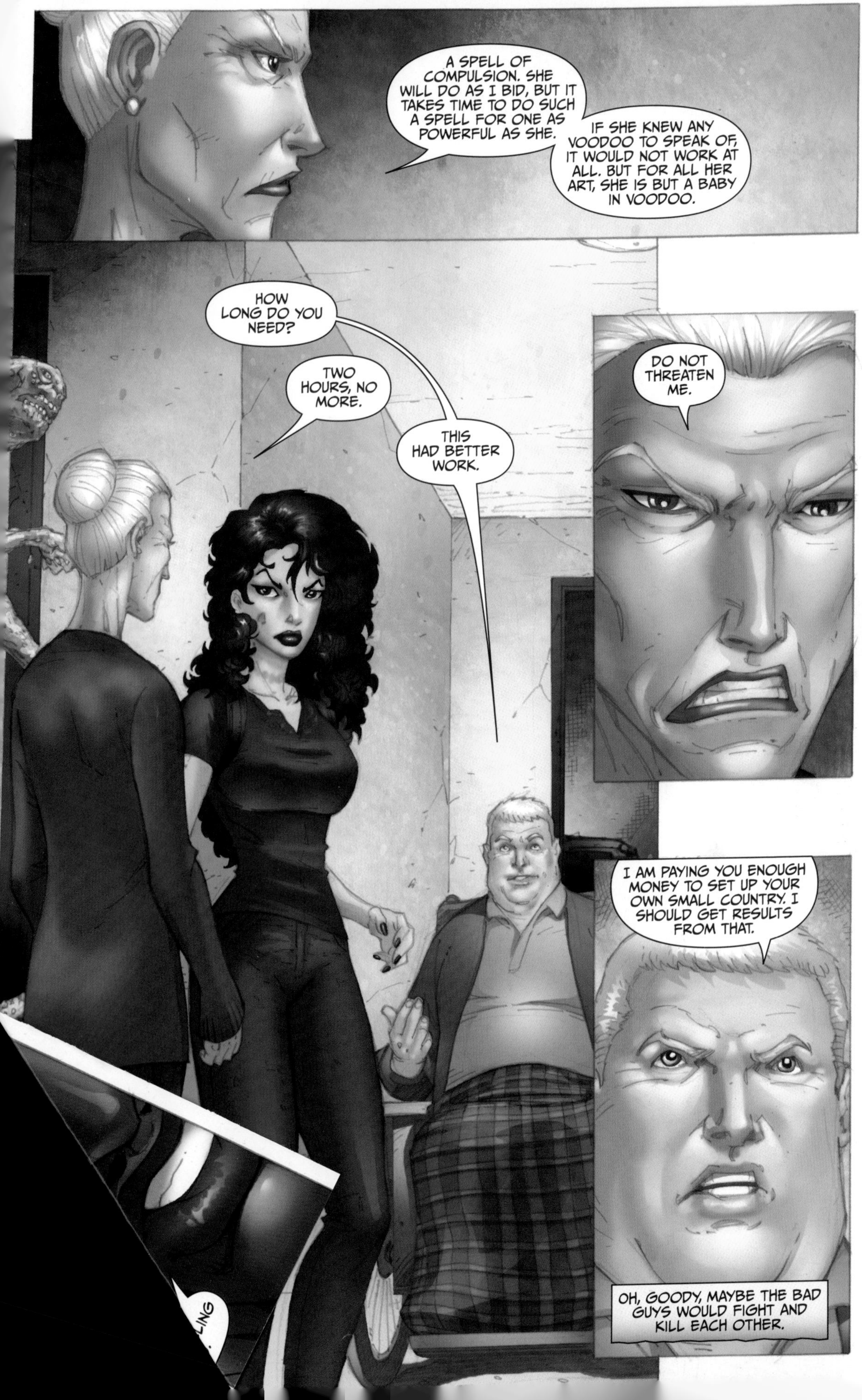
A SPELL OF COMPULSION. SHE WILL DO AS I BID, BUT IT TAKES TIME TO DO SUCH A SPELL FOR ONE AS POWERFUL AS SHE.
IF SHE KNEW ANY VOODOO TO SPEAK OF, IT WOULD NOT WORK AT ALL. BUT FOR ALL HER ART, SHE IS BUT A BABY IN VOODOO.
HOW LONG DO YOU NEED?
TWO HOURS, NO MORE.
THIS HAD BETTER WORK.
DO NOT THREATEN ME.
I AM PAYING YOU ENOUGH MONEY TO SET UP YOUR OWN SMALL COUNTRY. I SHOULD GET RESULTS FROM THAT.
OH, GOODY, MAYBE THE BAD GUYS WOULD FIGHT AND KILL EACH OTHER.

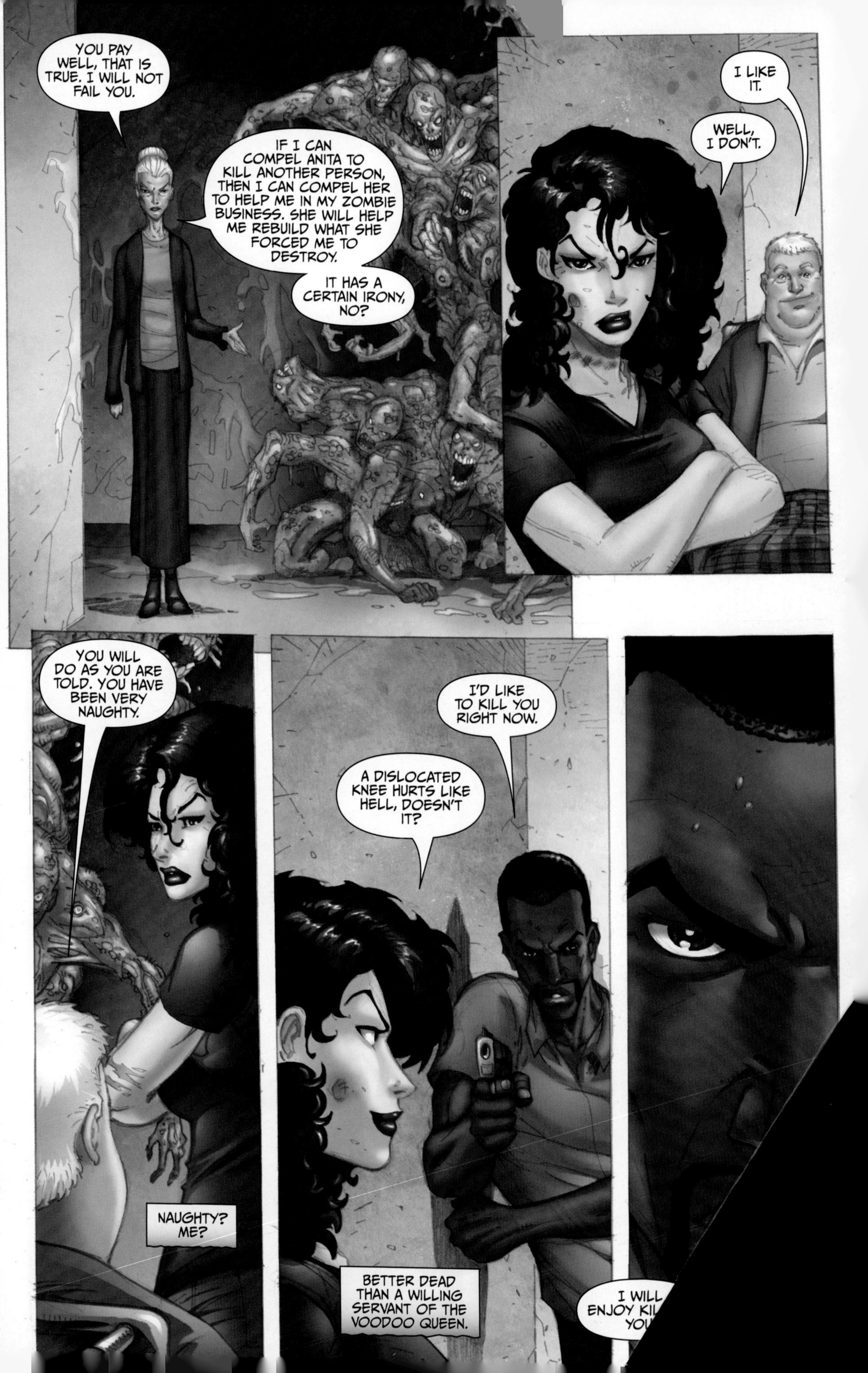
YOU PAY WELL, THAT IS TRUE. I WILL NOT FAIL YOU.
IF I CAN COMPEL ANITA TO KILL ANOTHER PERSON, THEN I CAN COMPEL HER TO HELP ME IN MY ZOMBIE BUSINESS. SHE WILL HELP ME REBUILD WHAT SHE FORCED ME TO DESTROY.
IT HAS A CERTAIN IRONY, NO?
I LIKE IT.
WELL, I DON'T.
YOU WILL DO AS YOU ARE TOLD. YOU HAVE BEEN VERY NAUGHTY.
NAUGHTY? ME?
I'D LIKE TO KILL YOU RIGHT NOW.
A DISLOCATED KNEE HURTS LIKE HELL, DOESN'T IT?
BETTER DEAD THAN A WILLING SERVANT OF THE VOODOO QUEEN.

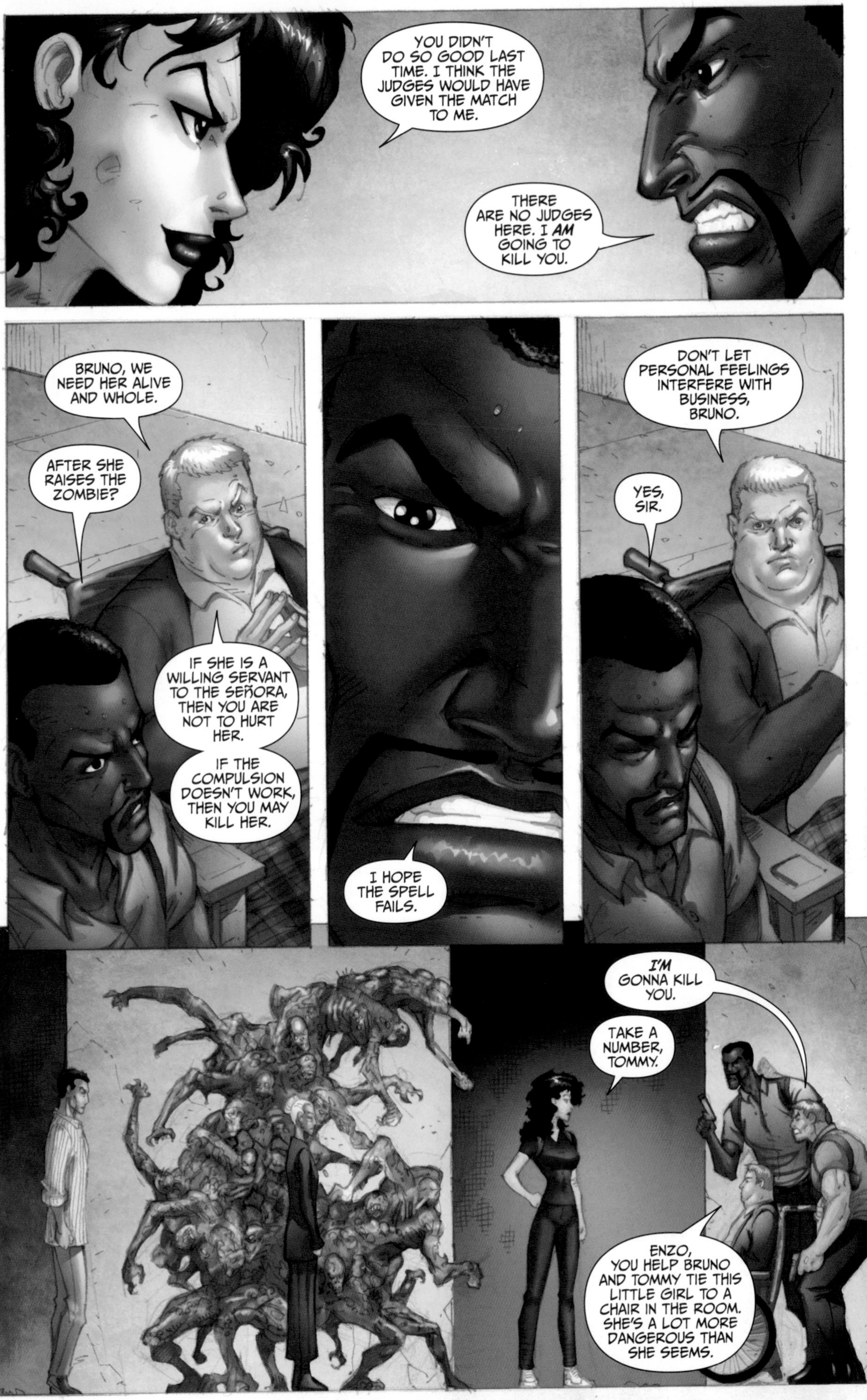
YOU DIDN'T DO SO GOOD LAST TIME. I THINK THE JUDGES WOULD HAVE GIVEN THE MATCH TO ME.
THERE ARE NO JUDGES HERE. I *AM* GOING TO KILL YOU.
BRUNO, WE NEED HER ALIVE AND WHOLE.
AFTER SHE RAISES THE ZOMBIE?
IF SHE IS A WILLING SERVANT TO THE SEÑORA, THEN YOU ARE NOT TO HURT HER.
IF THE COMPULSION DOESN'T WORK, THEN YOU MAY KILL HER.
I HOPE THE SPELL FAILS.
DON'T LET PERSONAL FEELINGS INTERFERE WITH BUSINESS, BRUNO.
YES, SIR.
I'M GONNA KILL YOU.
TAKE A NUMBER, TOMMY.
ENZO, YOU HELP BRUNO AND TOMMY TIE THIS LITTLE GIRL TO A CHAIR IN THE ROOM. SHE'S A LOT MORE DANGEROUS THAN SHE SEEMS.

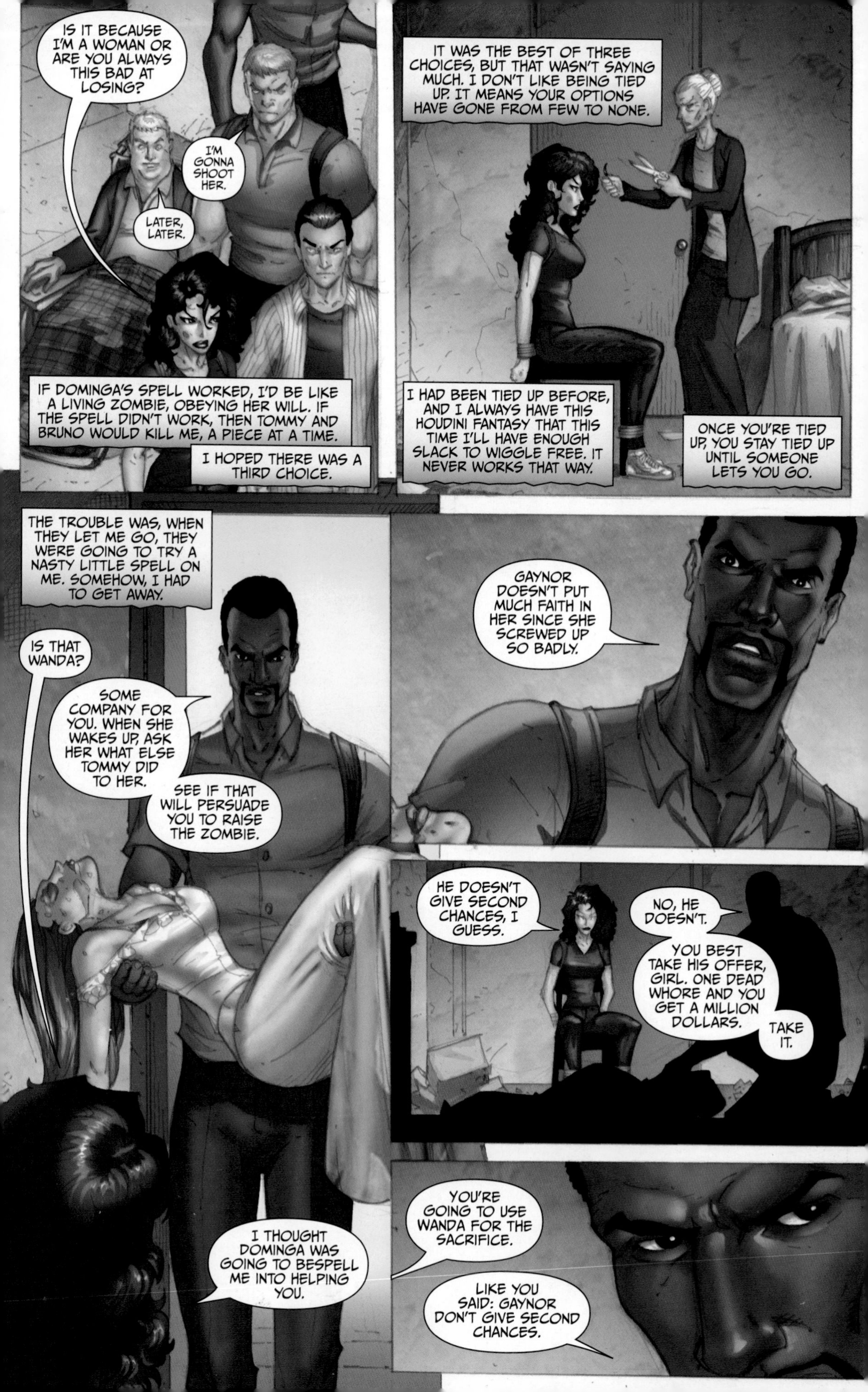
IS IT BECAUSE I'M A WOMAN OR ARE YOU ALWAYS THIS BAD AT LOSING?
I'M GONNA SHOOT HER.
LATER, LATER.
IF DOMINGA'S SPELL WORKED, I'D BE LIKE A LIVING ZOMBIE, OBEYING HER WILL. IF THE SPELL DIDN'T WORK, THEN TOMMY AND BRUNO WOULD KILL ME, A PIECE AT A TIME.
I HOPED THERE WAS A THIRD CHOICE.
IT WAS THE BEST OF THREE CHOICES, BUT THAT WASN'T SAYING MUCH. I DON'T LIKE BEING TIED UP. IT MEANS YOUR OPTIONS HAVE GONE FROM FEW TO NONE.
I HAD BEEN TIED UP BEFORE, AND I ALWAYS HAVE THIS HOUDINI FANTASY THAT THIS TIME I'LL HAVE ENOUGH SLACK TO WIGGLE FREE. IT NEVER WORKS THAT WAY.
ONCE YOU'RE TIED UP, YOU STAY TIED UP UNTIL SOMEONE LETS YOU GO.
THE TROUBLE WAS, WHEN THEY LET ME GO, THEY WERE GOING TO TRY A NASTY LITTLE SPELL ON ME. SOMEHOW, I HAD TO GET AWAY.
IS THAT WANDA?
SOME COMPANY FOR YOU. WHEN SHE WAKES UP, ASK HER WHAT ELSE TOMMY DID TO HER.
SEE IF THAT WILL PERSUADE YOU TO RAISE THE ZOMBIE.
GAYNOR DOESN'T PUT MUCH FAITH IN HER SINCE SHE SCREWED UP SO BADLY.
HE DOESN'T GIVE SECOND CHANCES, I GUESS.
NO, HE DOESN'T.
YOU BEST TAKE HIS OFFER, GIRL. ONE DEAD WHORE AND YOU GET A MILLION DOLLARS.
TAKE IT.
I THOUGHT DOMINGA WAS GOING TO BESPELL ME INTO HELPING YOU.
YOU'RE GOING TO USE WANDA FOR THE SACRIFICE.
LIKE YOU SAID: GAYNOR DON'T GIVE SECOND CHANCES.

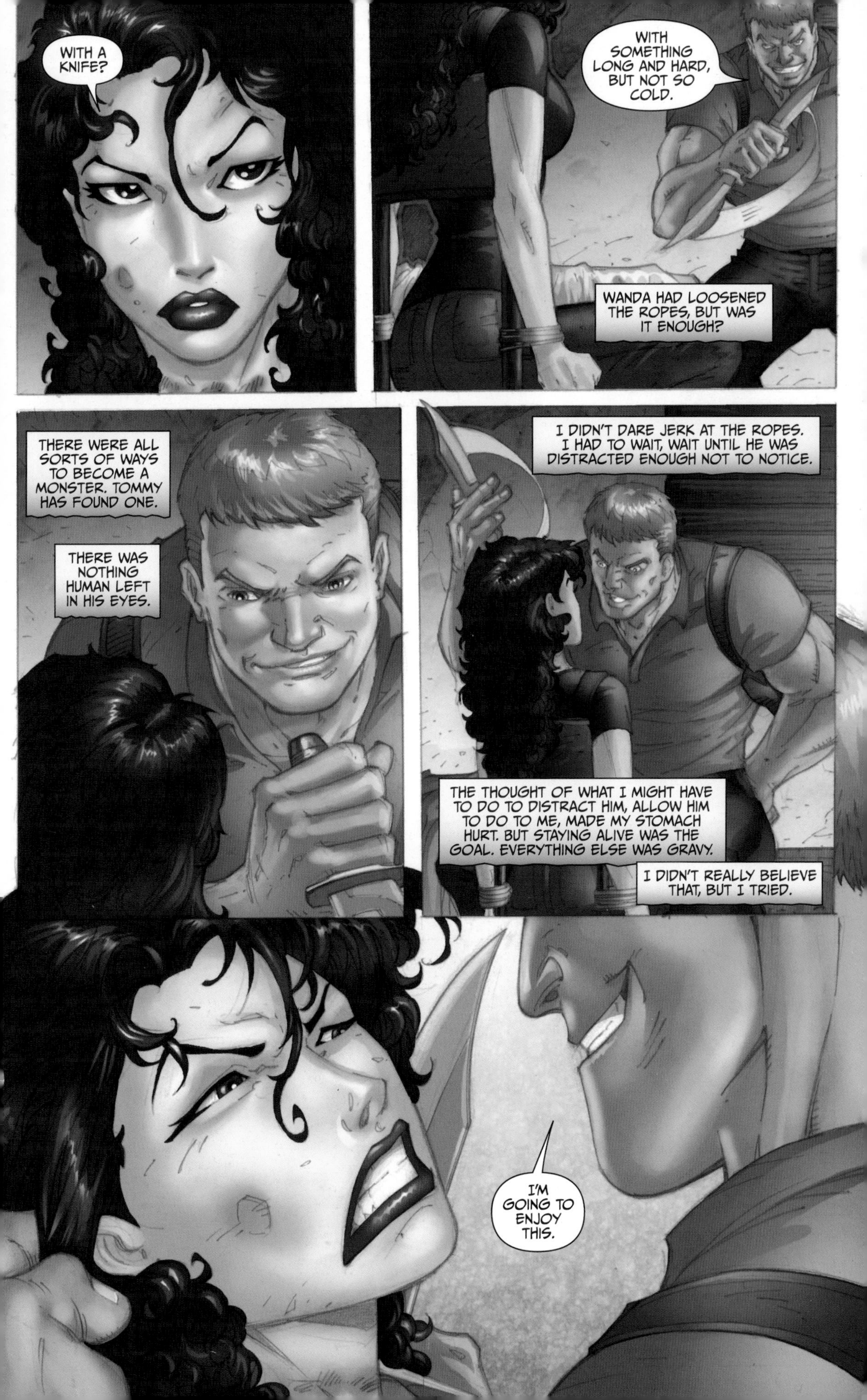
WITH A KNIFE?
WITH SOMETHING LONG AND HARD, BUT NOT SO COLD.
WANDA HAD LOOSENED THE ROPES, BUT WAS IT ENOUGH?
THERE WERE ALL SORTS OF WAYS TO BECOME A MONSTER. TOMMY HAS FOUND ONE.
THERE WAS NOTHING HUMAN LEFT IN HIS EYES.
I DIDN'T DARE JERK AT THE ROPES. I HAD TO WAIT, WAIT UNTIL HE WAS DISTRACTED ENOUGH NOT TO NOTICE.
THE THOUGHT OF WHAT I MIGHT HAVE TO DO TO DISTRACT HIM, ALLOW HIM TO DO TO ME, MADE MY STOMACH HURT. BUT STAYING ALIVE WAS THE GOAL. EVERYTHING ELSE WAS GRAVY.
I DIDN'T REALLY BELIEVE THAT, BUT I TRIED.
I'M GOING TO ENJOY THIS.

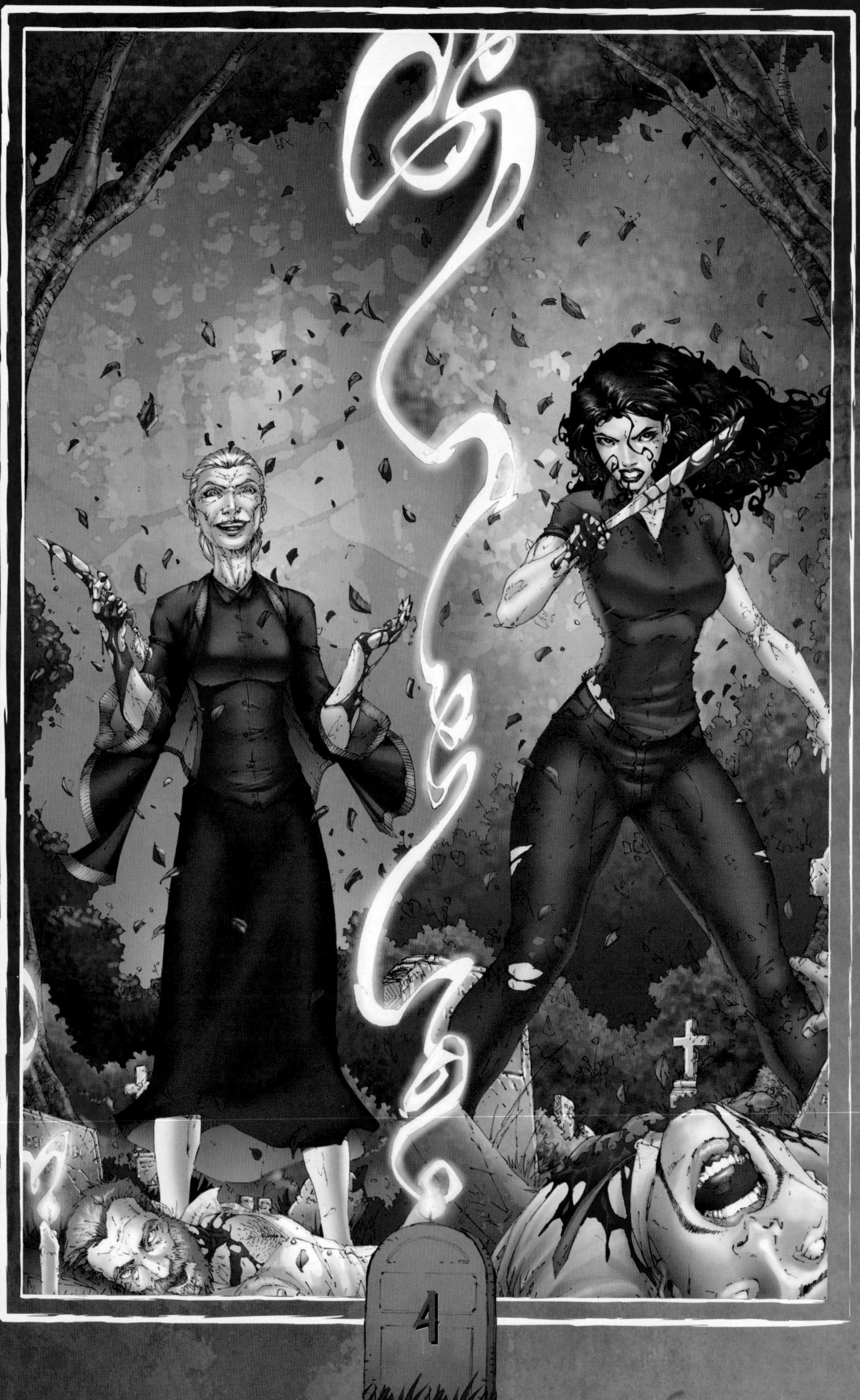
4

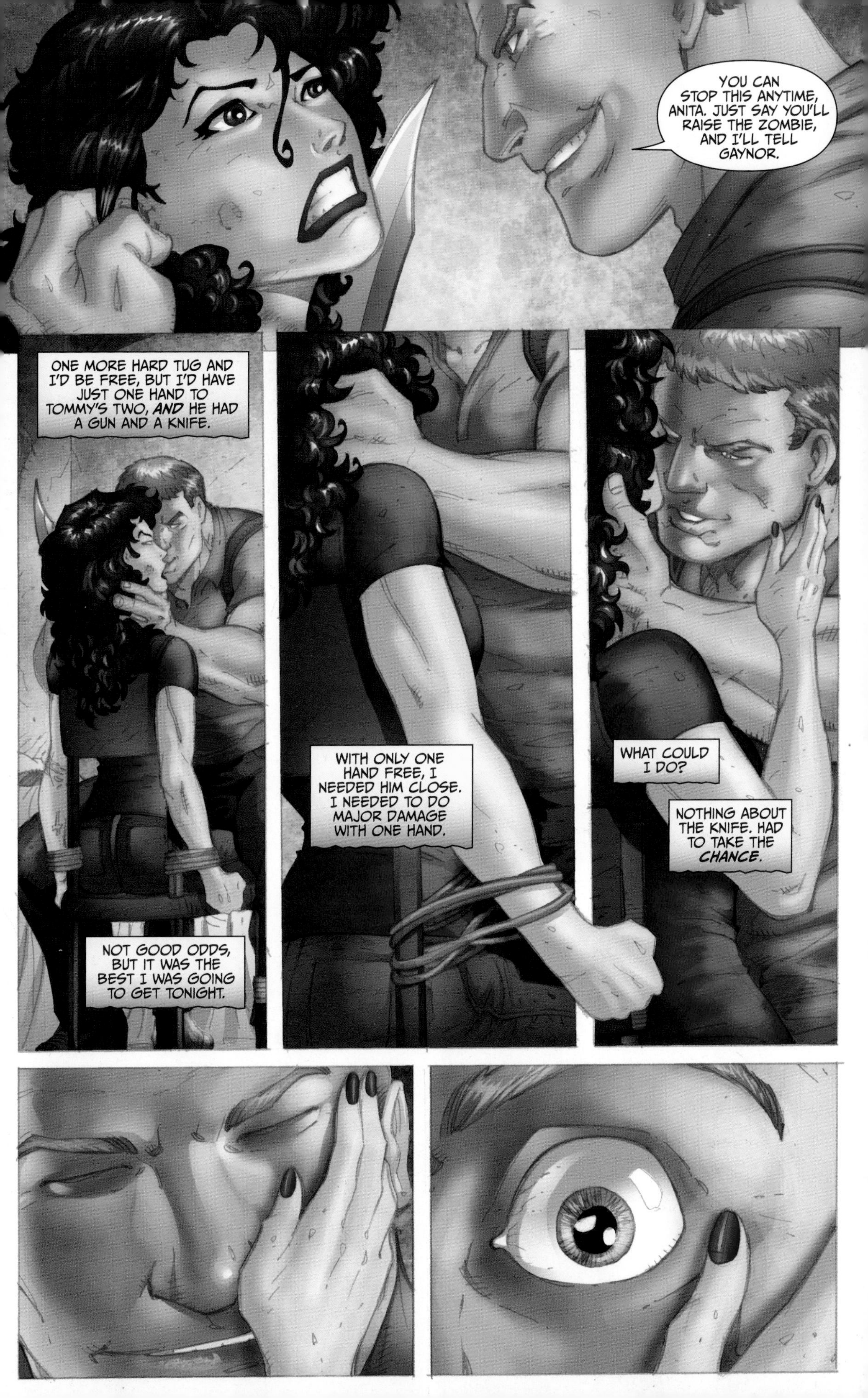
YOU CAN STOP THIS ANYTIME, ANITA. JUST SAY YOU'LL RAISE THE ZOMBIE, AND I'LL TELL GAYNOR.
ONE MORE HARD TUG AND I'D BE FREE, BUT I'D HAVE JUST ONE HAND TO TOMMY'S TWO, *AND* HE HAD A GUN AND A KNIFE.
NOT GOOD ODDS, BUT IT WAS THE BEST I WAS GOING TO GET TONIGHT.
WITH ONLY ONE HAND FREE, I NEEDED HIM CLOSE. I NEEDED TO DO MAJOR DAMAGE WITH ONE HAND.
WHAT COULD I DO?
NOTHING ABOUT THE KNIFE. HAD TO TAKE THE *CHANCE*.

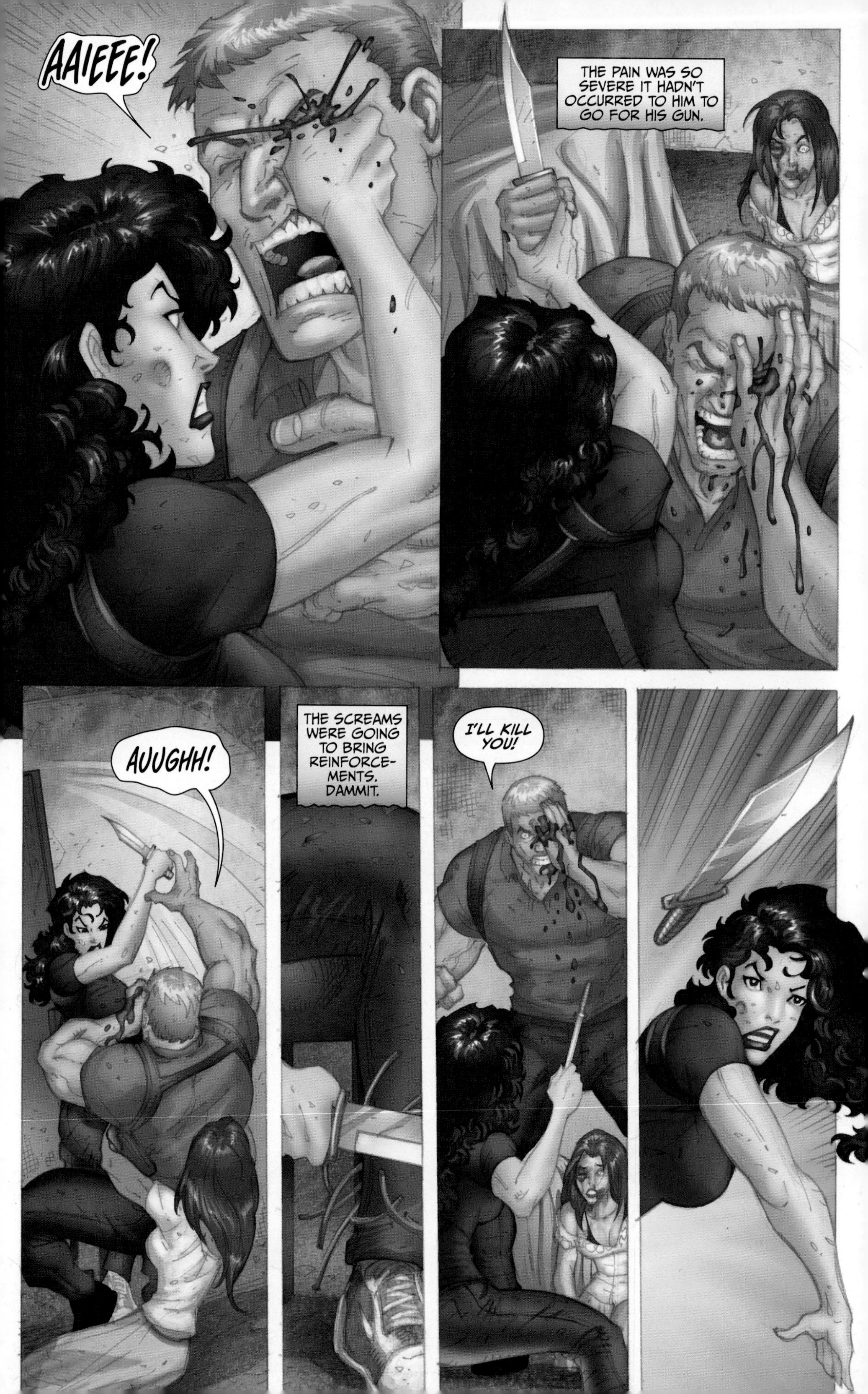
AAIEEE!
THE PAIN WAS SO SEVERE IT HADN'T OCCURRED TO HIM TO GO FOR HIS GUN.
AUUGHH!
THE SCREAMS WERE GOING TO BRING REINFORCE-MENTS. DAMMIT.
I'LL KILL YOU!

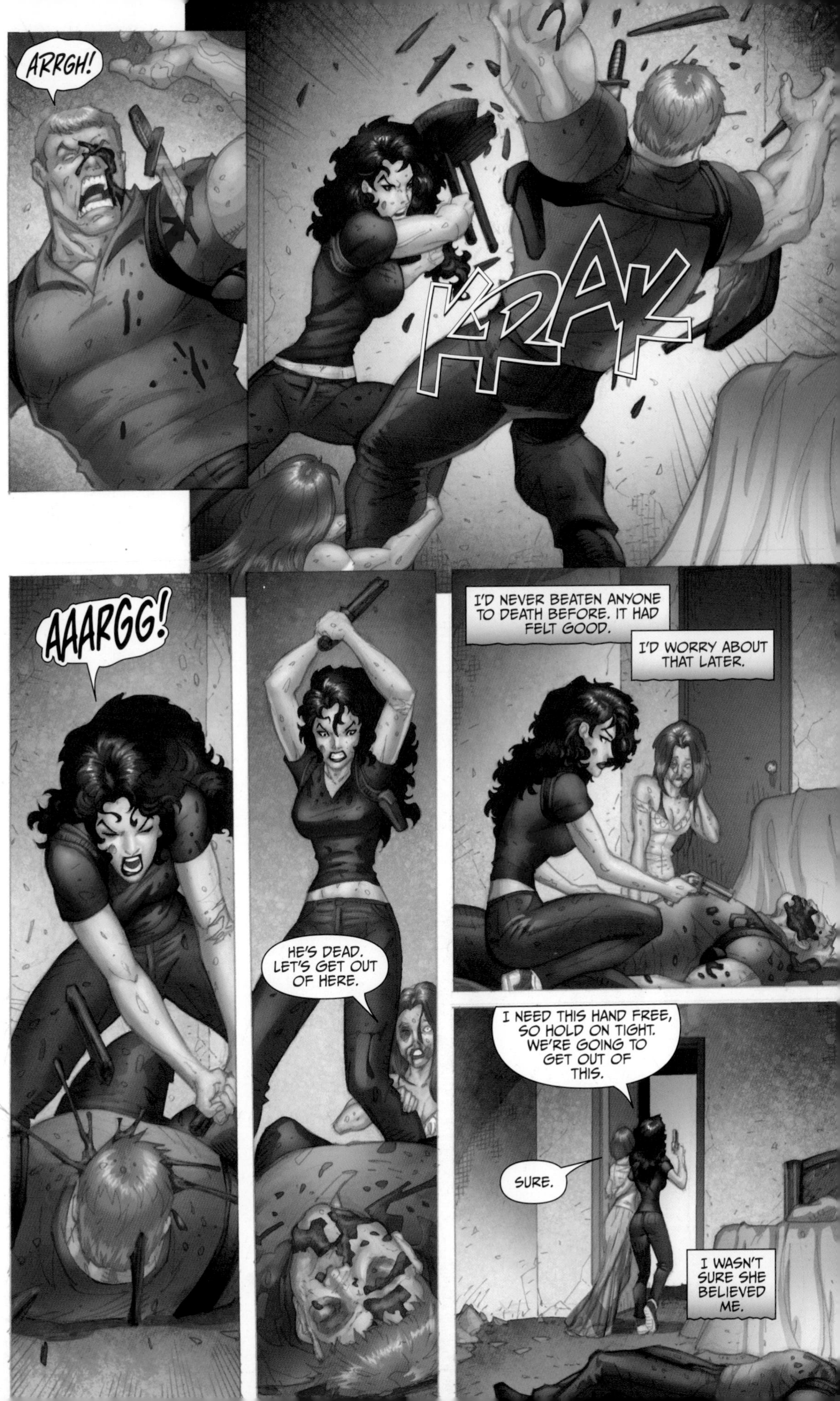
ARRGH!
KRAK
AAARGG!
HE'S DEAD. LET'S GET OUT OF HERE.
I'D NEVER BEATEN ANYONE TO DEATH BEFORE. IT HAD FELT GOOD.
I'D WORRY ABOUT THAT LATER.
I NEED THIS HAND FREE, SO HOLD ON TIGHT. WE'RE GOING TO GET OUT OF THIS.
SURE.
I WASN'T SURE SHE BELIEVED ME.

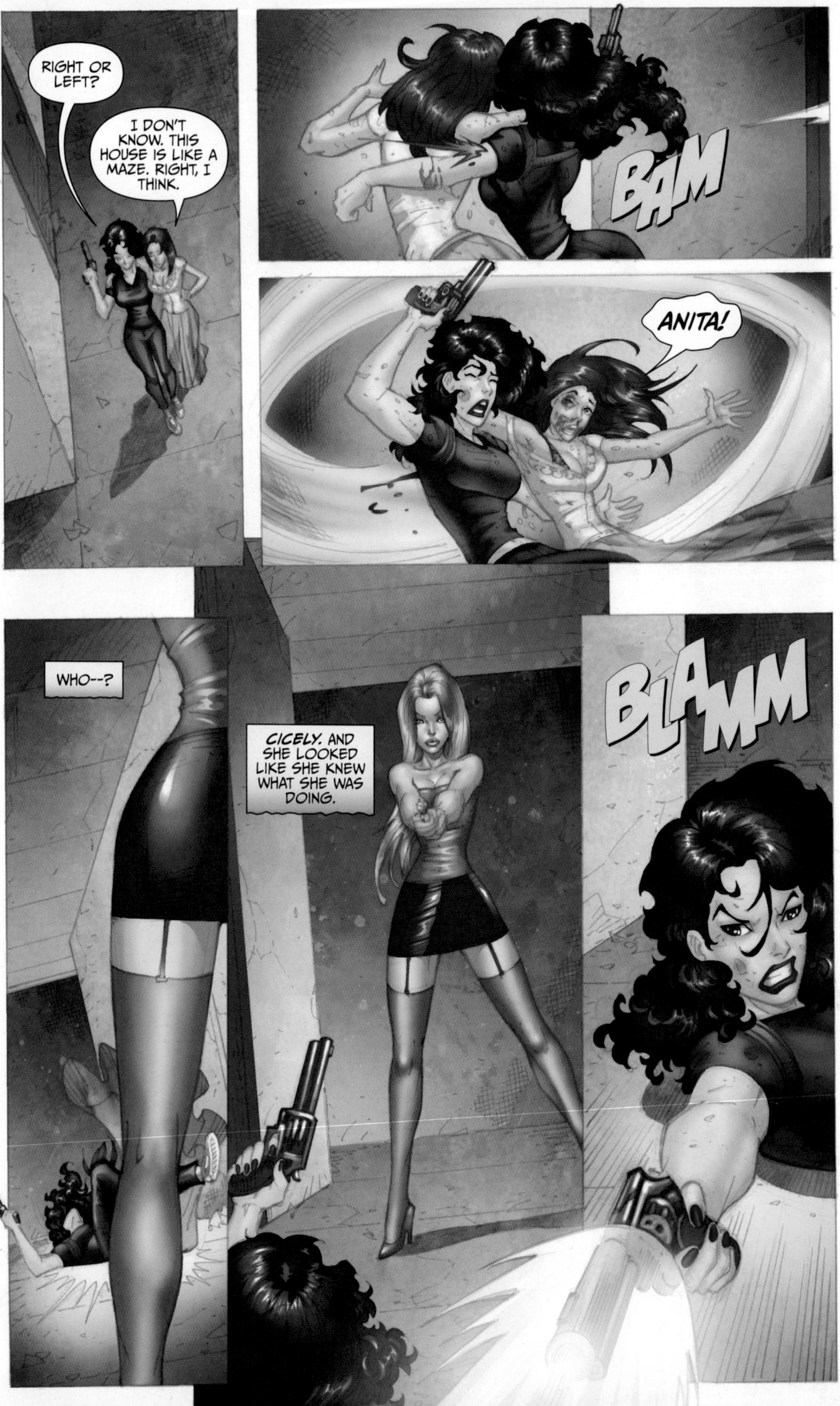
RIGHT OR LEFT?
I DON'T KNOW. THIS HOUSE IS LIKE A MAZE. RIGHT, I THINK.
BAM
ANITA!
WHO--?
CICELY. AND SHE LOOKED LIKE SHE KNEW WHAT SHE WAS DOING.
BLAMM

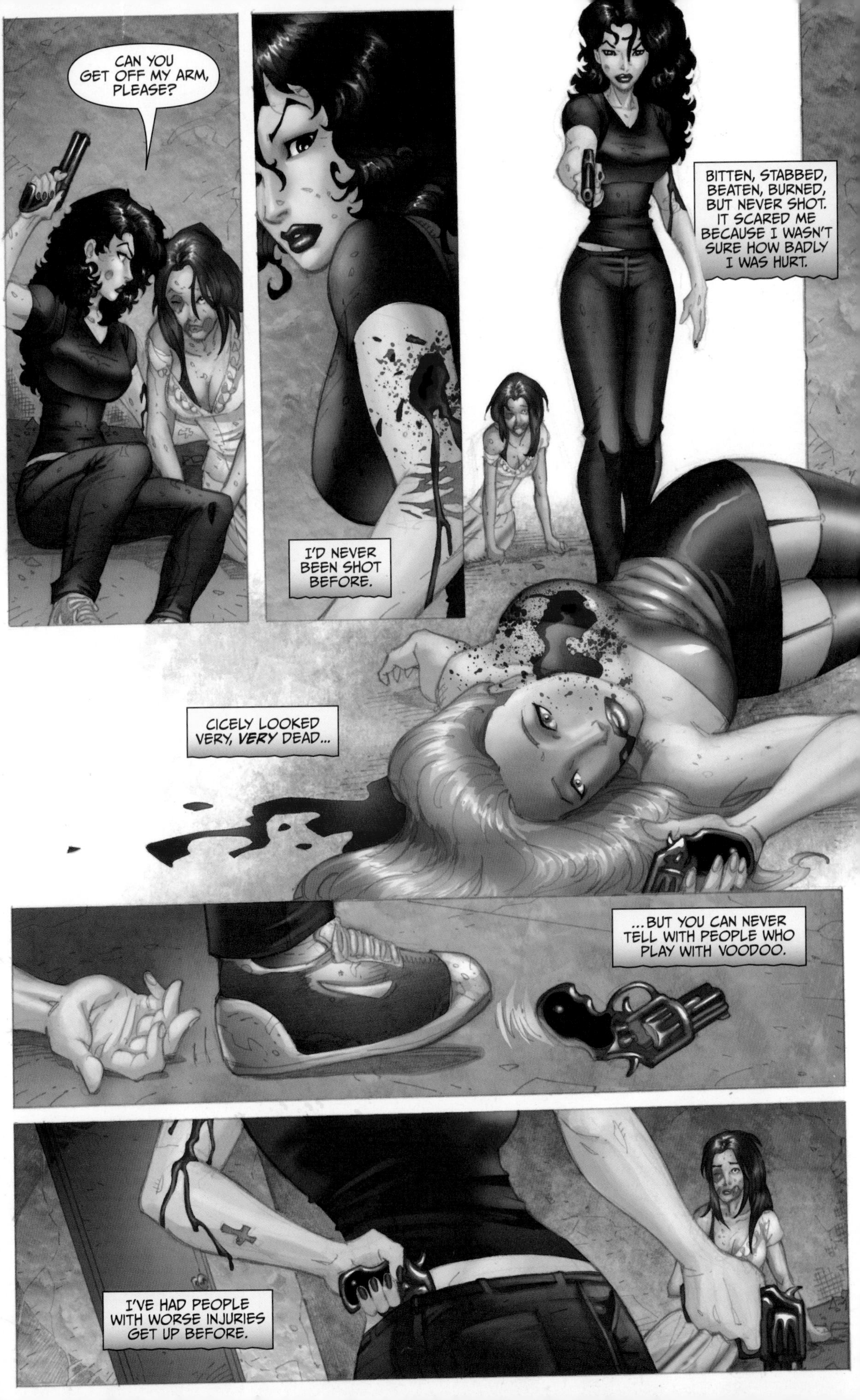

CAN YOU GET OFF MY ARM, PLEASE?
I'D NEVER BEEN SHOT BEFORE.
BITTEN, STABBED, BEATEN, BURNED, BUT NEVER SHOT. IT SCARED ME BECAUSE I WASN'T SURE HOW BADLY I WAS HURT.
CICELY LOOKED VERY, *VERY* DEAD...
...BUT YOU CAN NEVER TELL WITH PEOPLE WHO PLAY WITH VOODOO.
I'VE HAD PEOPLE WITH WORSE INJURIES GET UP BEFORE.

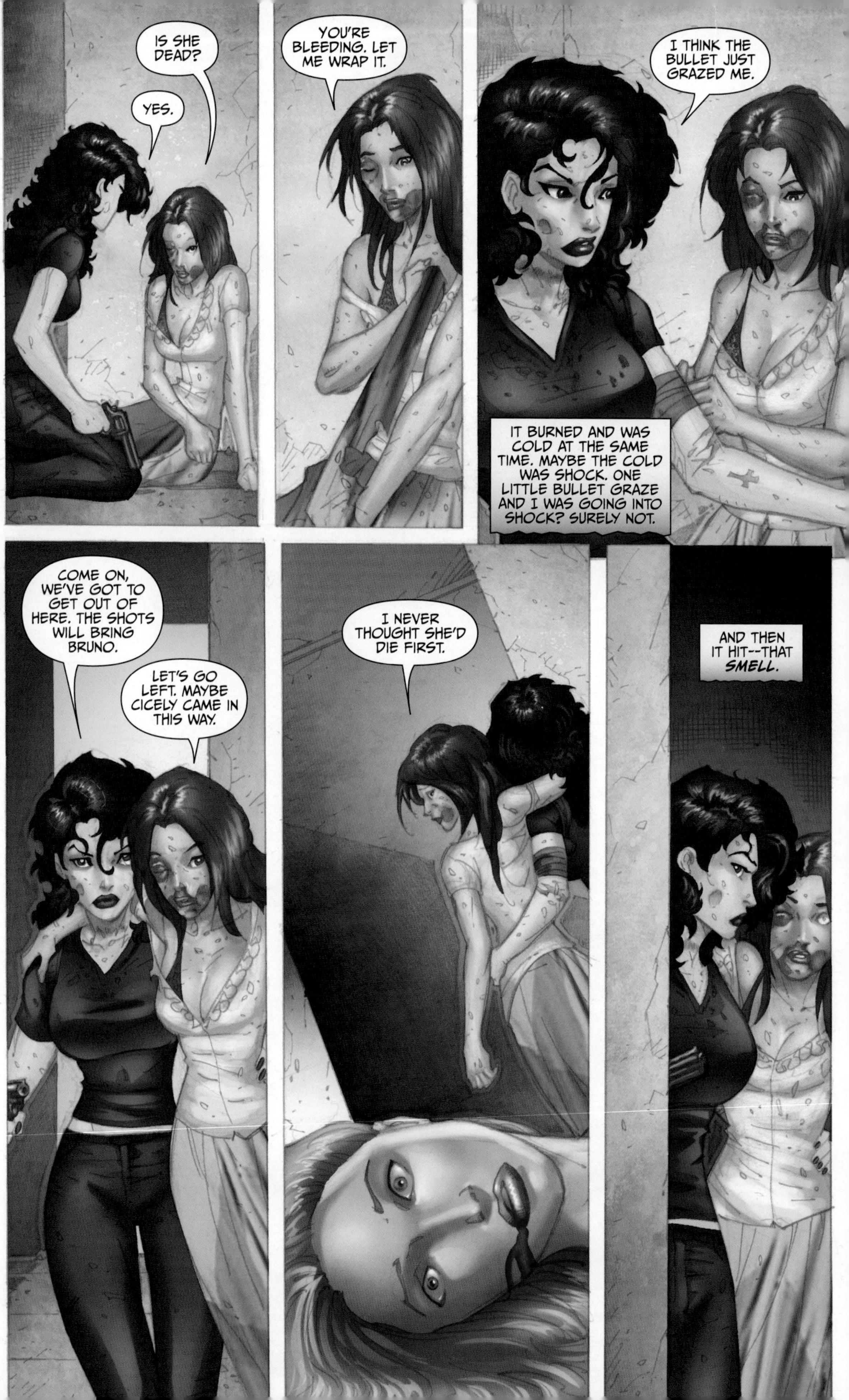
IS SHE DEAD?
YES.
YOU'RE BLEEDING. LET ME WRAP IT.
I THINK THE BULLET JUST GRAZED ME.
IT BURNED AND WAS COLD AT THE SAME TIME. MAYBE THE COLD WAS SHOCK. ONE LITTLE BULLET GRAZE AND I WAS GOING INTO SHOCK? SURELY NOT.
COME ON, WE'VE GOT TO GET OUT OF HERE. THE SHOTS WILL BRING BRUNO.
LET'S GO LEFT. MAYBE CICELY CAME IN THIS WAY.
I NEVER THOUGHT SHE'D DIE FIRST.
AND THEN IT HIT--THAT SMELL.

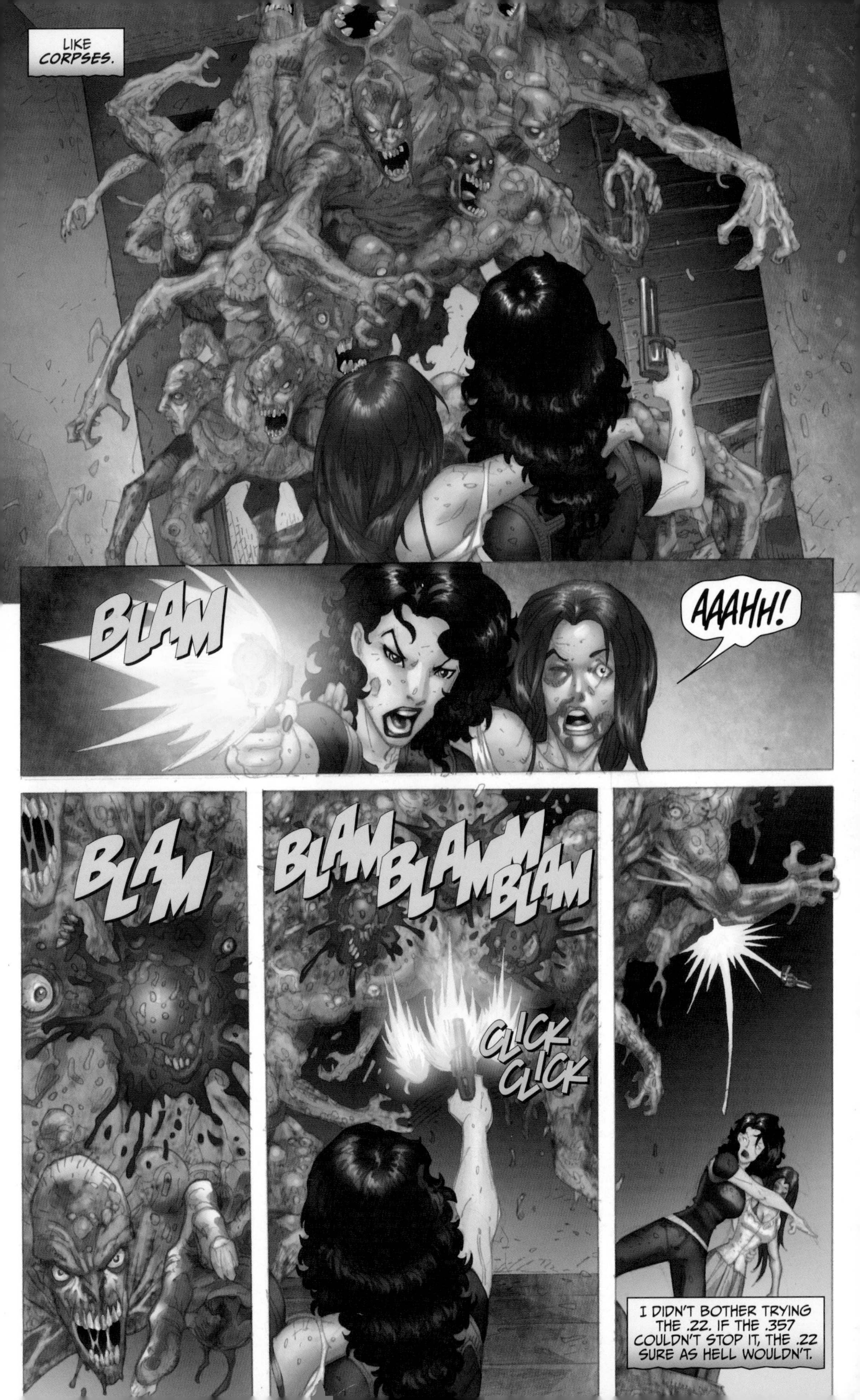
LIKE CORPSES.
BLAM
AAAHH!
BLAM
BLAM BLAMM BLAM
CLICK CLICK
I DIDN'T BOTHER TRYING THE .22. IF THE .357 COULDN'T STOP IT, THE .22 SURE AS HELL WOULDN'T.

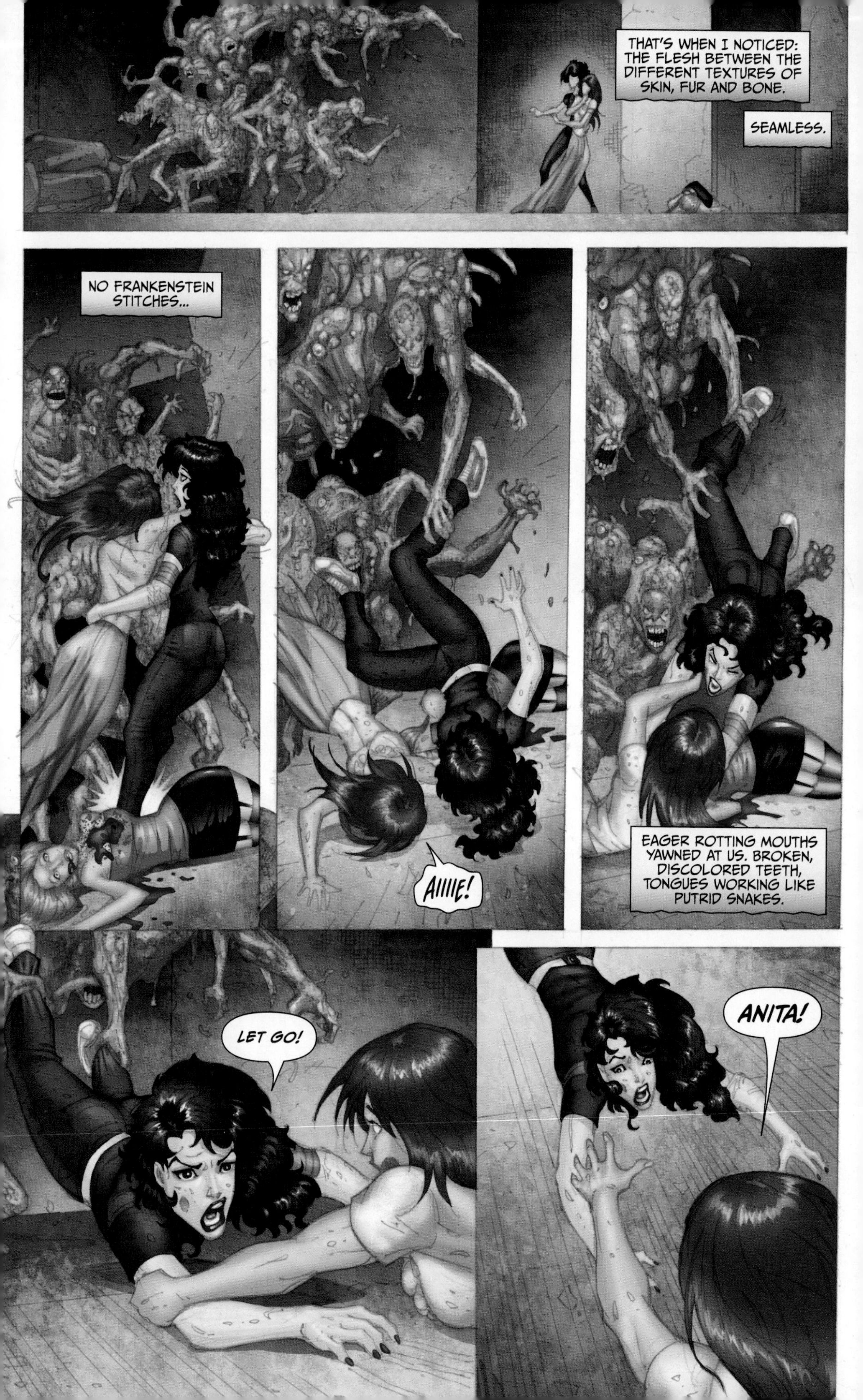
THAT'S WHEN I NOTICED: THE FLESH BETWEEN THE DIFFERENT TEXTURES OF SKIN, FUR AND BONE.
SEAMLESS.
NO FRANKENSTEIN STITCHES...
AIIIIE!
EAGER ROTTING MOUTHS YAWNED AT US. BROKEN, DISCOLORED TEETH, TONGUES WORKING LIKE PUTRID SNAKES.
LET GO!
ANITA!

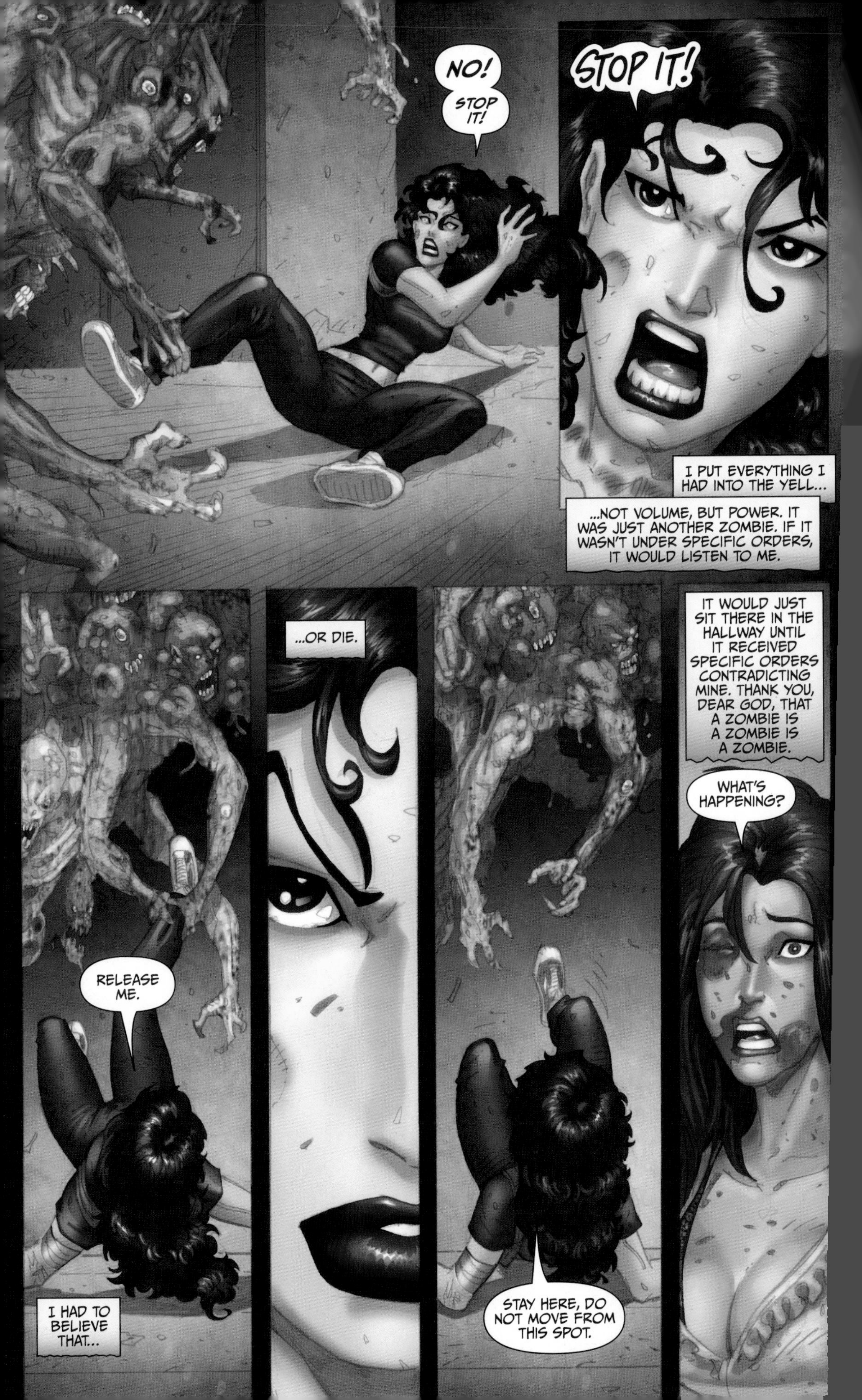
NO! STOP IT!
STOP IT!
I PUT EVERYTHING I HAD INTO THE YELL...
...NOT VOLUME, BUT POWER. IT WAS JUST ANOTHER ZOMBIE. IF IT WASN'T UNDER SPECIFIC ORDERS, IT WOULD LISTEN TO ME.
RELEASE ME.
I HAD TO BELIEVE THAT...
...OR DIE.
STAY HERE, DO NOT MOVE FROM THIS SPOT.
IT WOULD JUST SIT THERE IN THE HALLWAY UNTIL IT RECEIVED SPECIFIC ORDERS CONTRADICTING MINE. THANK YOU, DEAR GOD, THAT A ZOMBIE IS A ZOMBIE IS A ZOMBIE.
WHAT'S HAPPENING?

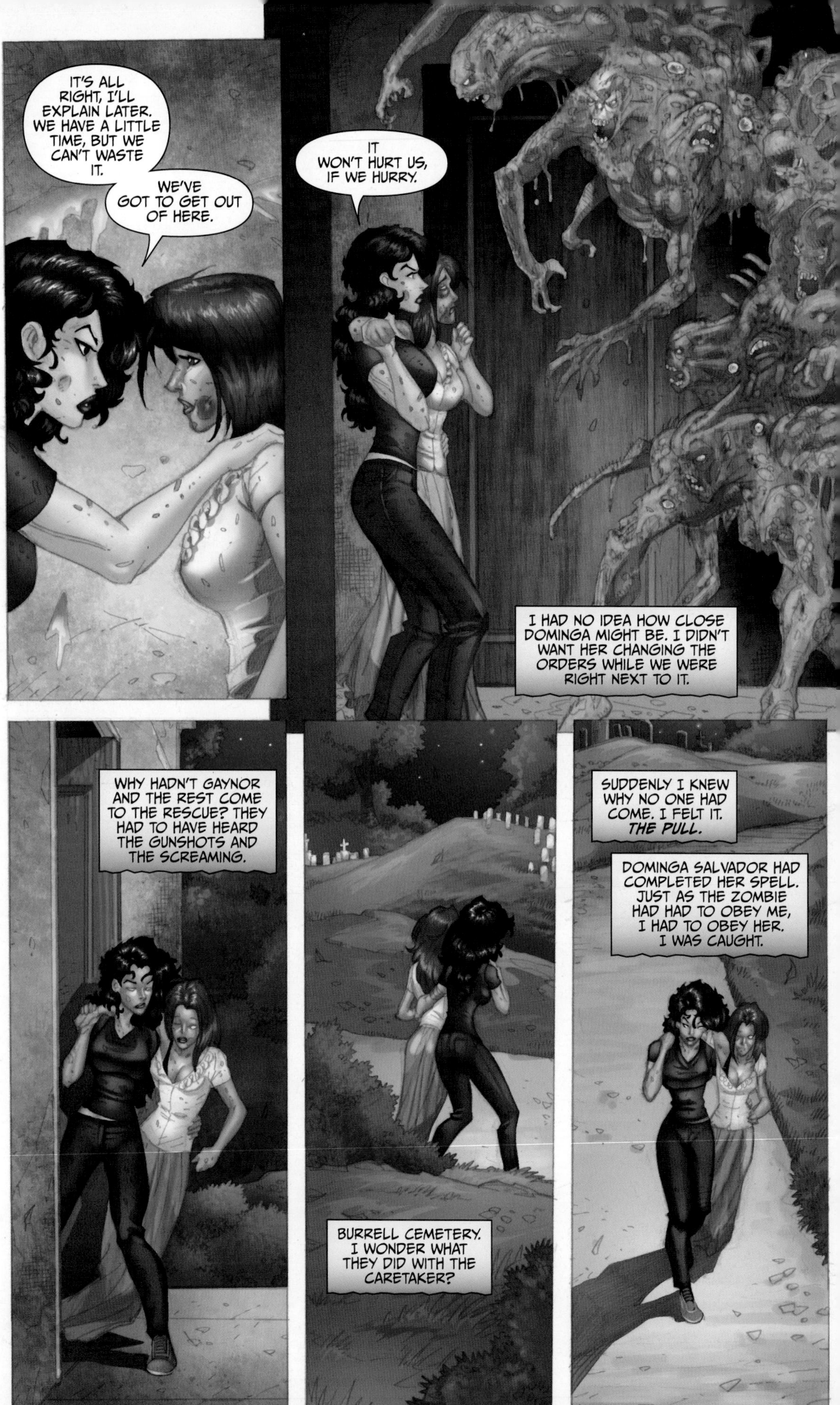
IT'S ALL RIGHT, I'LL EXPLAIN LATER. WE HAVE A LITTLE TIME, BUT WE CAN'T WASTE IT.
WE'VE GOT TO GET OUT OF HERE.
IT WON'T HURT US, IF WE HURRY.
I HAD NO IDEA HOW CLOSE DOMINGA MIGHT BE. I DIDN'T WANT HER CHANGING THE ORDERS WHILE WE WERE RIGHT NEXT TO IT.
WHY HADN'T GAYNOR AND THE REST COME TO THE RESCUE? THEY HAD TO HAVE HEARD THE GUNSHOTS AND THE SCREAMING.
BURRELL CEMETERY. I WONDER WHAT THEY DID WITH THE CARETAKER?
SUDDENLY I KNEW WHY NO ONE HAD COME. I FELT IT. *THE PULL.*
DOMINGA SALVADOR HAD COMPLETED HER SPELL. JUST AS THE ZOMBIE HAD HAD TO OBEY ME, I HAD TO OBEY HER. I WAS CAUGHT.

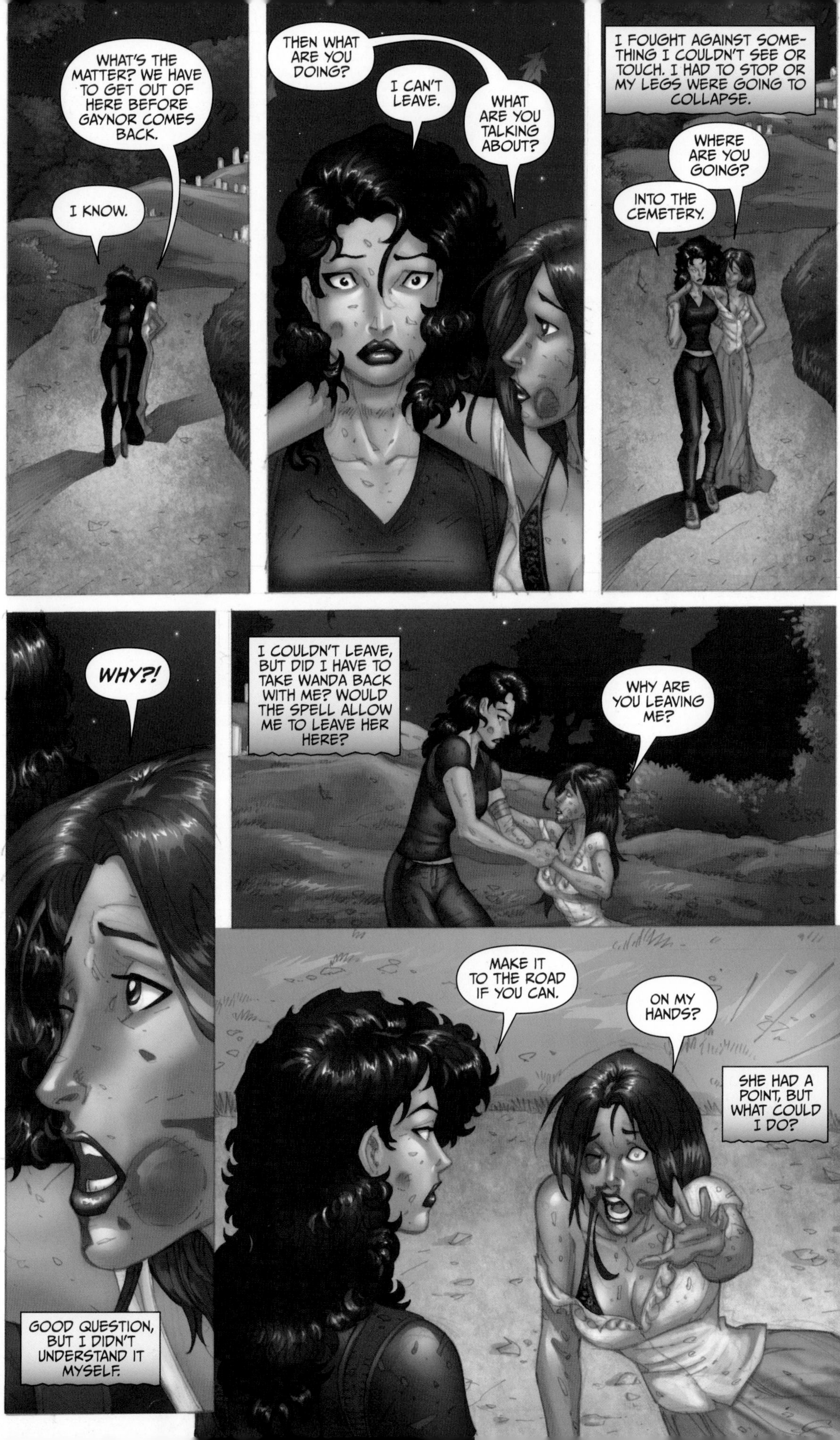
WHAT'S THE MATTER? WE HAVE TO GET OUT OF HERE BEFORE GAYNOR COMES BACK.
I KNOW.
THEN WHAT ARE YOU DOING?
I CAN'T LEAVE.
WHAT ARE YOU TALKING ABOUT?
I FOUGHT AGAINST SOMETHING I COULDN'T SEE OR TOUCH. I HAD TO STOP OR MY LEGS WERE GOING TO COLLAPSE.
WHERE ARE YOU GOING?
INTO THE CEMETERY.
WHY?!
GOOD QUESTION, BUT I DIDN'T UNDERSTAND IT MYSELF.
I COULDN'T LEAVE, BUT DID I HAVE TO TAKE WANDA BACK WITH ME? WOULD THE SPELL ALLOW ME TO LEAVE HER HERE?
WHY ARE YOU LEAVING ME?
MAKE IT TO THE ROAD IF YOU CAN.
ON MY HANDS?
SHE HAD A POINT, BUT WHAT COULD I DO?

CAN YOU USE A GUN?

NO.

IT'S LOADED AND READY TO FIRE. SINCE YOU DON'T KNOW ANYTHING ABOUT GUNS, KEEP IT HIDDEN UNTIL ENZO OR BRUNO IS RIGHT ON TOP OF YOU, THEN FIRE.

YOU CAN'T MISS AT POINT-BLANK RANGE.

WHY ARE YOU LEAVING ME?

SHOULD I LEAVE HER THE GUN, OR TAKE IT WITH ME AND MAYBE GET A CHANCE TO KILL DOMINGA? IF THIS WORKED LIKE ORDERING A ZOMBIE, I COULD KILL HER IF SHE DIDN'T SPECIFICALLY FORBID ME TO DO IT.

THEY'D CALL ME, THEN SEND SOMEONE BACK FOR WANDA. SHE WAS TO BE THE SACRIFICE.

A SPELL, I THINK.

WHAT KIND OF SPELL?

ONE THAT ALLOWS THEM TO ORDER ME TO COME TO THEM. ONE THAT FORBIDS ME TO LEAVE.

OH GOD.

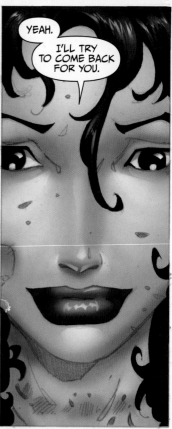

YEAH. I'LL TRY TO COME BACK FOR YOU.

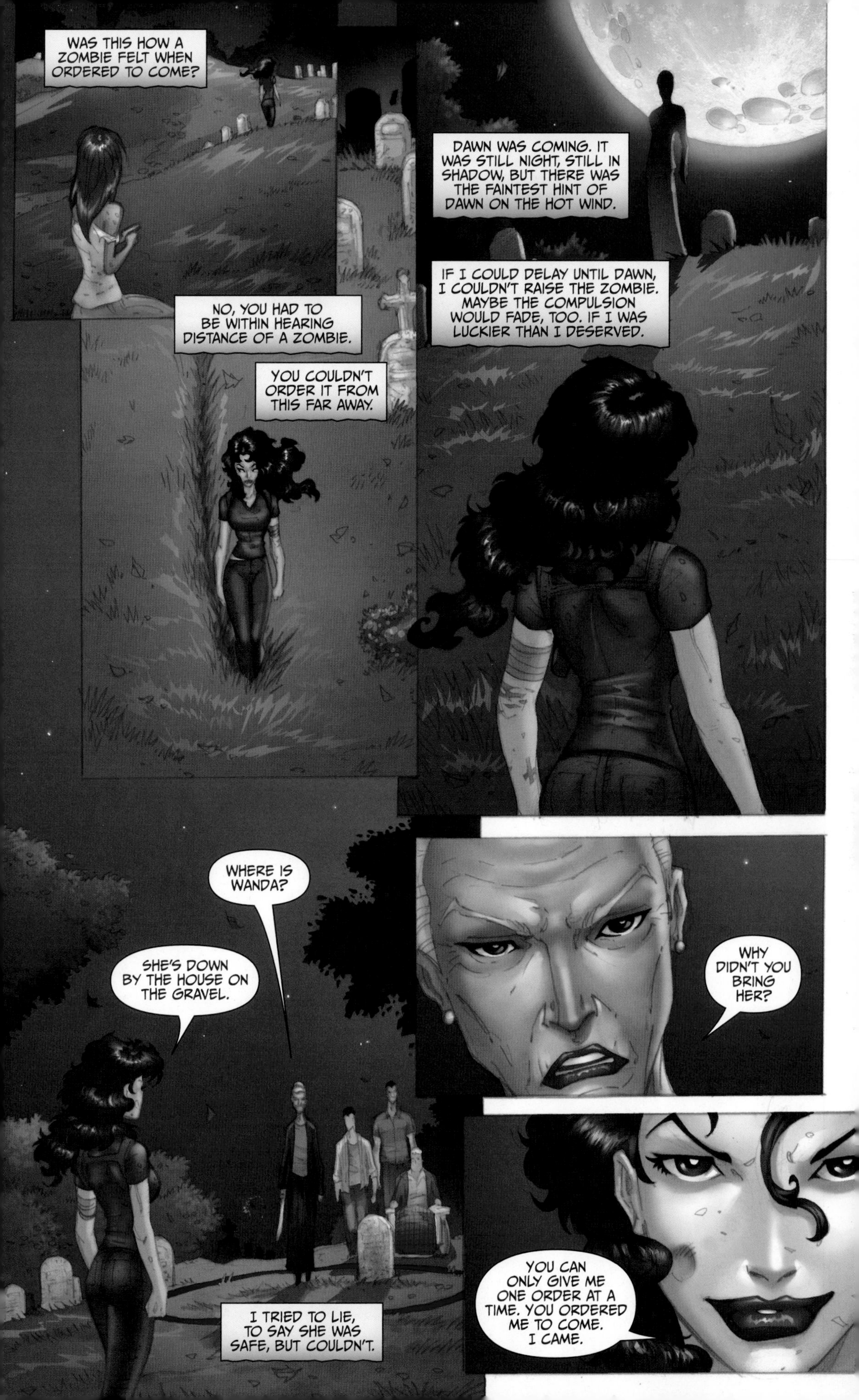
WAS THIS HOW A ZOMBIE FELT WHEN ORDERED TO COME?
NO, YOU HAD TO BE WITHIN HEARING DISTANCE OF A ZOMBIE.
YOU COULDN'T ORDER IT FROM THIS FAR AWAY.
DAWN WAS COMING. IT WAS STILL NIGHT, STILL IN SHADOW, BUT THERE WAS THE FAINTEST HINT OF DAWN ON THE HOT WIND.
IF I COULD DELAY UNTIL DAWN, I COULDN'T RAISE THE ZOMBIE. MAYBE THE COMPULSION WOULD FADE, TOO. IF I WAS LUCKIER THAN I DESERVED.
WHERE IS WANDA?
SHE'S DOWN BY THE HOUSE ON THE GRAVEL.
I TRIED TO LIE, TO SAY SHE WAS SAFE, BUT COULDN'T.
WHY DIDN'T YOU BRING HER?
YOU CAN ONLY GIVE ME ONE ORDER AT A TIME. YOU ORDERED ME TO COME. I CAME.

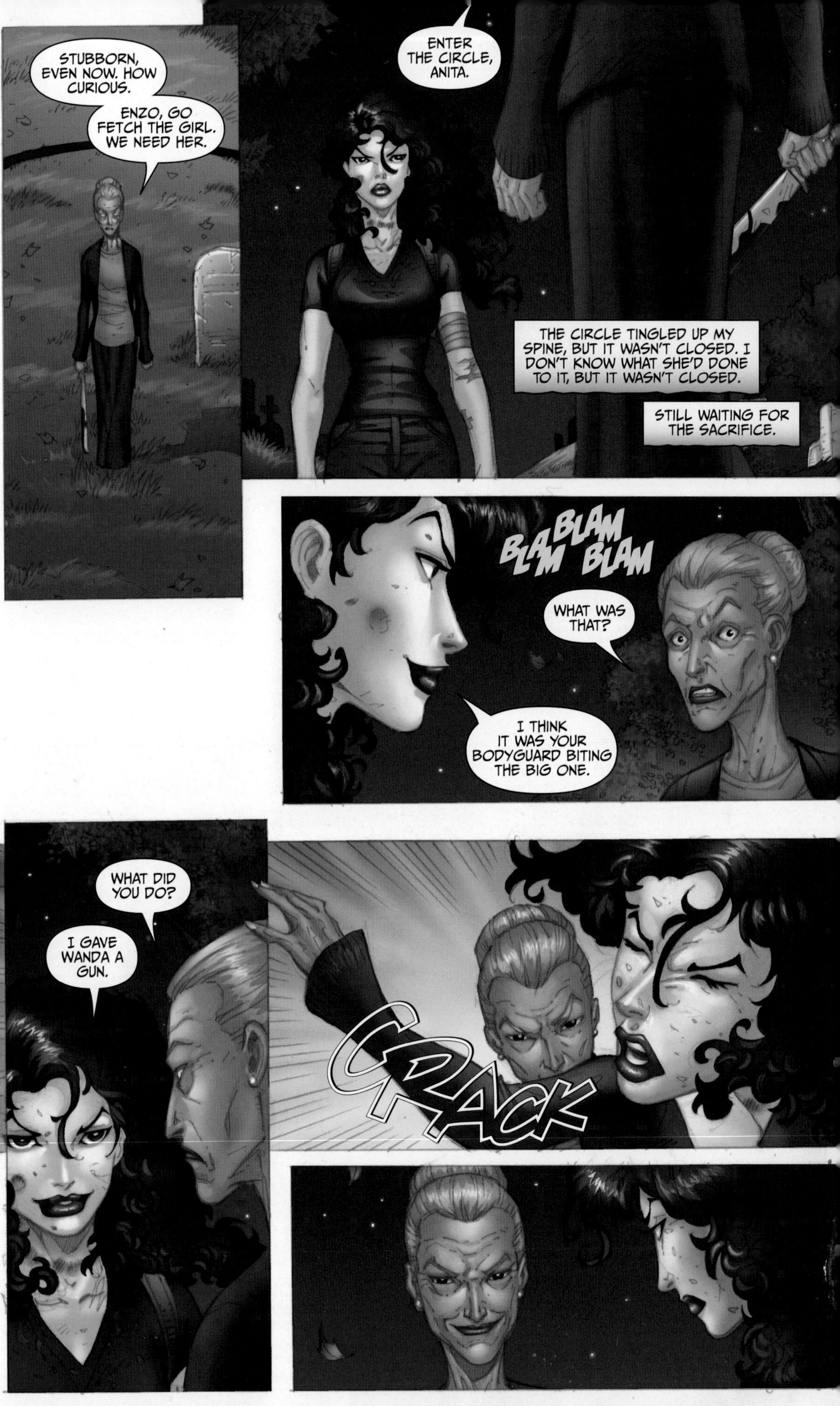
STUBBORN, EVEN NOW. HOW CURIOUS.
ENZO, GO FETCH THE GIRL. WE NEED HER.
ENTER THE CIRCLE, ANITA.
THE CIRCLE TINGLED UP MY SPINE, BUT IT WASN'T CLOSED. I DON'T KNOW WHAT SHE'D DONE TO IT, BUT IT WASN'T CLOSED.
STILL WAITING FOR THE SACRIFICE.
BLAM BLAM BLAM BLAM
WHAT WAS THAT?
I THINK IT WAS YOUR BODYGUARD BITING THE BIG ONE.
WHAT DID YOU DO?
I GAVE WANDA A GUN.
CRACK

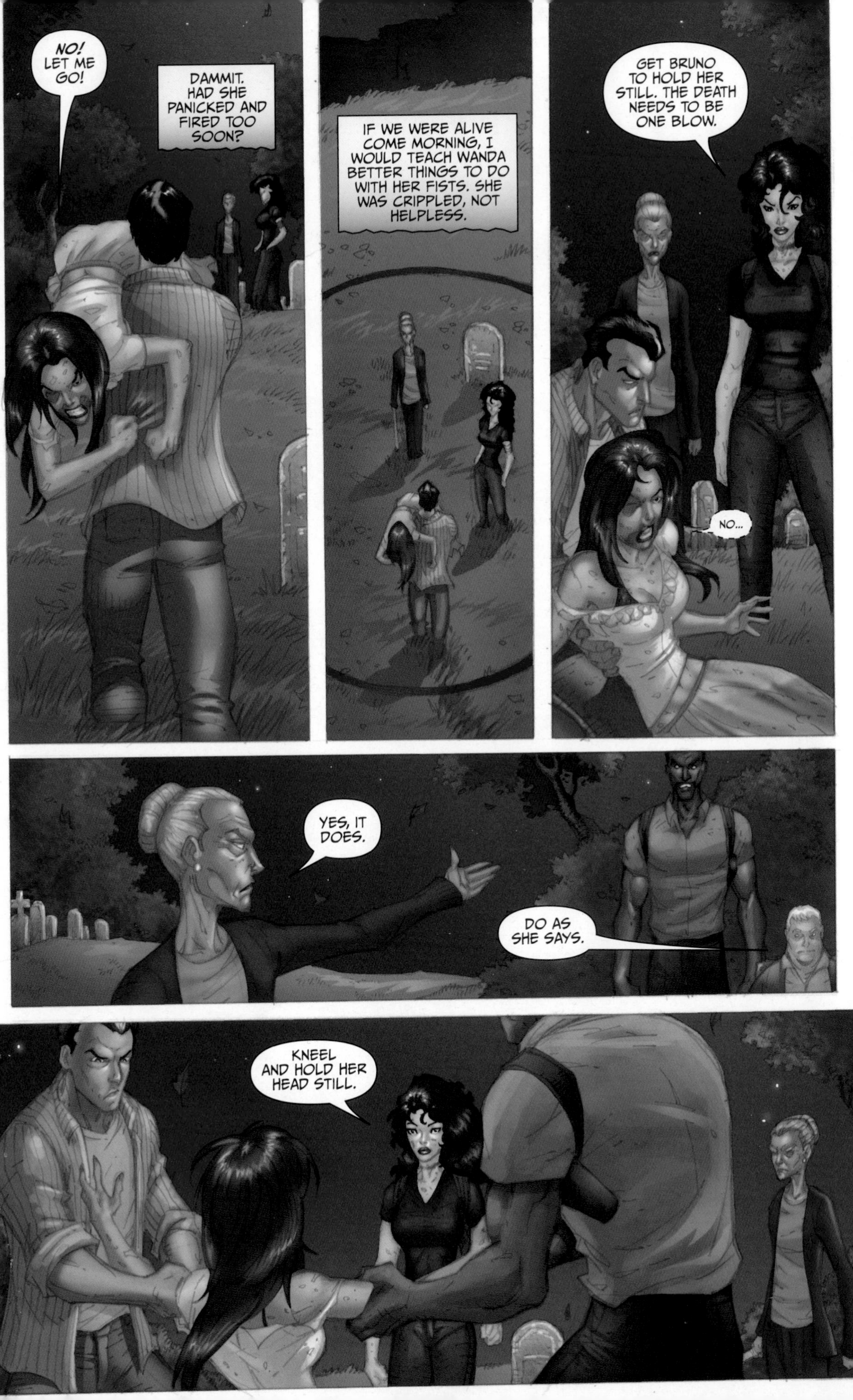
NO! LET ME GO!
DAMMIT. HAD SHE PANICKED AND FIRED TOO SOON?
IF WE WERE ALIVE COME MORNING, I WOULD TEACH WANDA BETTER THINGS TO DO WITH HER FISTS. SHE WAS CRIPPLED, NOT HELPLESS.
GET BRUNO TO HOLD HER STILL. THE DEATH NEEDS TO BE ONE BLOW.
NO...
YES, IT DOES.
DO AS SHE SAYS.
KNEEL AND HOLD HER HEAD STILL.

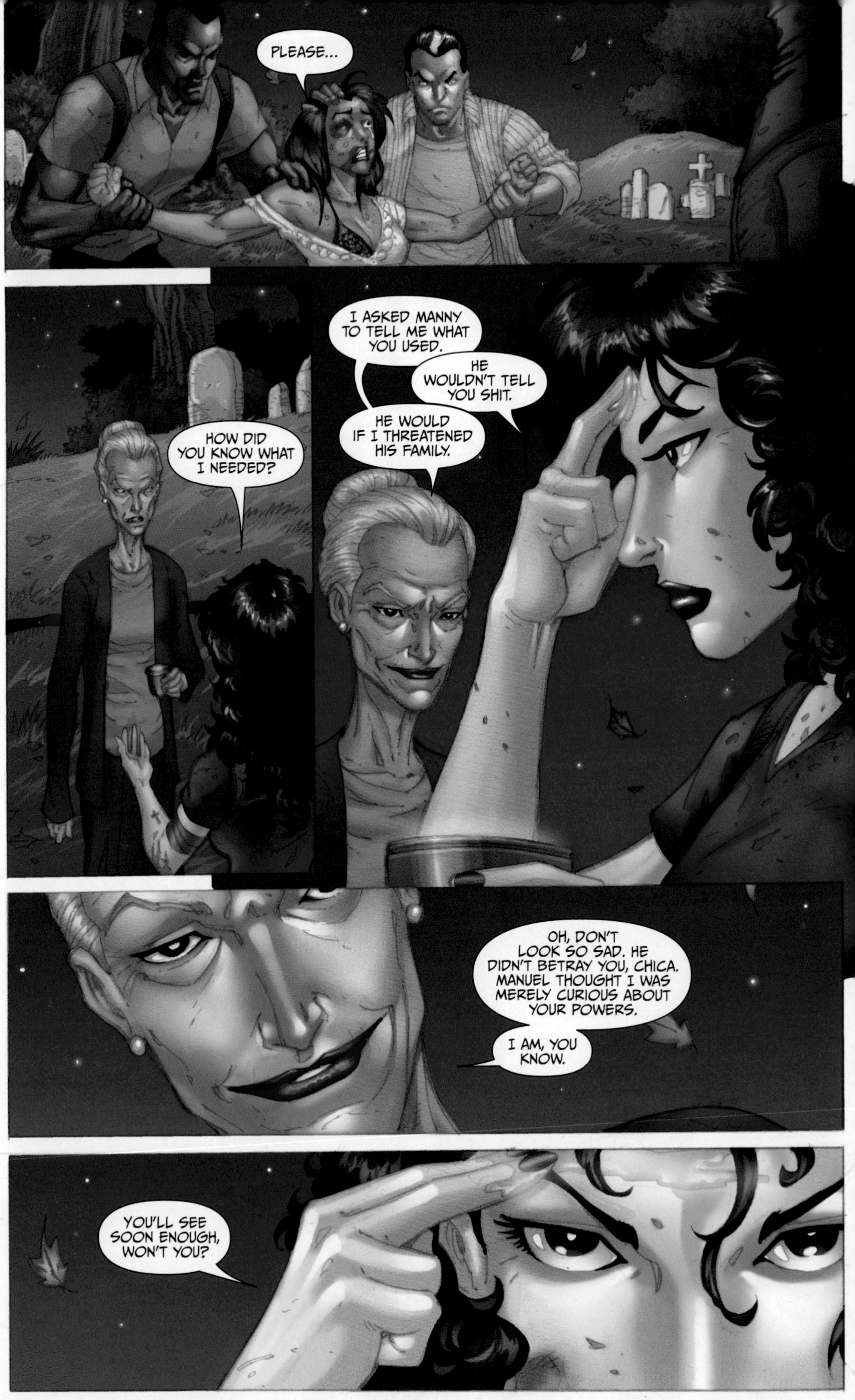
PLEASE...
HOW DID YOU KNOW WHAT I NEEDED?
I ASKED MANNY TO TELL ME WHAT YOU USED.
HE WOULDN'T TELL YOU SHIT.
HE WOULD IF I THREATENED HIS FAMILY.
OH, DON'T LOOK SO SAD. HE DIDN'T BETRAY YOU, CHICA. MANUEL THOUGHT I WAS MERELY CURIOUS ABOUT YOUR POWERS.
I AM, YOU KNOW.
YOU'LL SEE SOON ENOUGH, WON'T YOU?

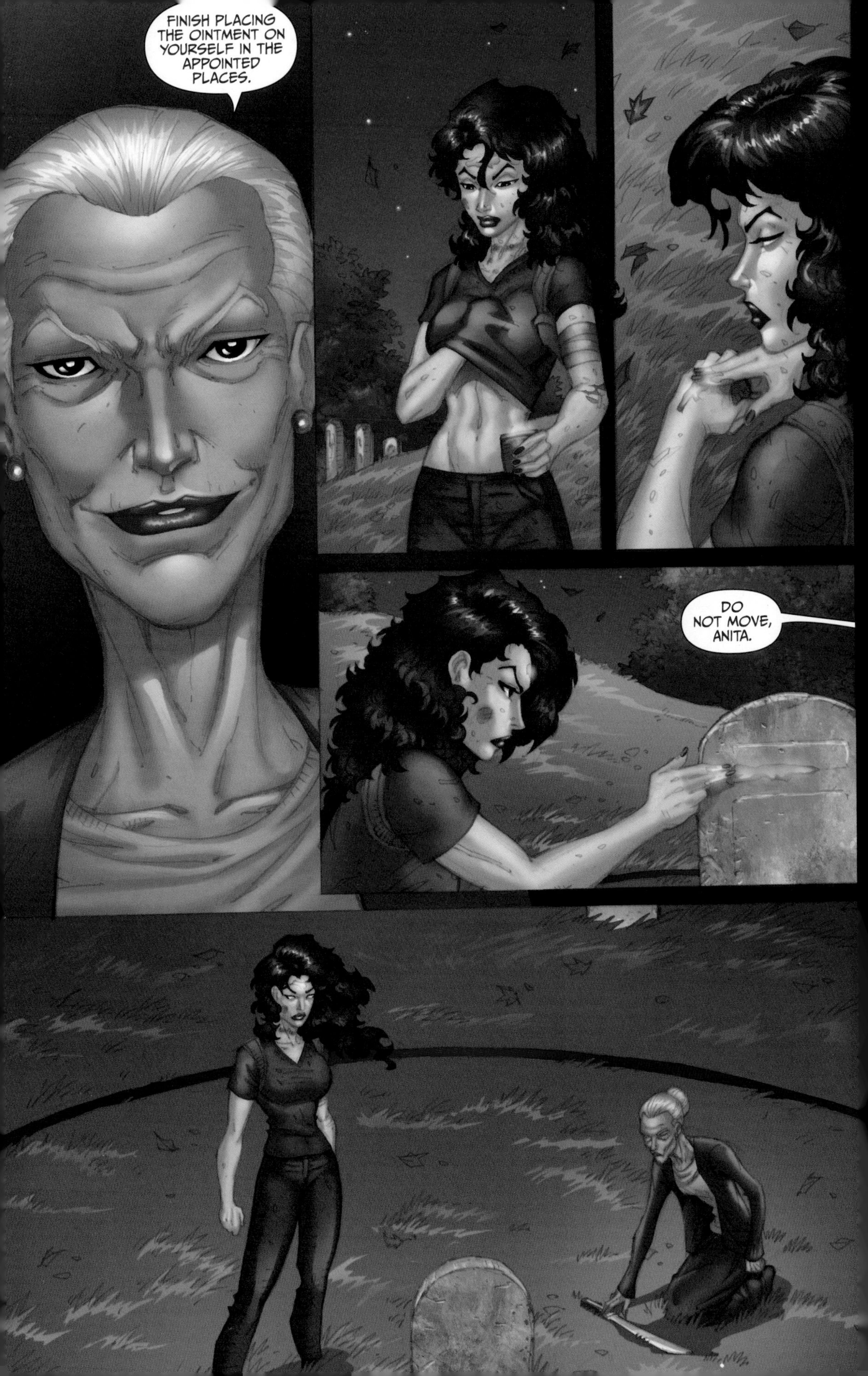
FINISH PLACING THE OINTMENT ON YOURSELF IN THE APPOINTED PLACES.
DO NOT MOVE, ANITA.

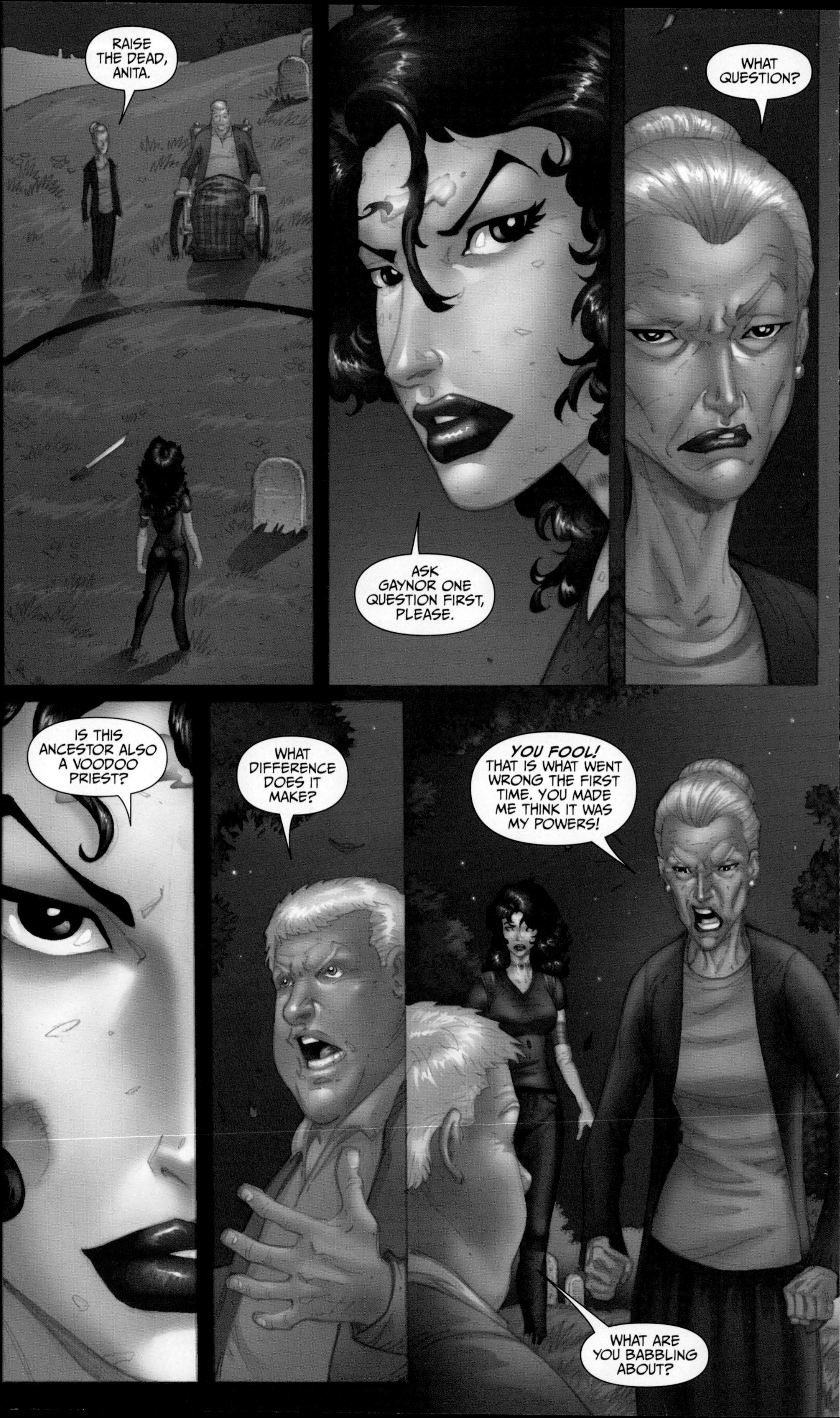
RAISE THE DEAD, ANITA.
ASK GAYNOR ONE QUESTION FIRST, PLEASE.
WHAT QUESTION?
IS THIS ANCESTOR ALSO A VOODOO PRIEST?
WHAT DIFFERENCE DOES IT MAKE?
YOU FOOL! THAT IS WHAT WENT WRONG THE FIRST TIME. YOU MADE ME THINK IT WAS MY POWERS!
WHAT ARE YOU BABBLING ABOUT?

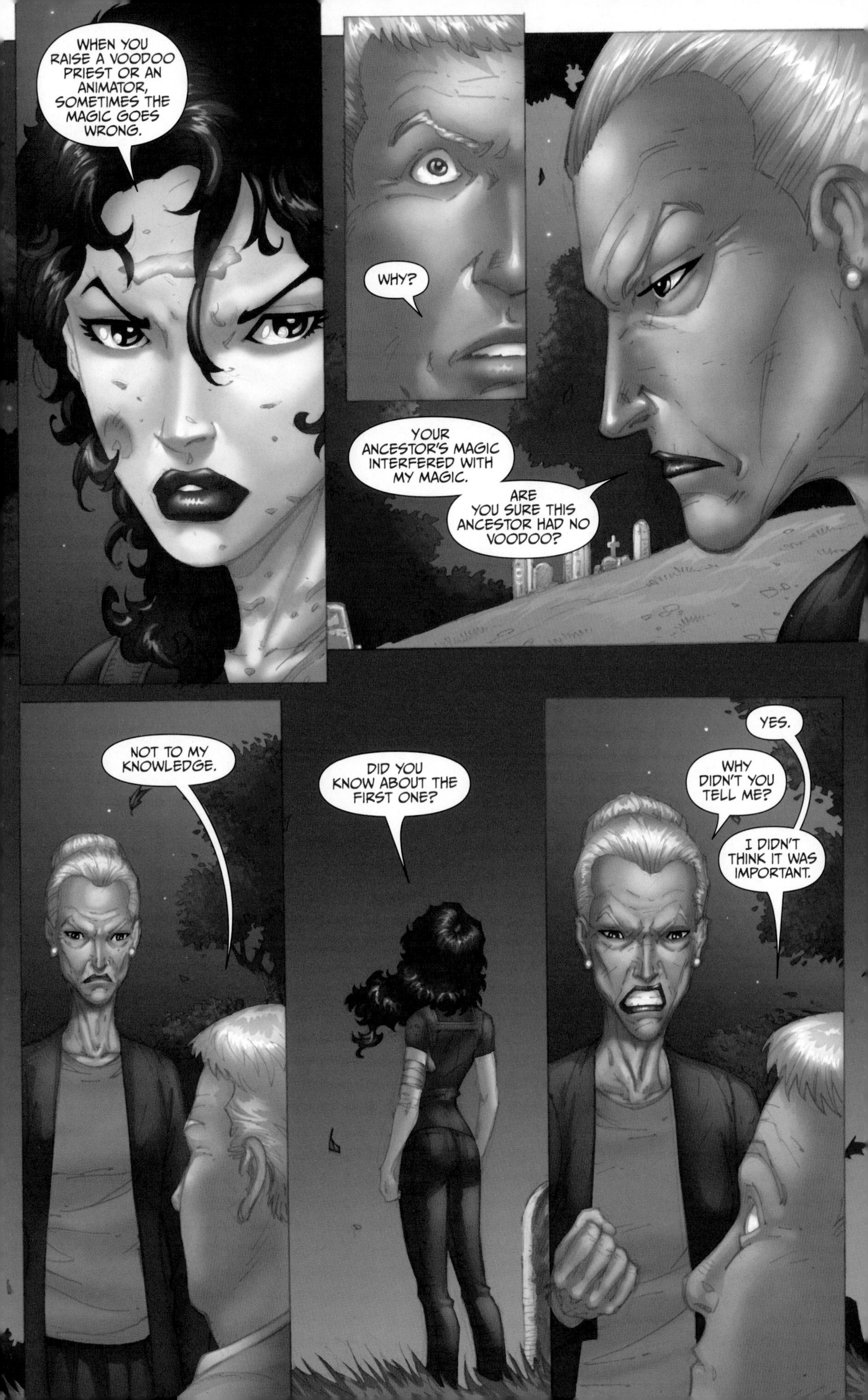

WHEN YOU RAISE A VOODOO PRIEST OR AN ANIMATOR, SOMETIMES THE MAGIC GOES WRONG.
WHY?
YOUR ANCESTOR'S MAGIC INTERFERED WITH MY MAGIC.
ARE YOU SURE THIS ANCESTOR HAD NO VOODOO?
NOT TO MY KNOWLEDGE.
DID YOU KNOW ABOUT THE FIRST ONE?
YES.
WHY DIDN'T YOU TELL ME?
I DIDN'T THINK IT WAS IMPORTANT.

GET ON WITH IT. OR DON'T YOU WANT YOUR MONEY?

DO NOT THREATEN ME!

PEACHY KEEN, THE BAD GUYS WERE GOING TO FIGHT AMONG THEMSELVES.

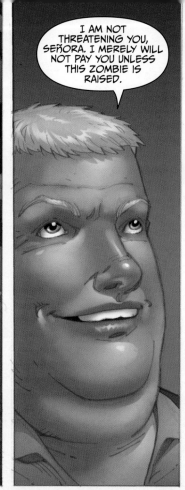

I AM NOT THREATENING YOU, SEÑORA. I MERELY WILL NOT PAY YOU UNLESS THIS ZOMBIE IS RAISED.

DO AS I ORDERED AND RAISE THE DEAD.

NO MORE DELAYS. RAISE THE DEAD, ANITA, NOW!

IT WAS LIKE BEATING AGAINST A WALL I COULDN'T FEEL.

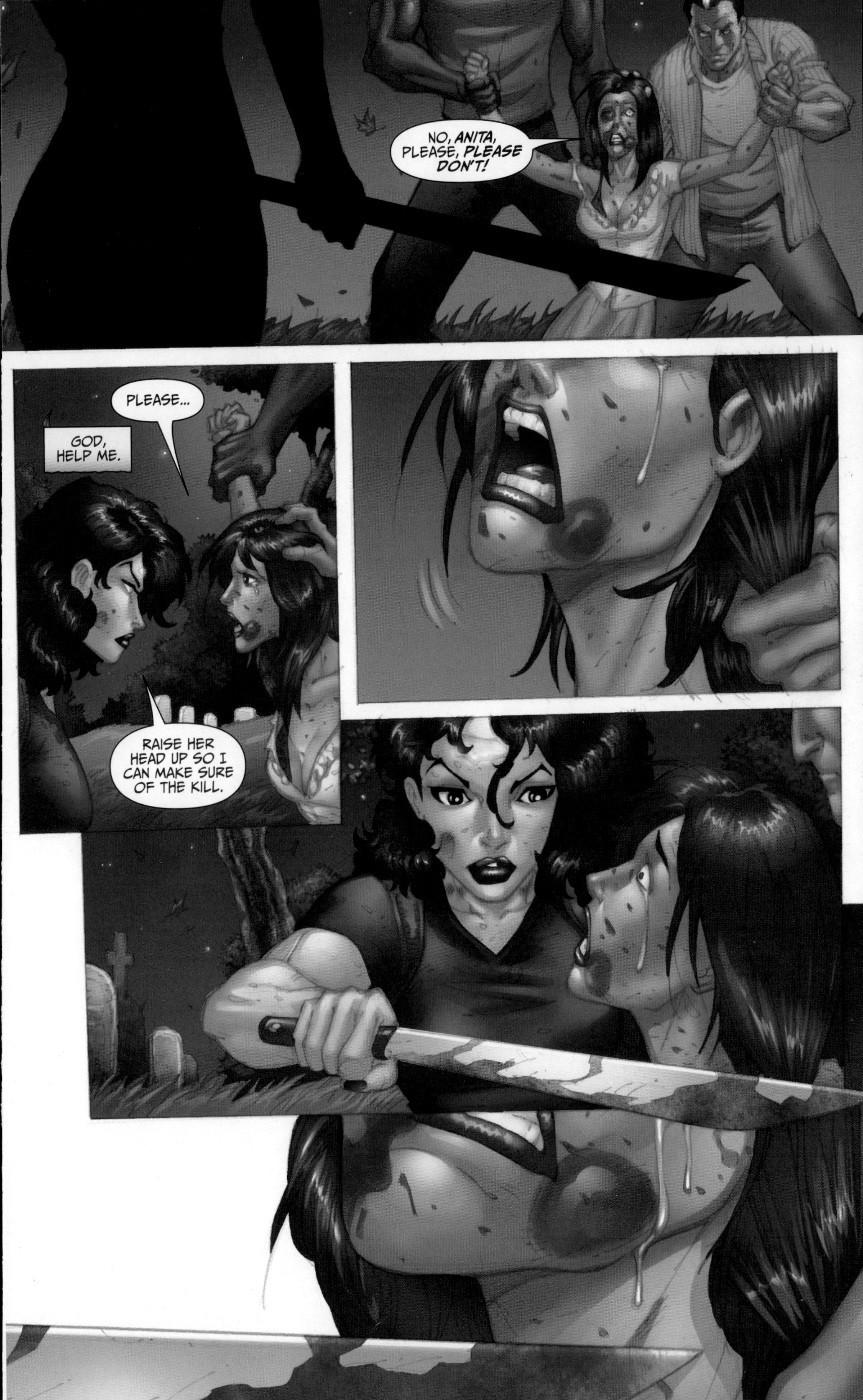
NO, ANITA, PLEASE, PLEASE DON'T!
PLEASE...
GOD, HELP ME.
RAISE HER HEAD UP SO I CAN MAKE SURE OF THE KILL.

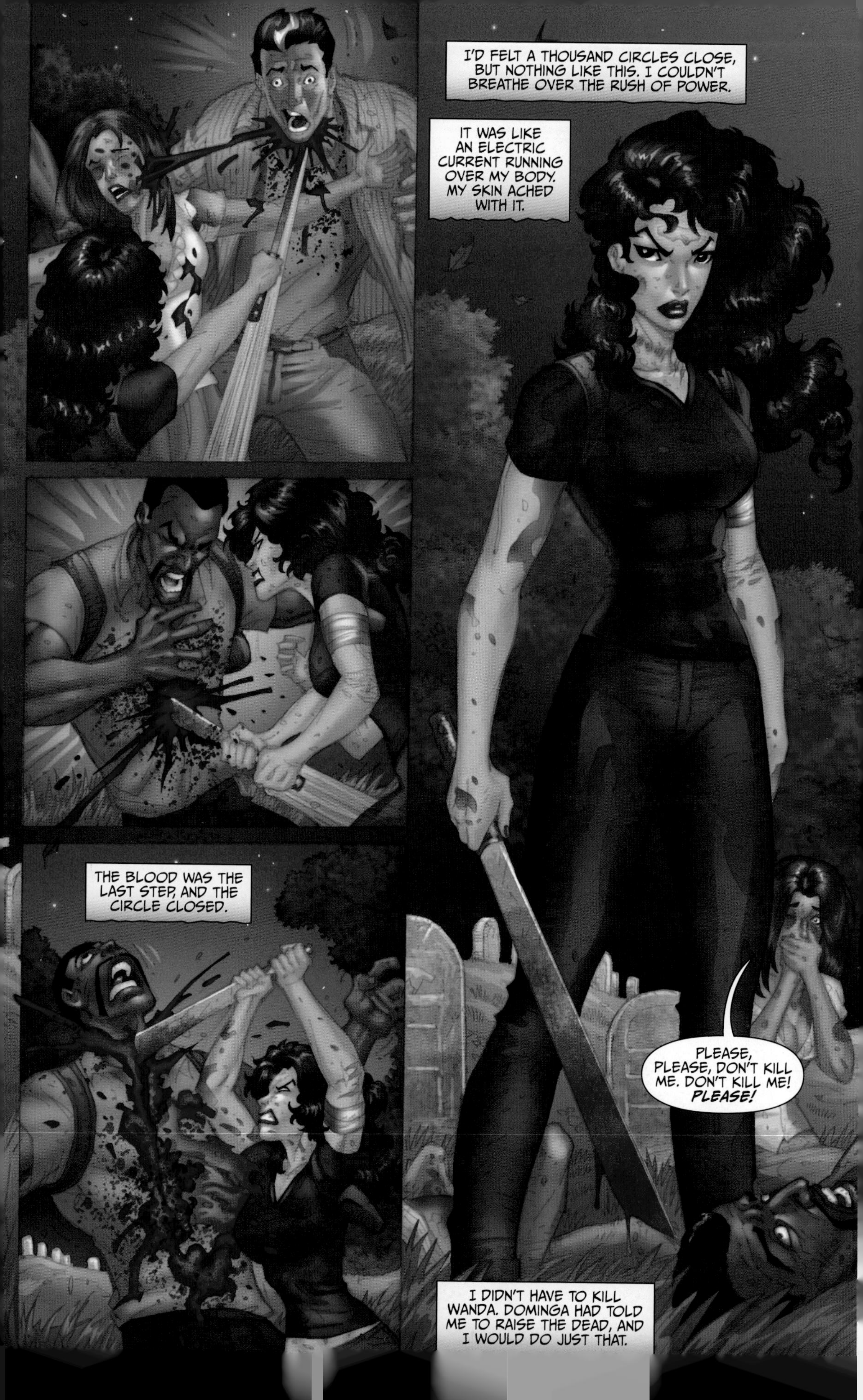
I'D FELT A THOUSAND CIRCLES CLOSE, BUT NOTHING LIKE THIS. I COULDN'T BREATHE OVER THE RUSH OF POWER.
IT WAS LIKE AN ELECTRIC CURRENT RUNNING OVER MY BODY. MY SKIN ACHED WITH IT.
THE BLOOD WAS THE LAST STEP, AND THE CIRCLE CLOSED.
PLEASE, PLEASE, DON'T KILL ME. DON'T KILL ME! *PLEASE!*
I DIDN'T HAVE TO KILL WANDA. DOMINGA HAD TOLD ME TO RAISE THE DEAD, AND I WOULD DO JUST THAT.

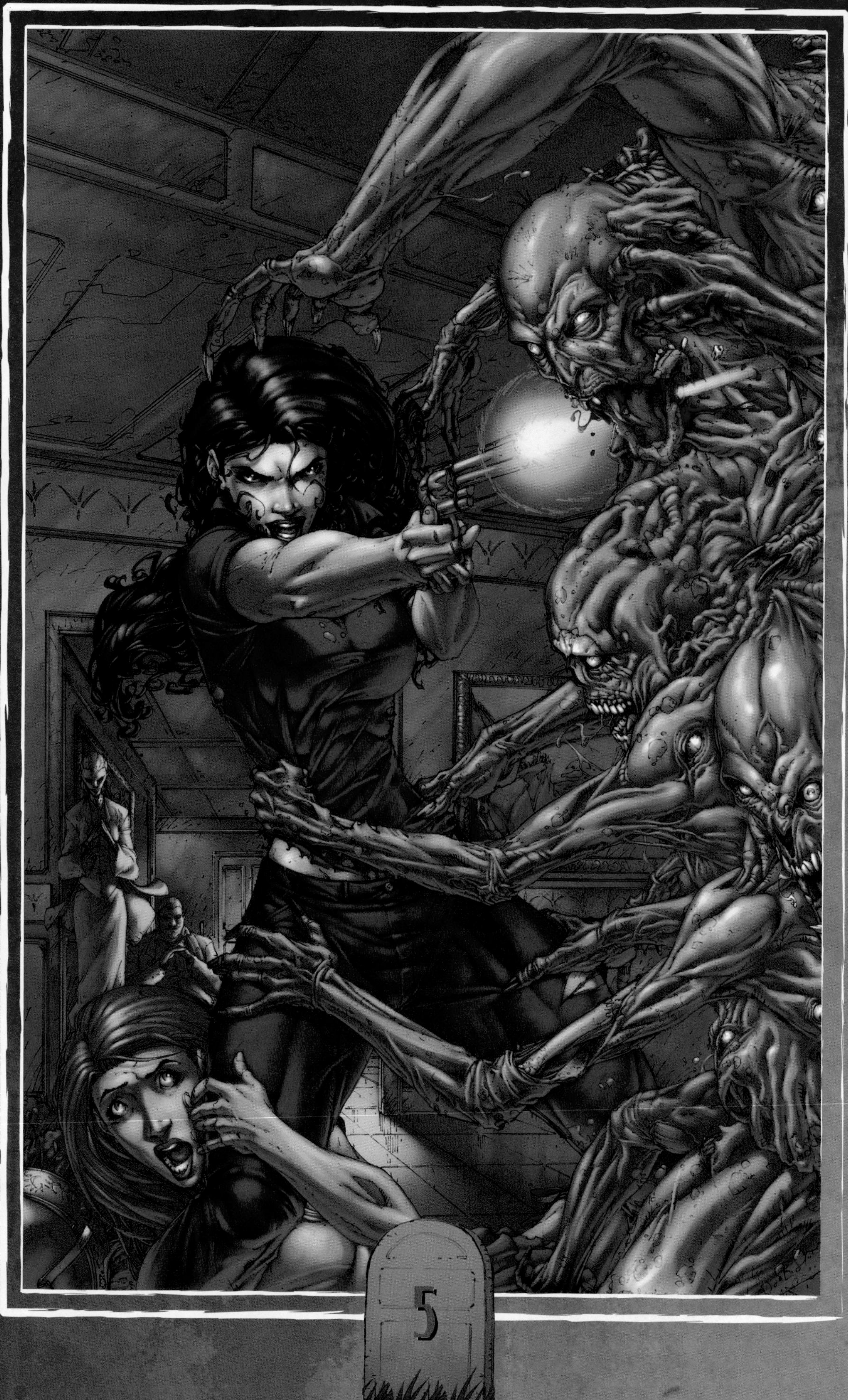
5

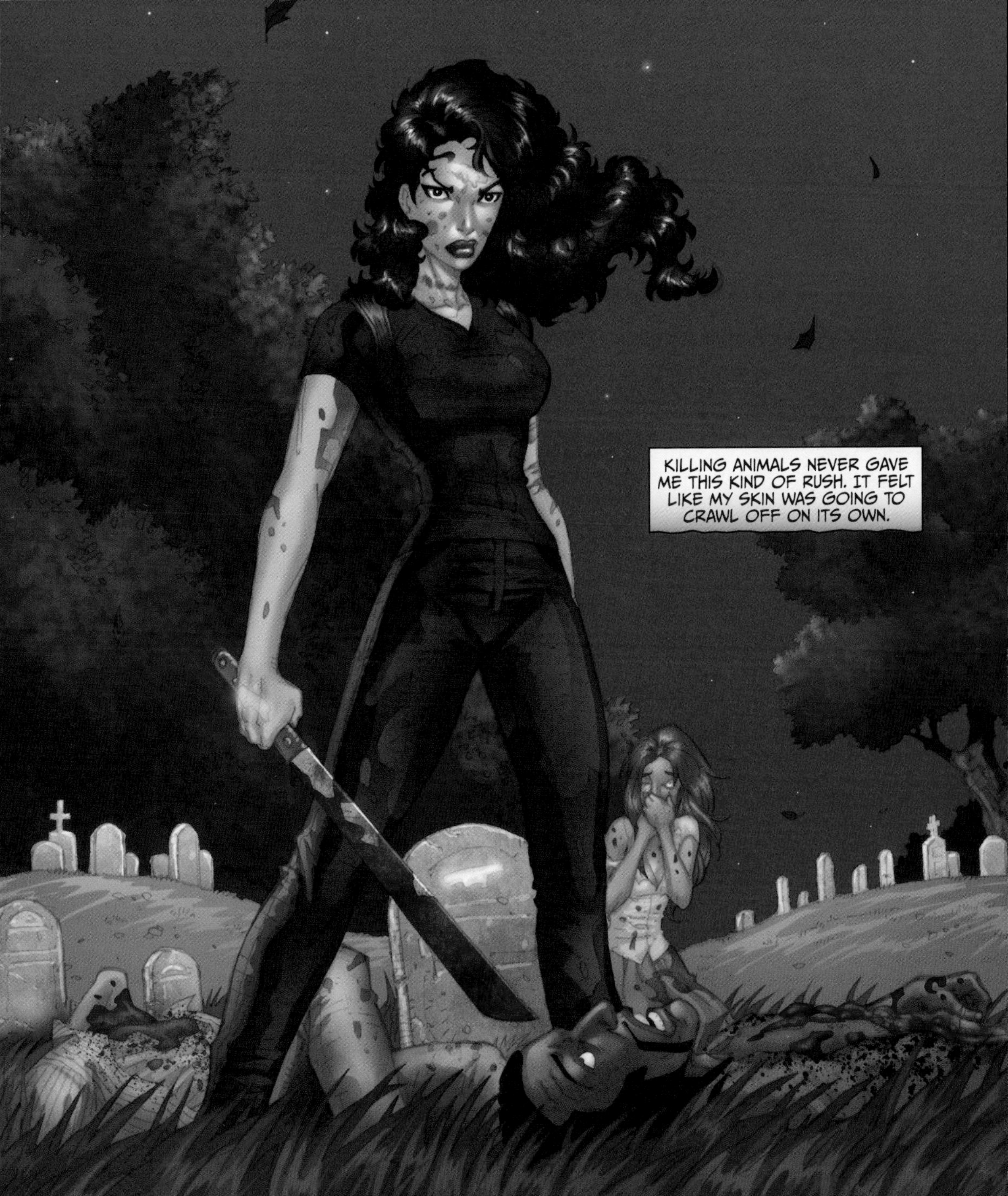
KILLING ANIMALS NEVER GAVE ME THIS KIND OF RUSH. IT FELT LIKE MY SKIN WAS GOING TO CRAWL OFF ON ITS OWN.

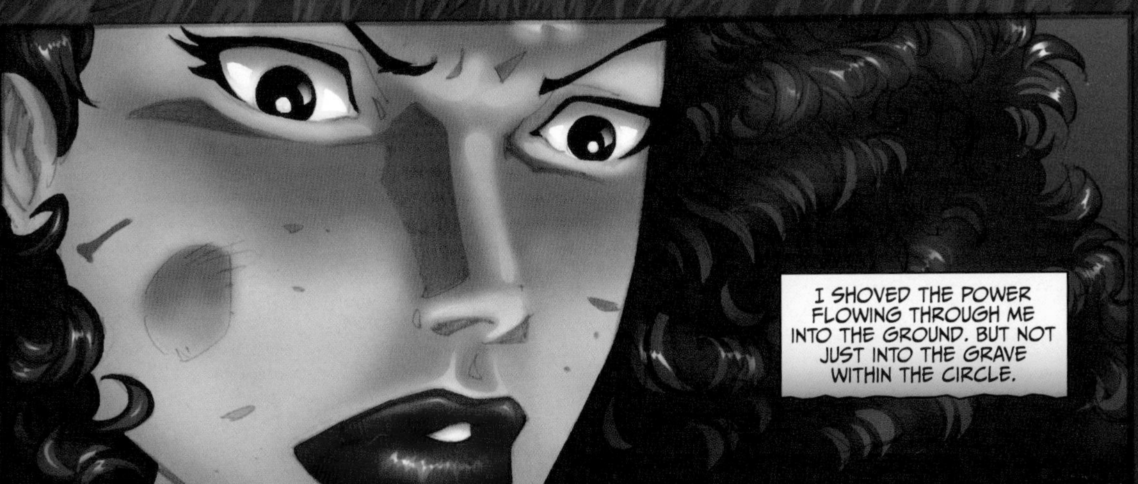
I SHOVED THE POWER FLOWING THROUGH ME INTO THE GROUND. BUT NOT JUST INTO THE GRAVE WITHIN THE CIRCLE.

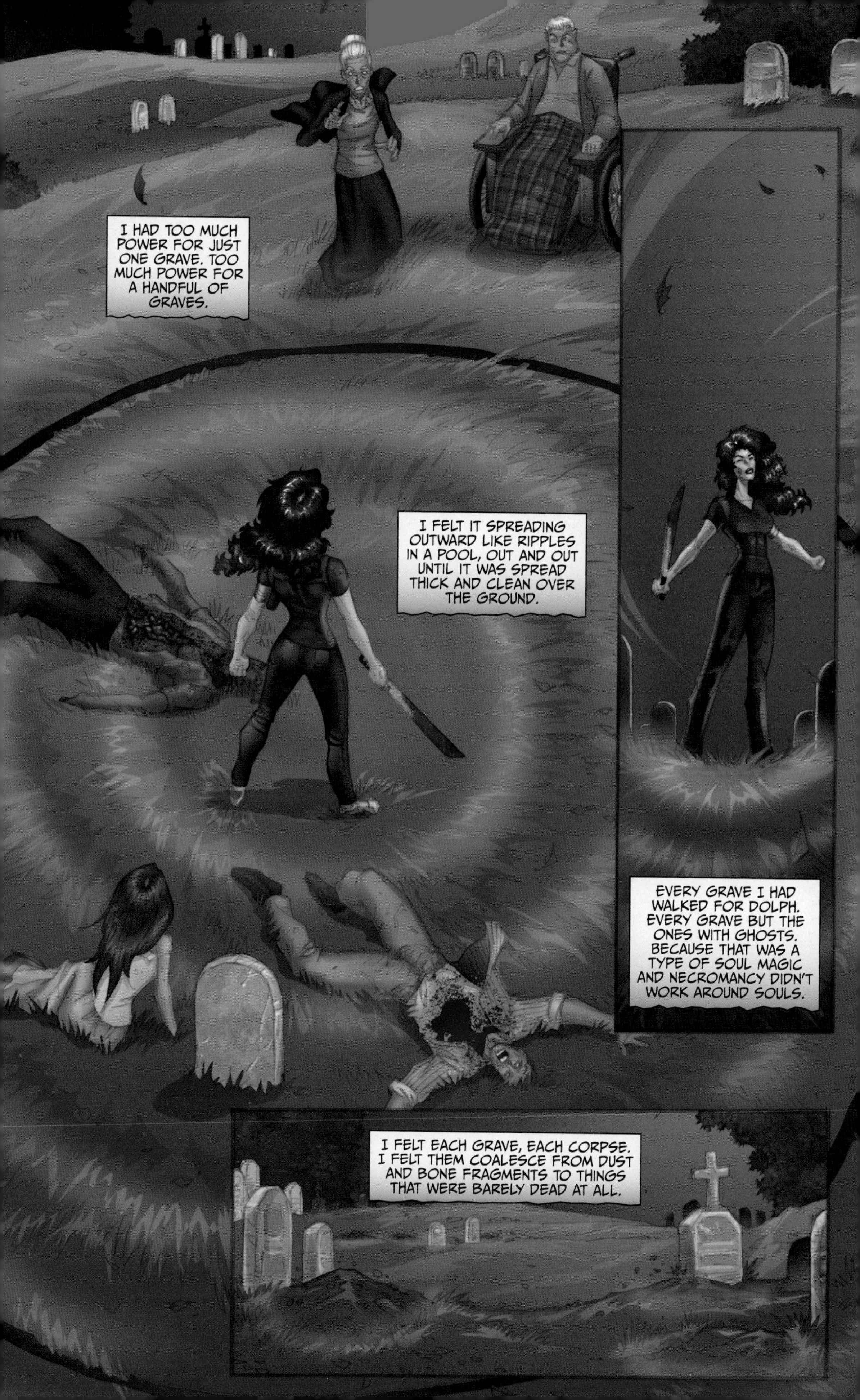
I HAD TOO MUCH POWER FOR JUST ONE GRAVE. TOO MUCH POWER FOR A HANDFUL OF GRAVES.
I FELT IT SPREADING OUTWARD LIKE RIPPLES IN A POOL, OUT AND OUT UNTIL IT WAS SPREAD THICK AND CLEAN OVER THE GROUND.
EVERY GRAVE I HAD WALKED FOR DOLPH. EVERY GRAVE BUT THE ONES WITH GHOSTS. BECAUSE THAT WAS A TYPE OF SOUL MAGIC AND NECROMANCY DIDN'T WORK AROUND SOULS.
I FELT EACH GRAVE, EACH CORPSE. I FELT THEM COALESCE FROM DUST AND BONE FRAGMENTS TO THINGS THAT WERE BARELY DEAD AT ALL.

ARISE FROM YOUR GRAVES ALL DEAD WITHIN SOUND OF MY CALL!
ARISE AND SERVE ME!
WITHOUT NAMING THEM ALL I SHOULDN'T HAVE BEEN ABLE TO CALL A SINGLE ONE FROM THE GRAVE, BUT THE POWER OF TWO HUMAN DEATHS WAS TOO MUCH FOR THE DEAD TO RESIST.
WHAT ARE YOU DOING?
RAISING THE DEAD, DOMINGA.

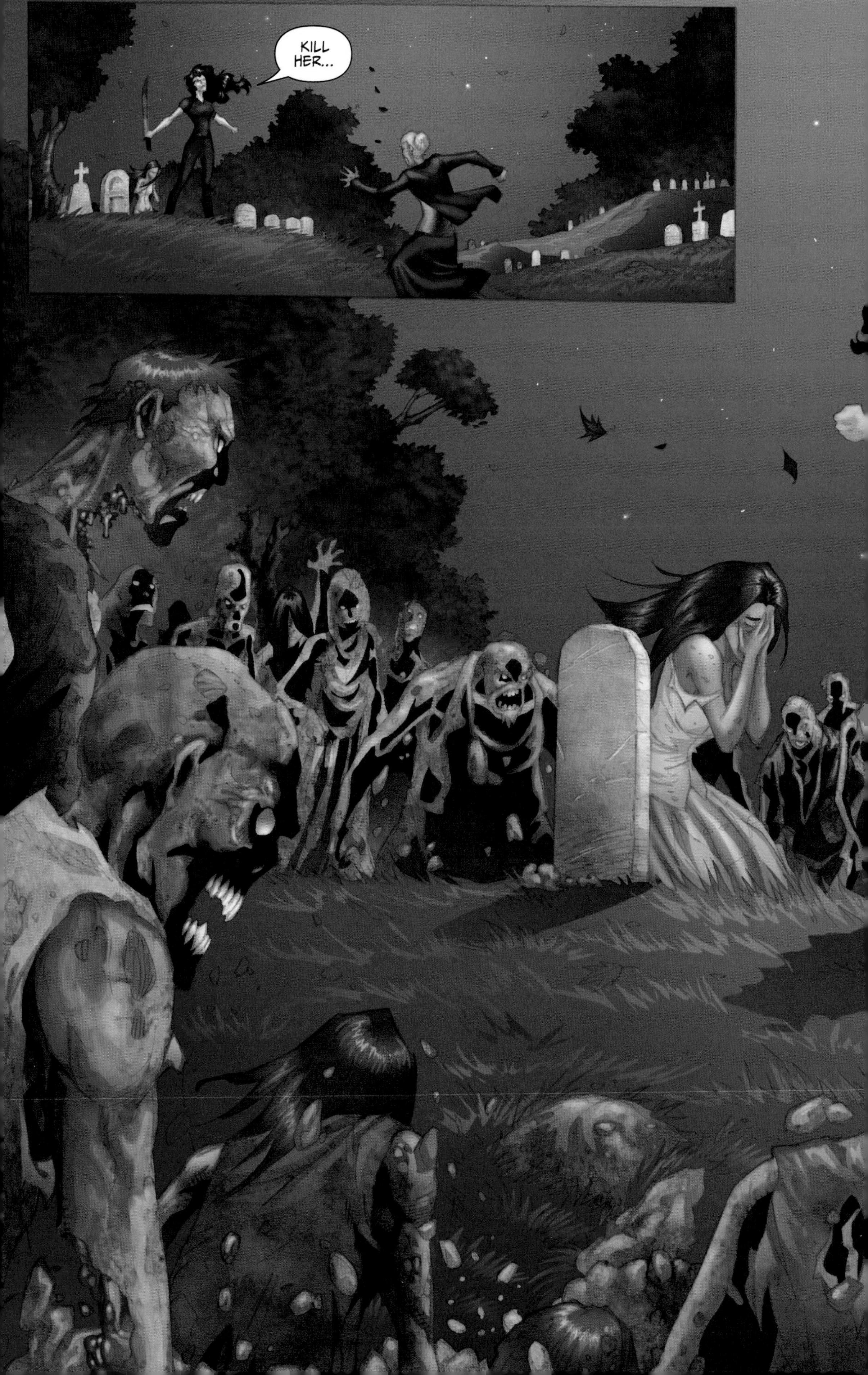
KILL HER...

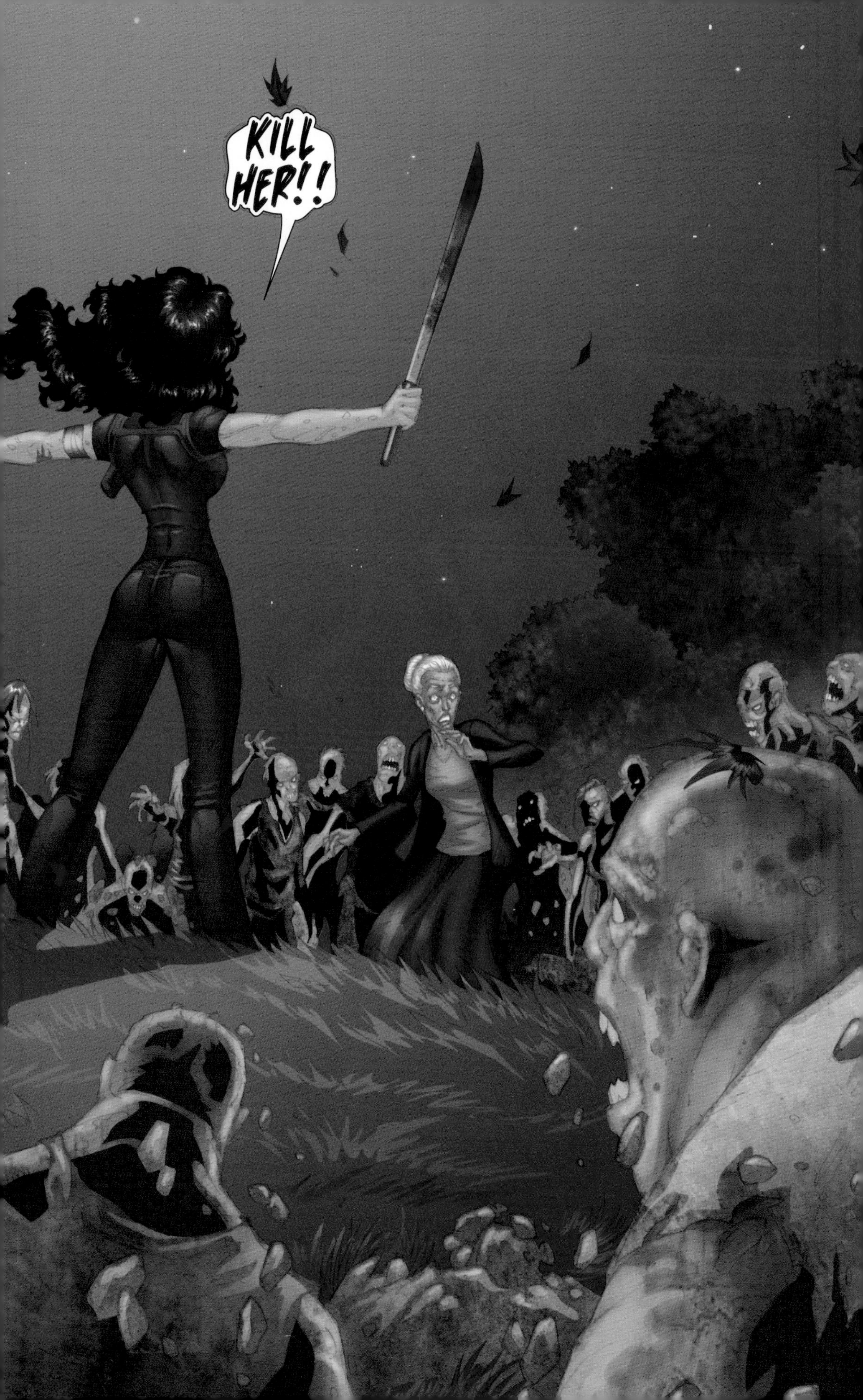
KILL HER!!

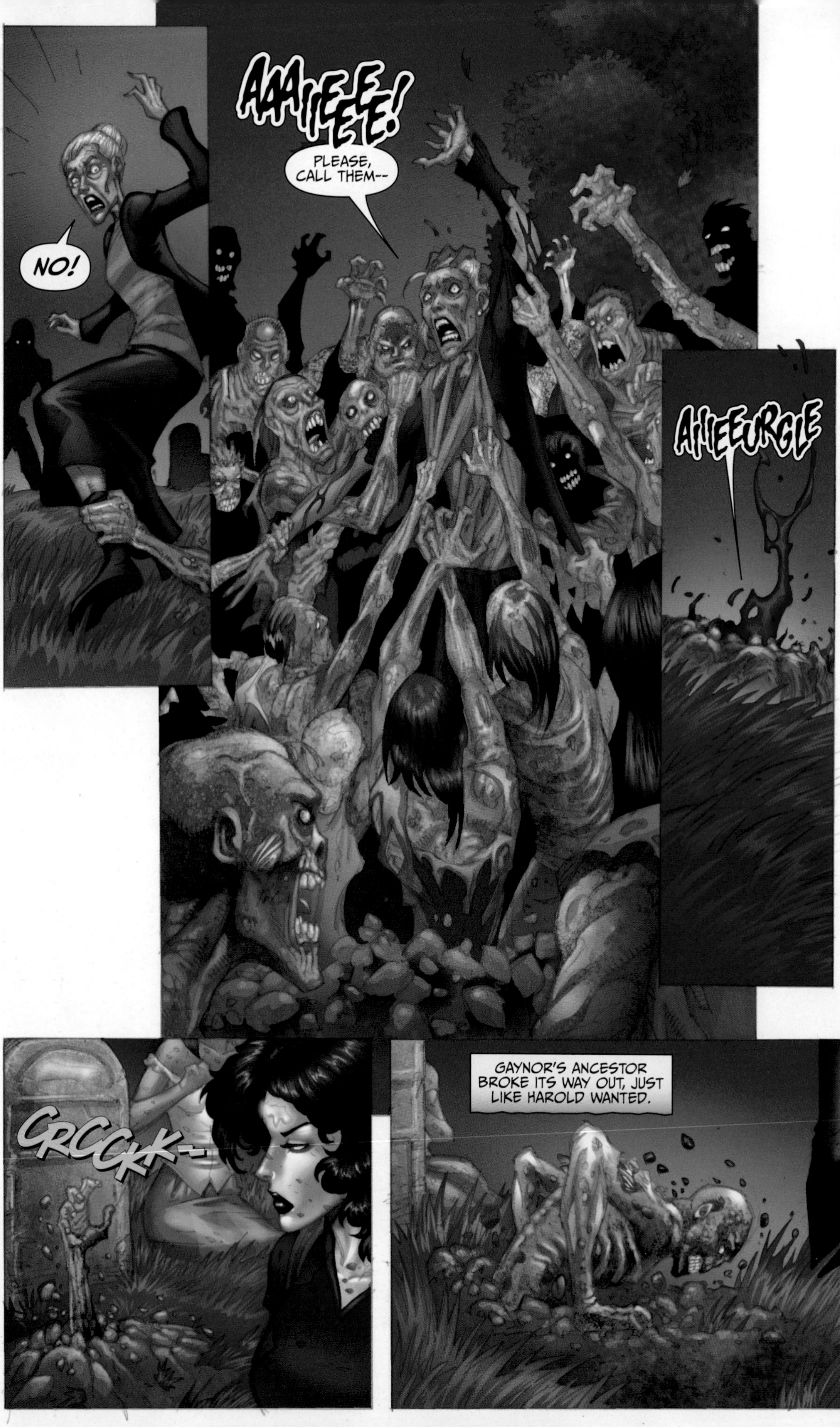
NO!
AAAIIEEEE!
PLEASE, CALL THEM--
AIIIEEURGLE
CRCCK--
GAYNOR'S ANCESTOR BROKE ITS WAY OUT, JUST LIKE HAROLD WANTED.

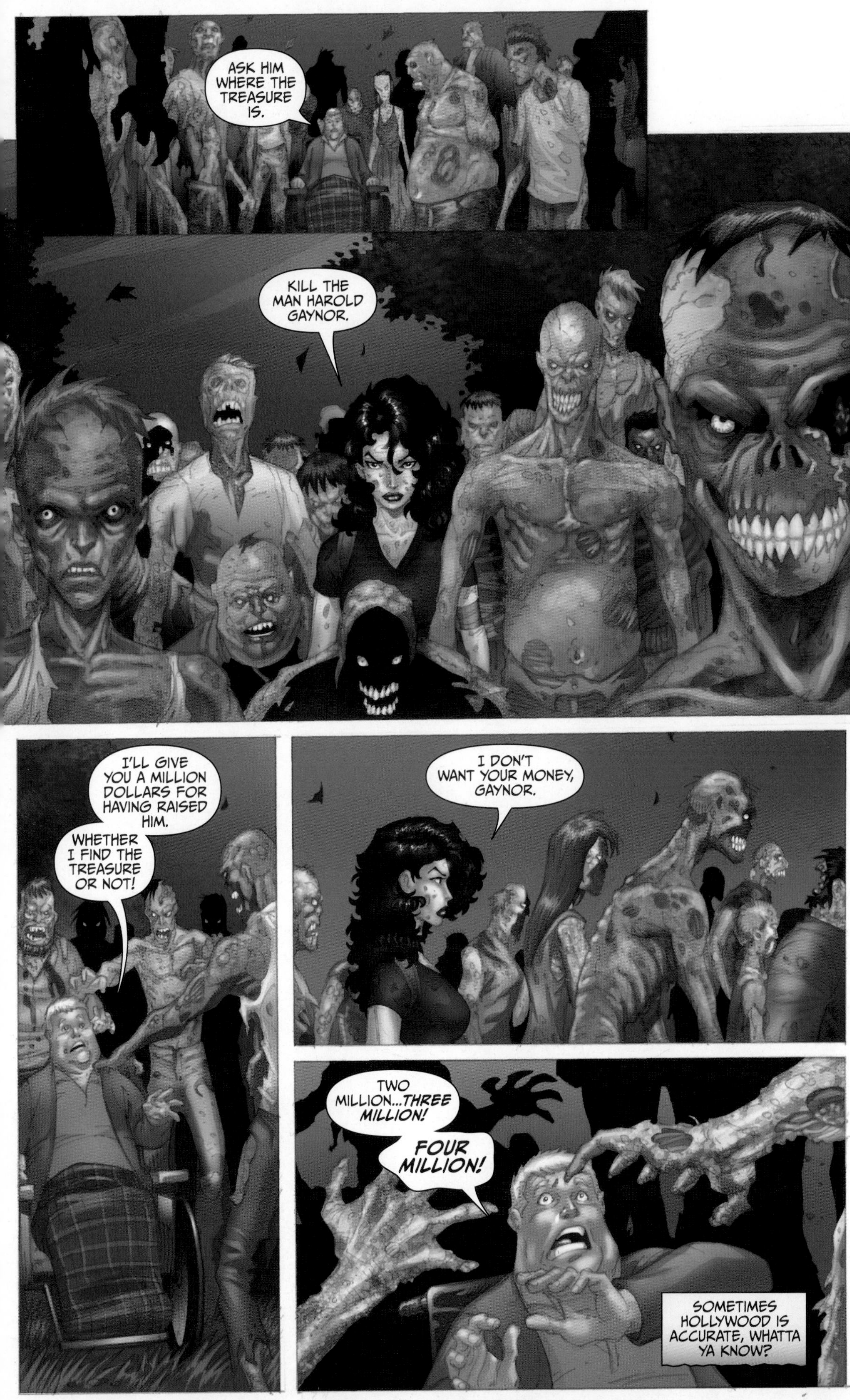
ASK HIM WHERE THE TREASURE IS.
KILL THE MAN HAROLD GAYNOR.
I'LL GIVE YOU A MILLION DOLLARS FOR HAVING RAISED HIM.
WHETHER I FIND THE TREASURE OR NOT!
I DON'T WANT YOUR MONEY, GAYNOR.
TWO MILLION...THREE MILLION!
FOUR MILLION!
SOMETIMES HOLLYWOOD IS ACCURATE, WHATTA YA KNOW?

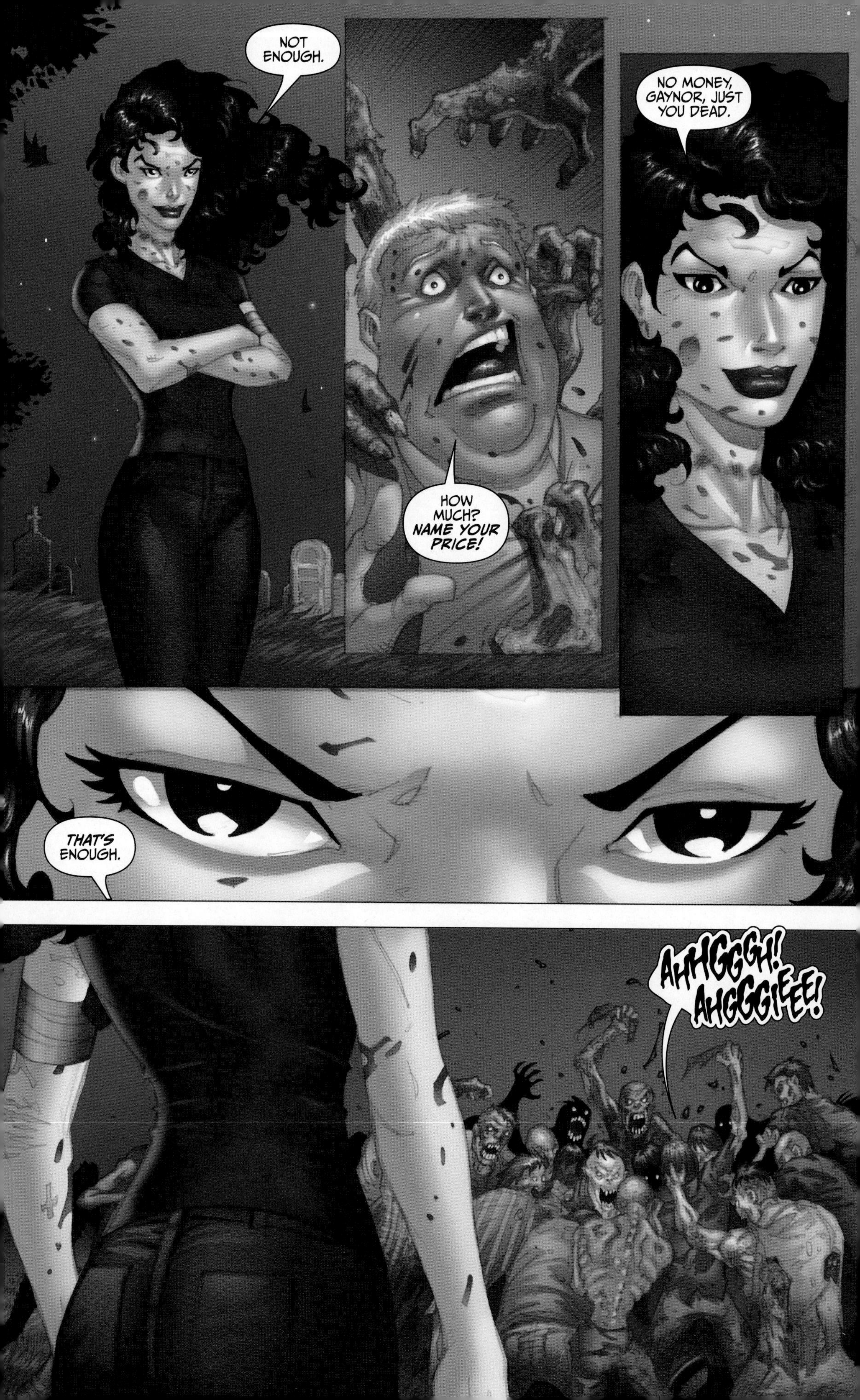
NOT ENOUGH.
HOW MUCH? *NAME YOUR PRICE!*
NO MONEY, GAYNOR, JUST YOU DEAD.
THAT'S ENOUGH.
AHHGGGH! AHGGGIEEE!

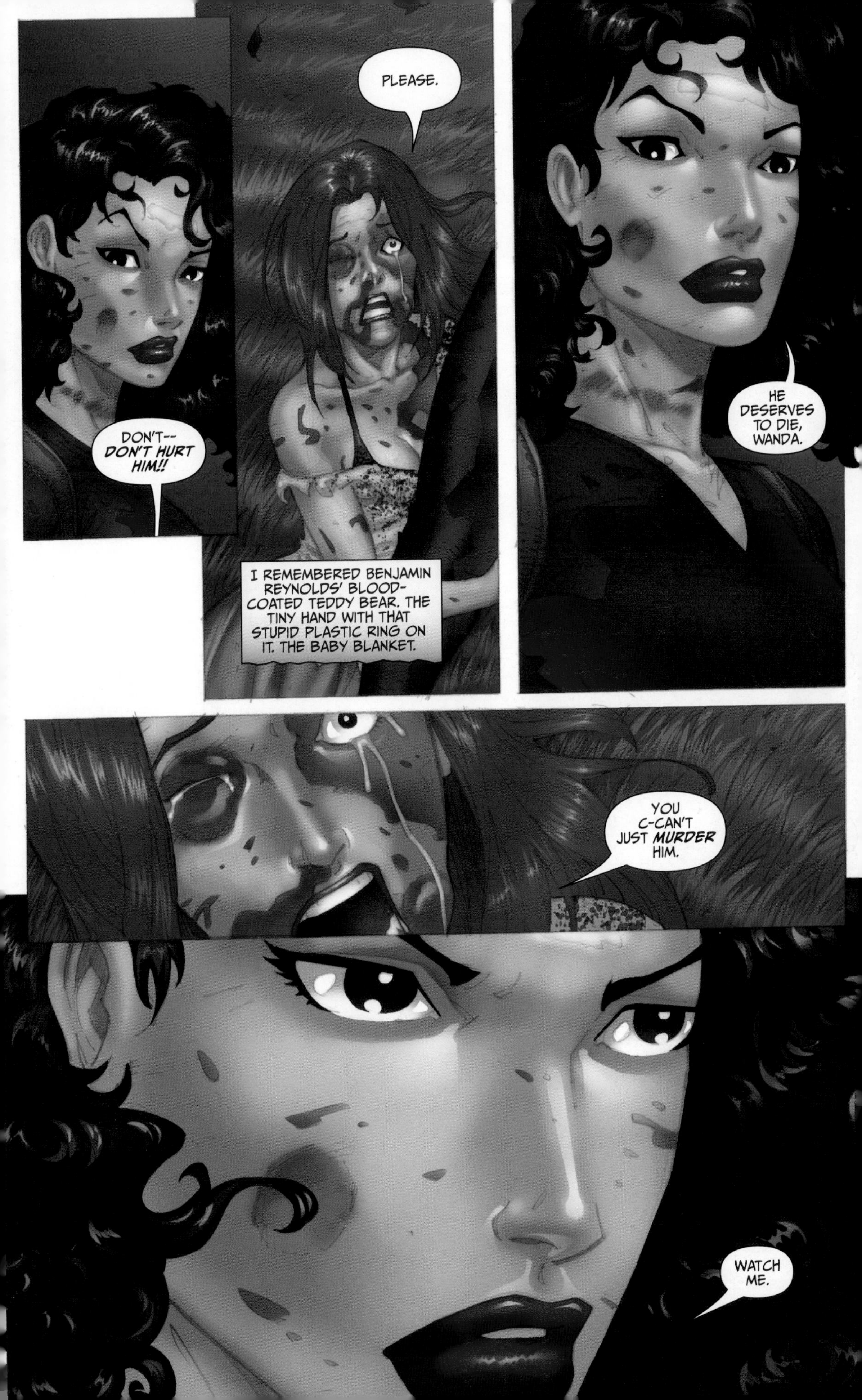
DON'T-- DON'T HURT HIM!!
PLEASE.
I REMEMBERED BENJAMIN REYNOLDS' BLOOD-COATED TEDDY BEAR. THE TINY HAND WITH THAT STUPID PLASTIC RING ON IT. THE BABY BLANKET.
HE DESERVES TO DIE, WANDA.
YOU C-CAN'T JUST MURDER HIM.
WATCH ME.

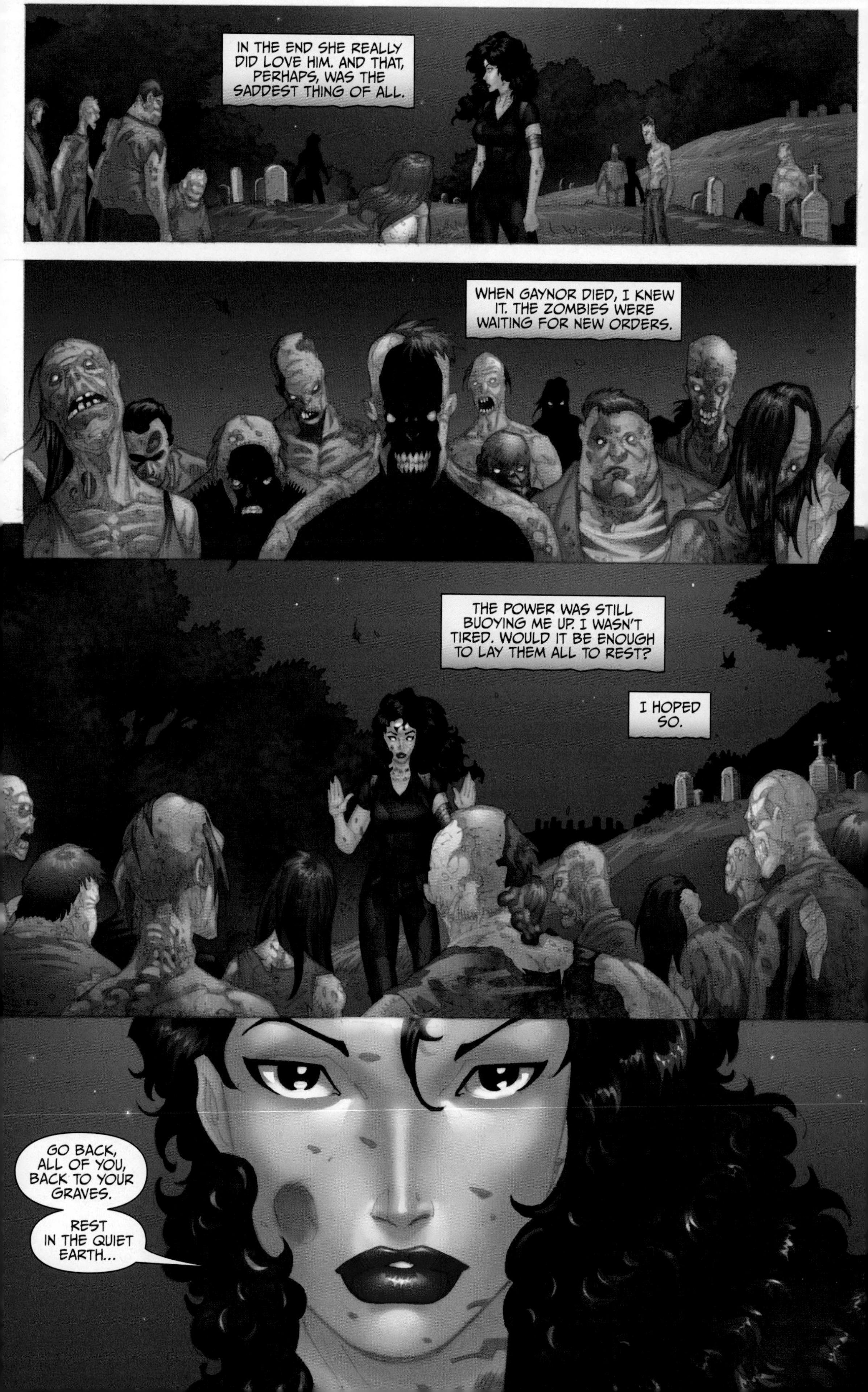
IN THE END SHE REALLY DID LOVE HIM. AND THAT, PERHAPS, WAS THE SADDEST THING OF ALL.
WHEN GAYNOR DIED, I KNEW IT. THE ZOMBIES WERE WAITING FOR NEW ORDERS.
THE POWER WAS STILL BUOYING ME UP. I WASN'T TIRED. WOULD IT BE ENOUGH TO LAY THEM ALL TO REST?
I HOPED SO.
GO BACK, ALL OF YOU, BACK TO YOUR GRAVES.
REST IN THE QUIET EARTH...

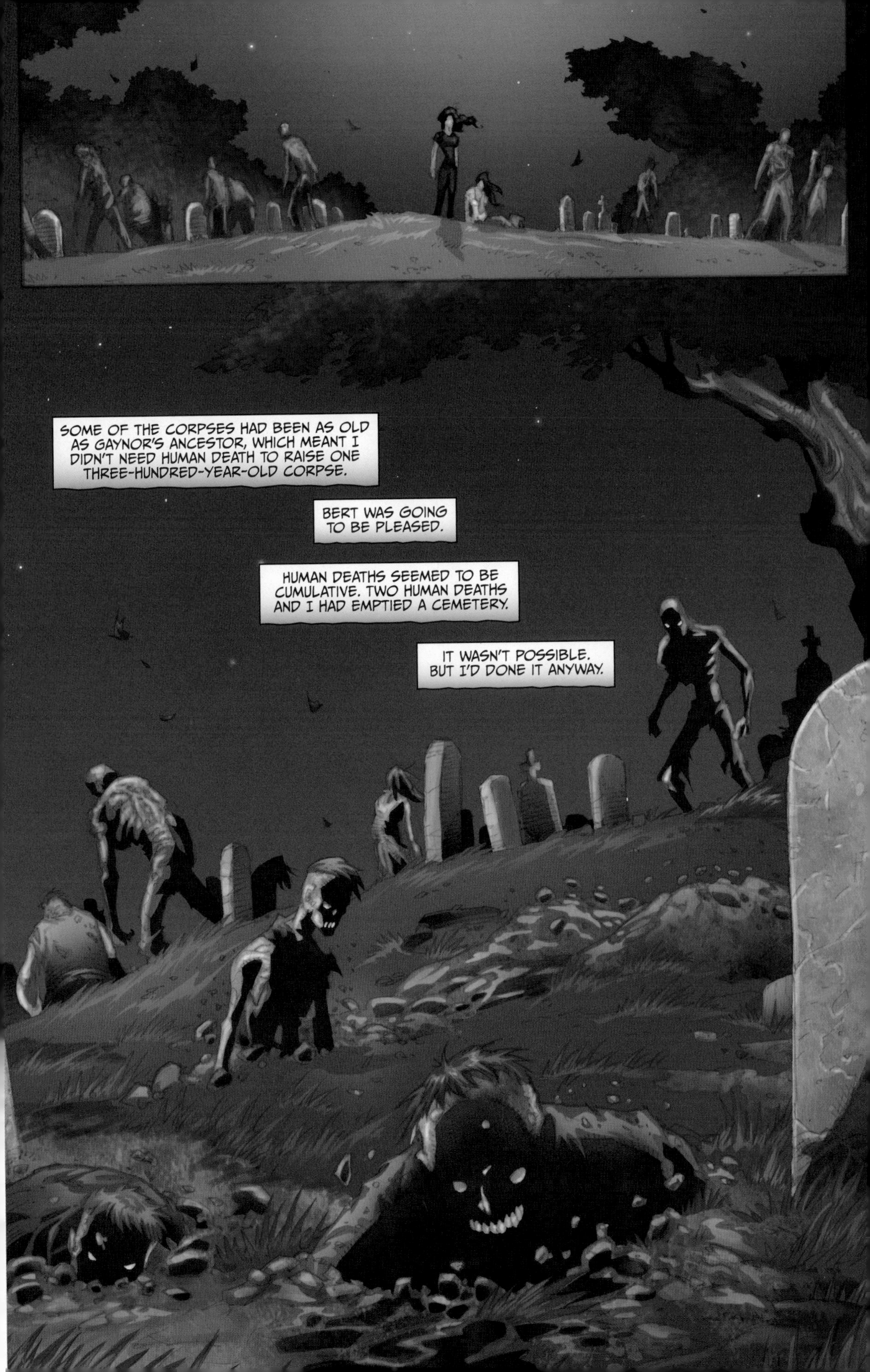
SOME OF THE CORPSES HAD BEEN AS OLD AS GAYNOR'S ANCESTOR, WHICH MEANT I DIDN'T NEED HUMAN DEATH TO RAISE ONE THREE-HUNDRED-YEAR-OLD CORPSE.
BERT WAS GOING TO BE PLEASED.
HUMAN DEATHS SEEMED TO BE CUMULATIVE. TWO HUMAN DEATHS AND I HAD EMPTIED A CEMETERY.
IT WASN'T POSSIBLE. BUT I'D DONE IT ANYWAY.

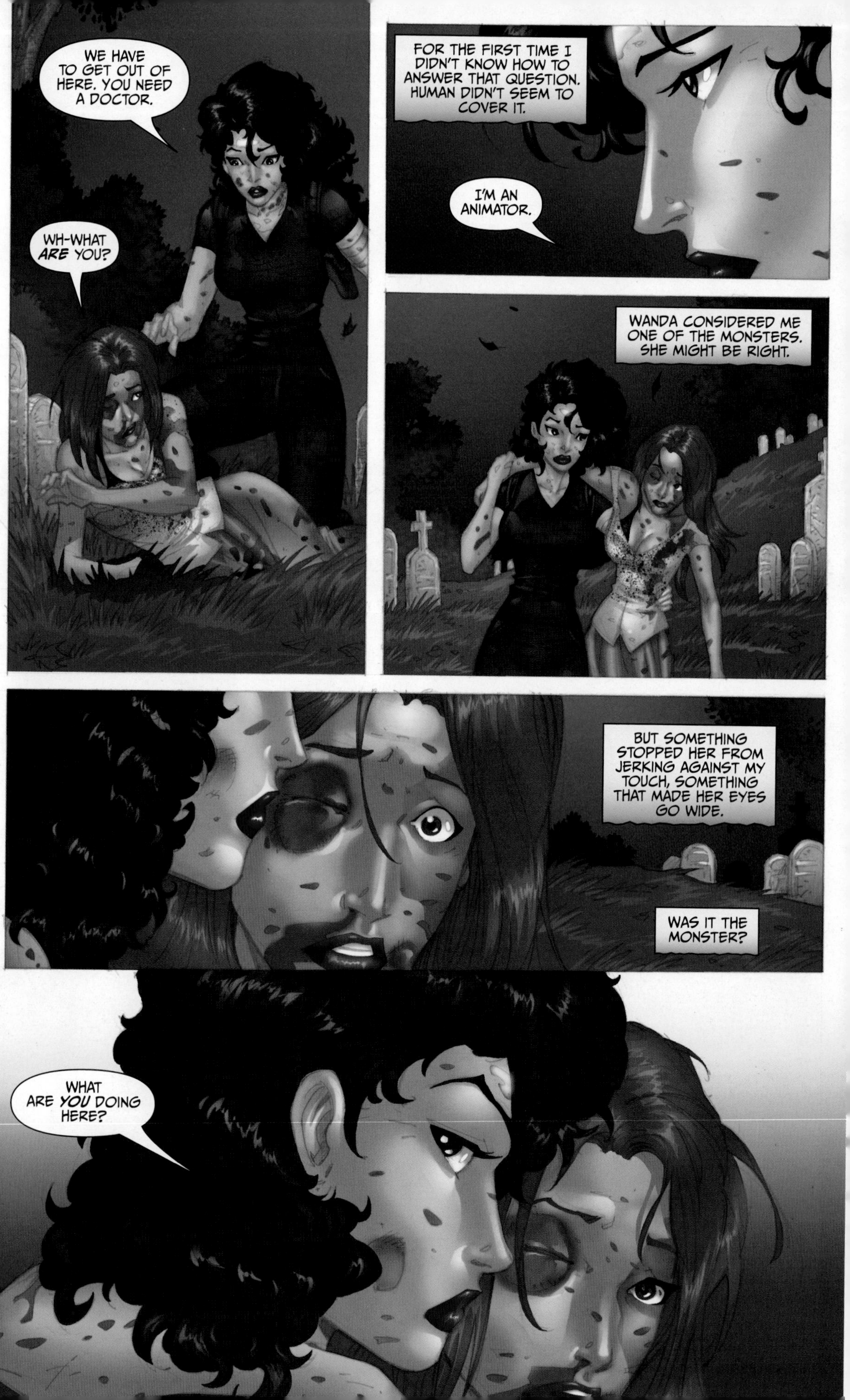
WE HAVE TO GET OUT OF HERE. YOU NEED A DOCTOR.
WH-WHAT ARE YOU?
FOR THE FIRST TIME I DIDN'T KNOW HOW TO ANSWER THAT QUESTION. HUMAN DIDN'T SEEM TO COVER IT.
I'M AN ANIMATOR.
WANDA CONSIDERED ME ONE OF THE MONSTERS. SHE MIGHT BE RIGHT.
BUT SOMETHING STOPPED HER FROM JERKING AGAINST MY TOUCH, SOMETHING THAT MADE HER EYES GO WIDE.
WAS IT THE MONSTER?
WHAT ARE YOU DOING HERE?

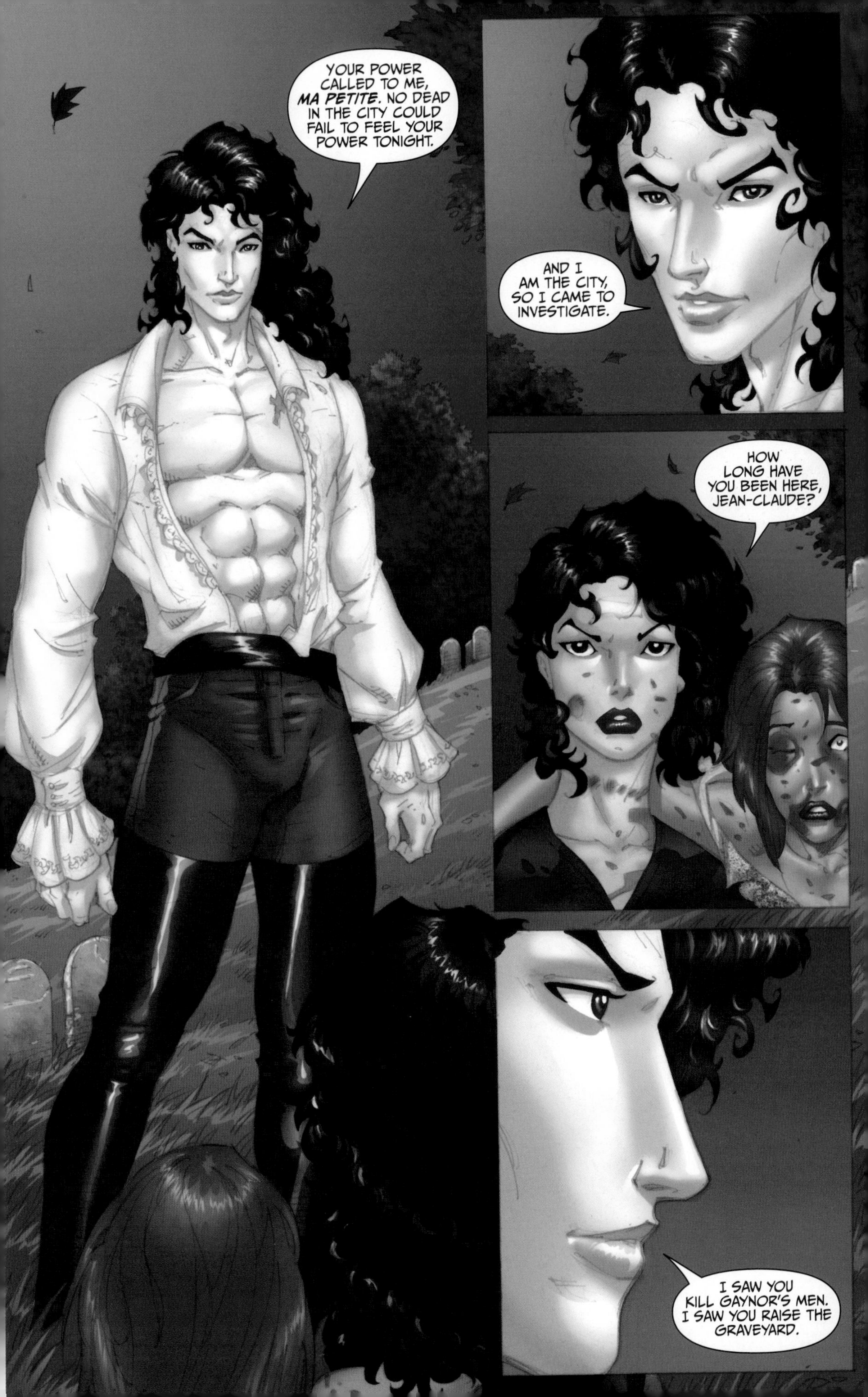
YOUR POWER CALLED TO ME, MA PETITE. NO DEAD IN THE CITY COULD FAIL TO FEEL YOUR POWER TONIGHT.
AND I AM THE CITY, SO I CAME TO INVESTIGATE.
HOW LONG HAVE YOU BEEN HERE, JEAN-CLAUDE?
I SAW YOU KILL GAYNOR'S MEN. I SAW YOU RAISE THE GRAVEYARD.

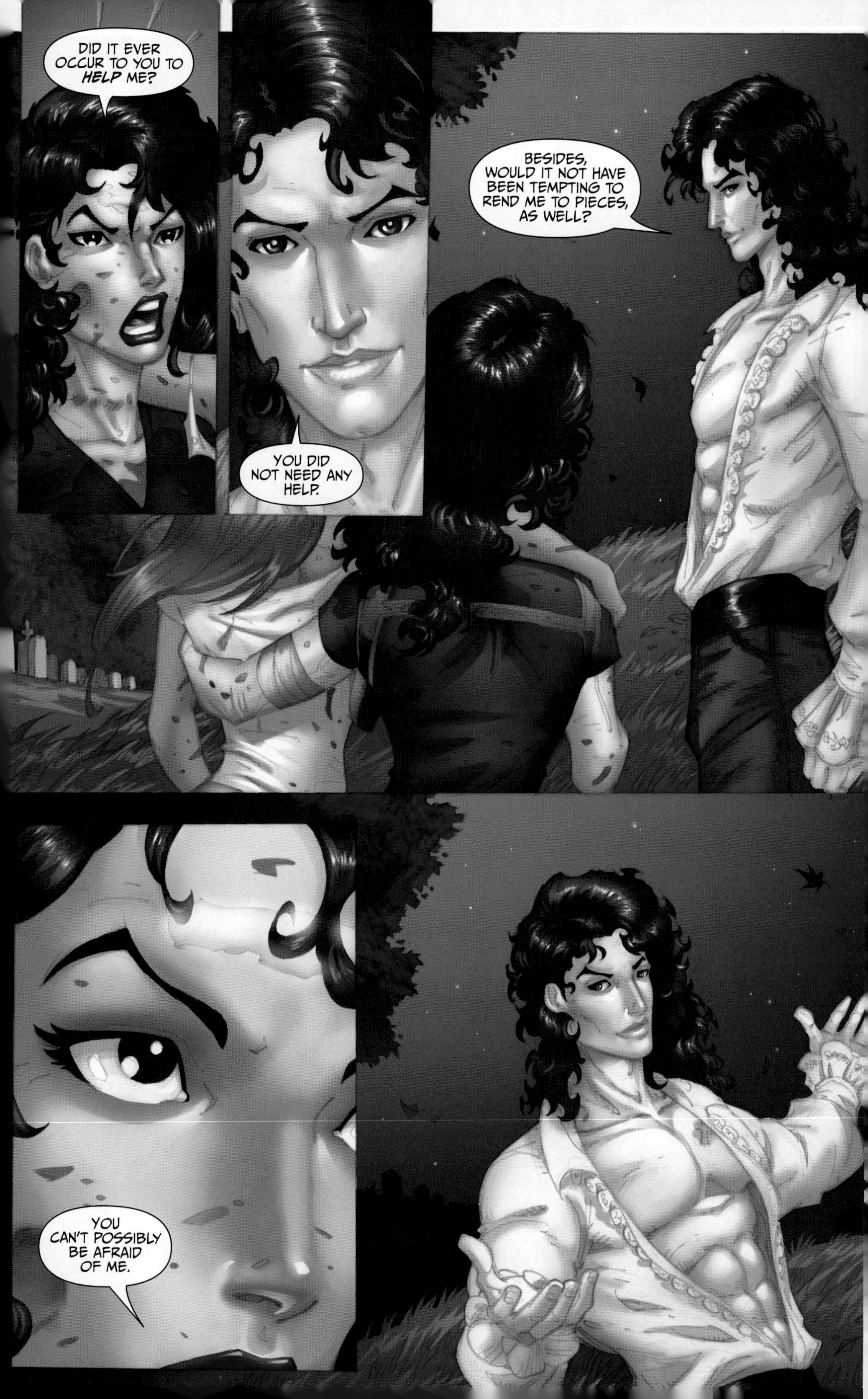
DID IT EVER OCCUR TO YOU TO *HELP* ME?
YOU DID NOT NEED ANY HELP.
BESIDES, WOULD IT NOT HAVE BEEN TEMPTING TO REND ME TO PIECES, AS WELL?
YOU CAN'T POSSIBLY BE AFRAID OF ME.

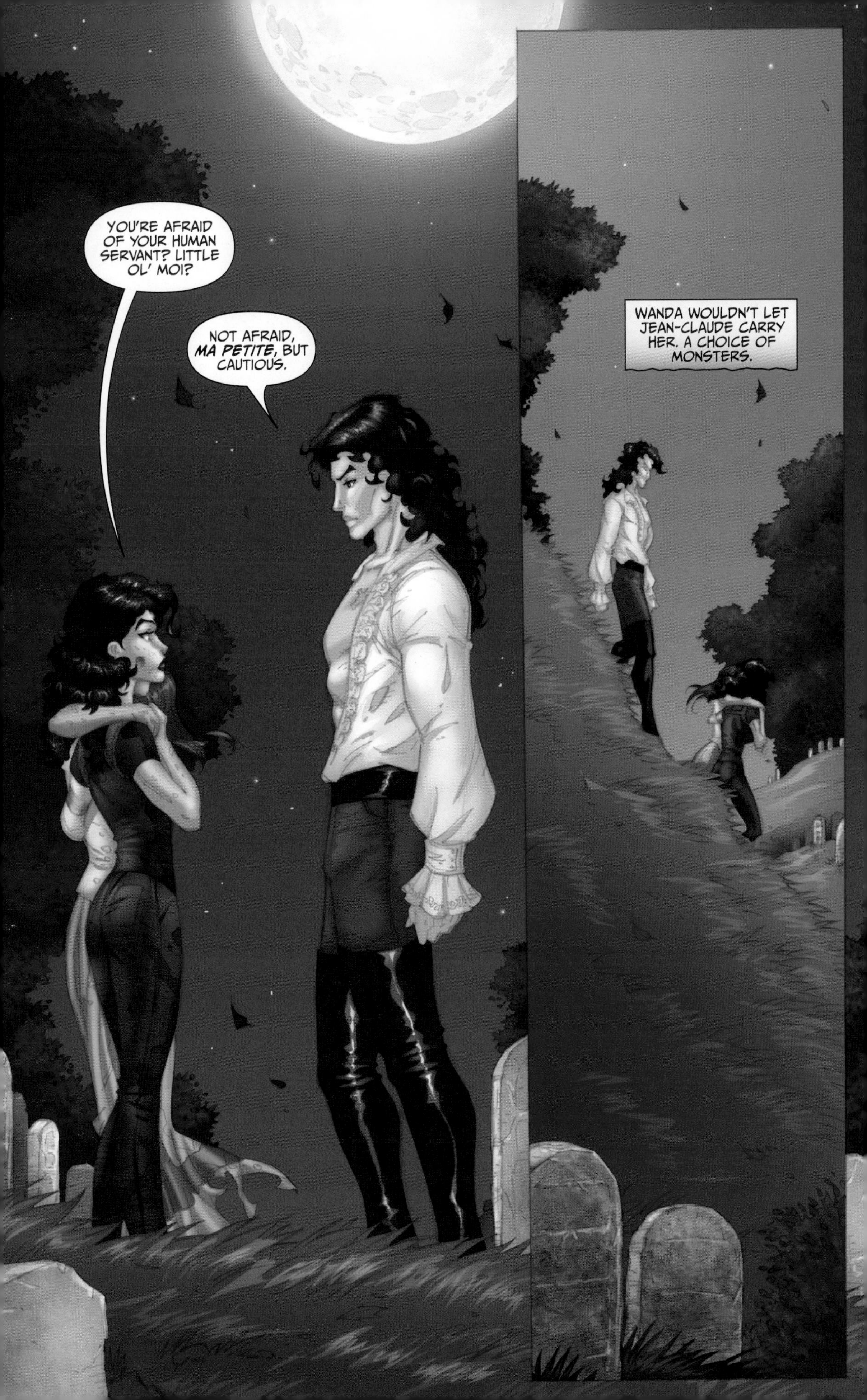
YOU'RE AFRAID OF YOUR HUMAN SERVANT? LITTLE OL' MOI?
NOT AFRAID, *MA PETITE*, BUT CAUTIOUS.
WANDA WOULDN'T LET JEAN-CLAUDE CARRY HER. A CHOICE OF MONSTERS.

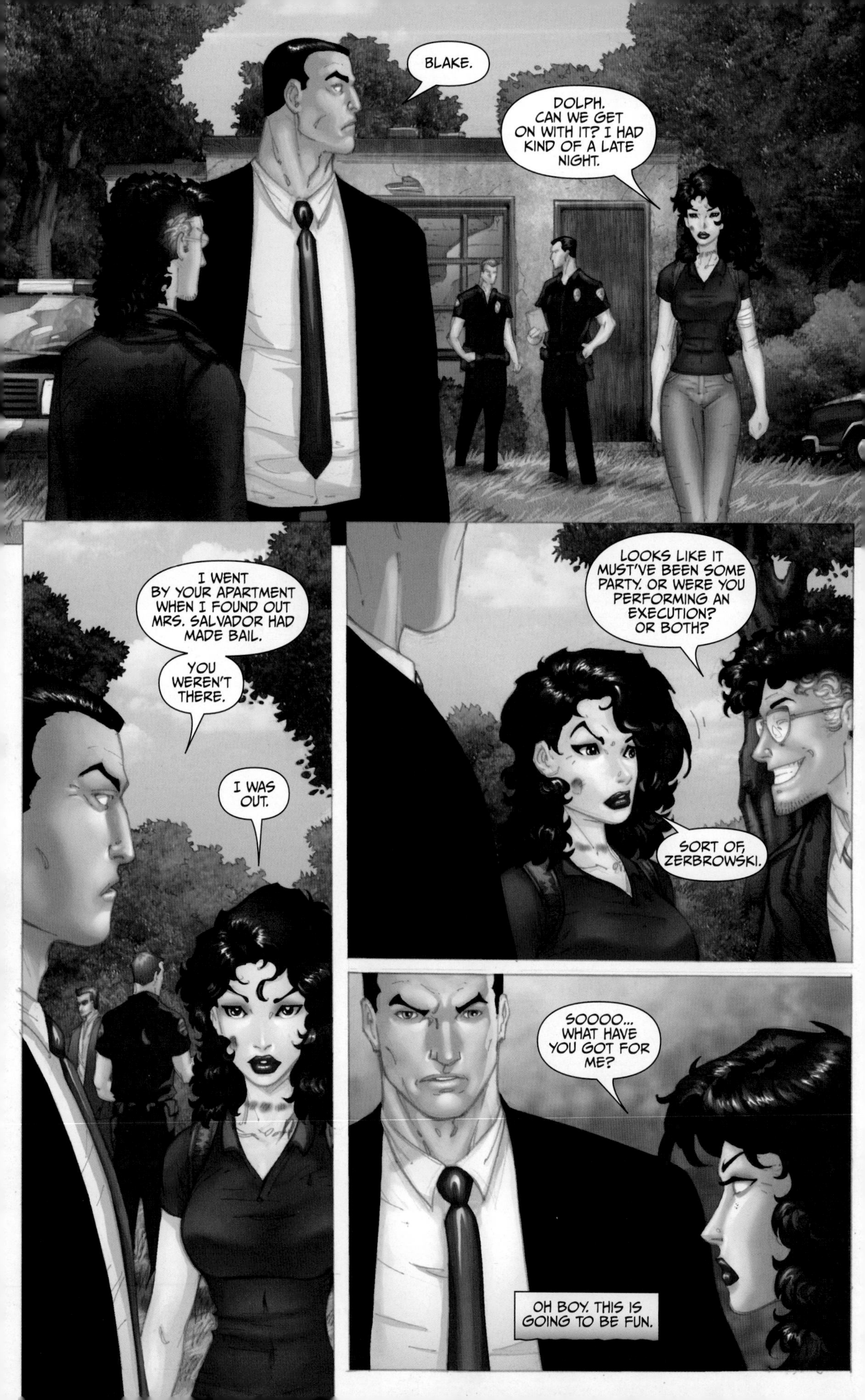
BLAKE.
DOLPH. CAN WE GET ON WITH IT? I HAD KIND OF A LATE NIGHT.
I WENT BY YOUR APARTMENT WHEN I FOUND OUT MRS. SALVADOR HAD MADE BAIL.
YOU WEREN'T THERE.
I WAS OUT.
LOOKS LIKE IT MUST'VE BEEN SOME PARTY. OR WERE YOU PERFORMING AN EXECUTION? OR BOTH?
SORT OF, ZERBROWSKI.
SOOOO... WHAT HAVE YOU GOT FOR ME?
OH BOY. THIS IS GOING TO BE FUN.

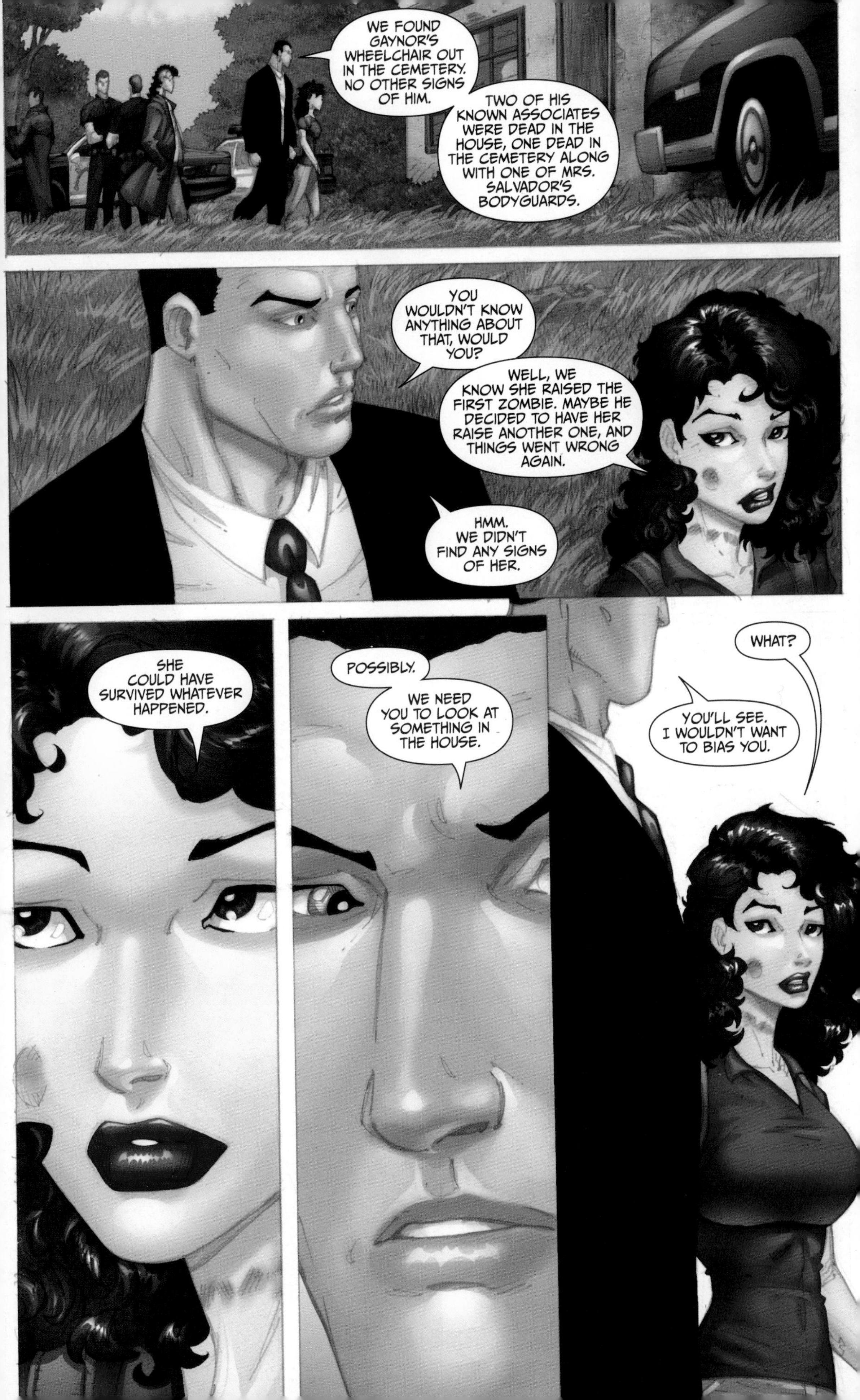
WE FOUND GAYNOR'S WHEELCHAIR OUT IN THE CEMETERY. NO OTHER SIGNS OF HIM.
TWO OF HIS KNOWN ASSOCIATES WERE DEAD IN THE HOUSE, ONE DEAD IN THE CEMETERY ALONG WITH ONE OF MRS. SALVADOR'S BODYGUARDS.
YOU WOULDN'T KNOW ANYTHING ABOUT THAT, WOULD YOU?
WELL, WE KNOW SHE RAISED THE FIRST ZOMBIE. MAYBE HE DECIDED TO HAVE HER RAISE ANOTHER ONE, AND THINGS WENT WRONG AGAIN.
HMM. WE DIDN'T FIND ANY SIGNS OF HER.
SHE COULD HAVE SURVIVED WHATEVER HAPPENED.
POSSIBLY.
WE NEED YOU TO LOOK AT SOMETHING IN THE HOUSE.
WHAT?
YOU'LL SEE. I WOULDN'T WANT TO BIAS YOU.

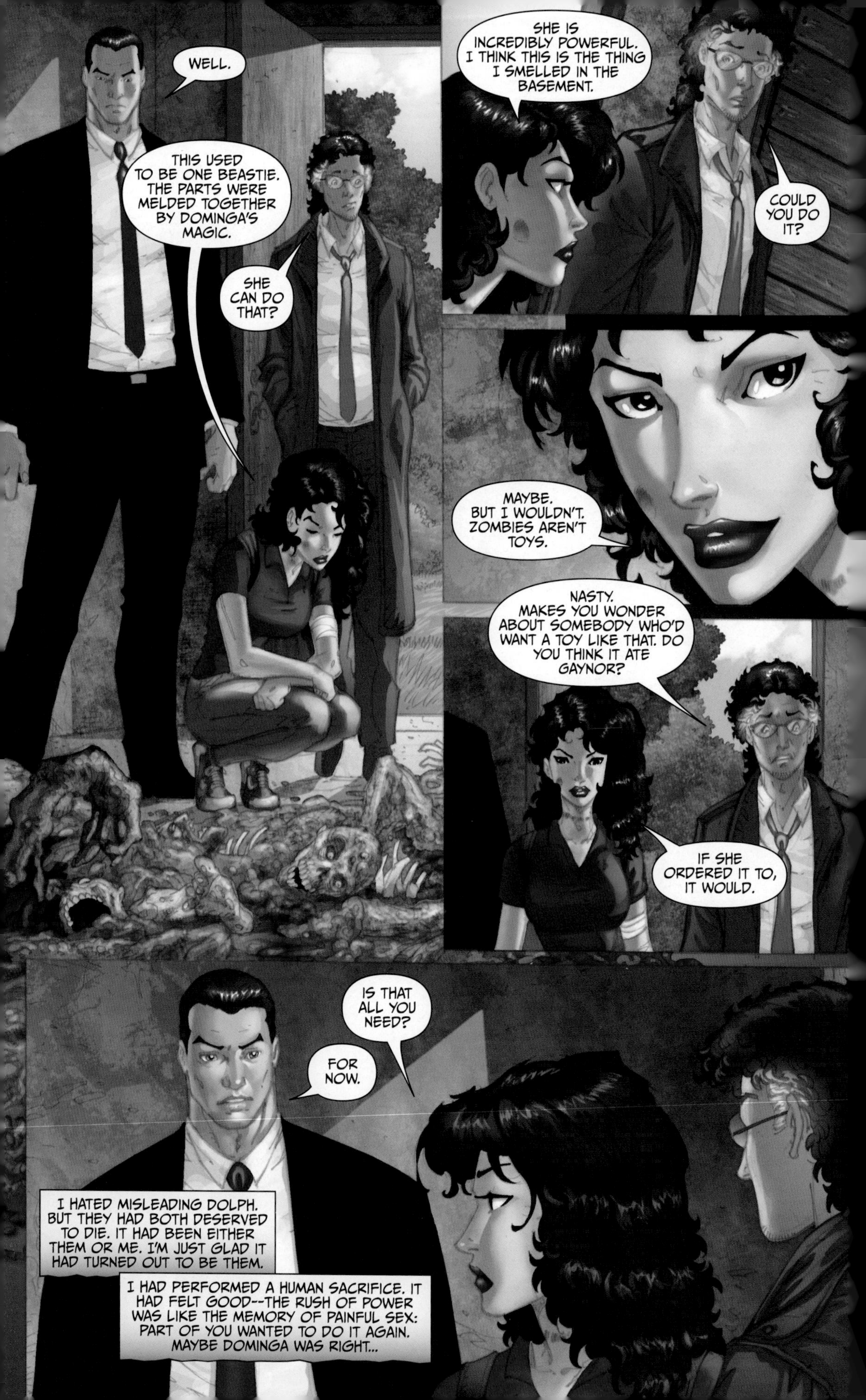
WELL.
THIS USED TO BE ONE BEASTIE. THE PARTS WERE MELDED TOGETHER BY DOMINGA'S MAGIC.
SHE CAN DO THAT?
SHE IS INCREDIBLY POWERFUL. I THINK THIS IS THE THING I SMELLED IN THE BASEMENT.
COULD YOU DO IT?
MAYBE. BUT I WOULDN'T. ZOMBIES AREN'T TOYS.
NASTY. MAKES YOU WONDER ABOUT SOMEBODY WHO'D WANT A TOY LIKE THAT. DO YOU THINK IT ATE GAYNOR?
IF SHE ORDERED IT TO, IT WOULD.
IS THAT ALL YOU NEED?
FOR NOW.
I HATED MISLEADING DOLPH. BUT THEY HAD BOTH DESERVED TO DIE. IT HAD BEEN EITHER THEM OR ME. I'M JUST GLAD IT HAD TURNED OUT TO BE THEM.
I HAD PERFORMED A HUMAN SACRIFICE. IT HAD FELT GOOD--THE RUSH OF POWER WAS LIKE THE MEMORY OF PAINFUL SEX: PART OF YOU WANTED TO DO IT AGAIN. MAYBE DOMINGA WAS RIGHT...

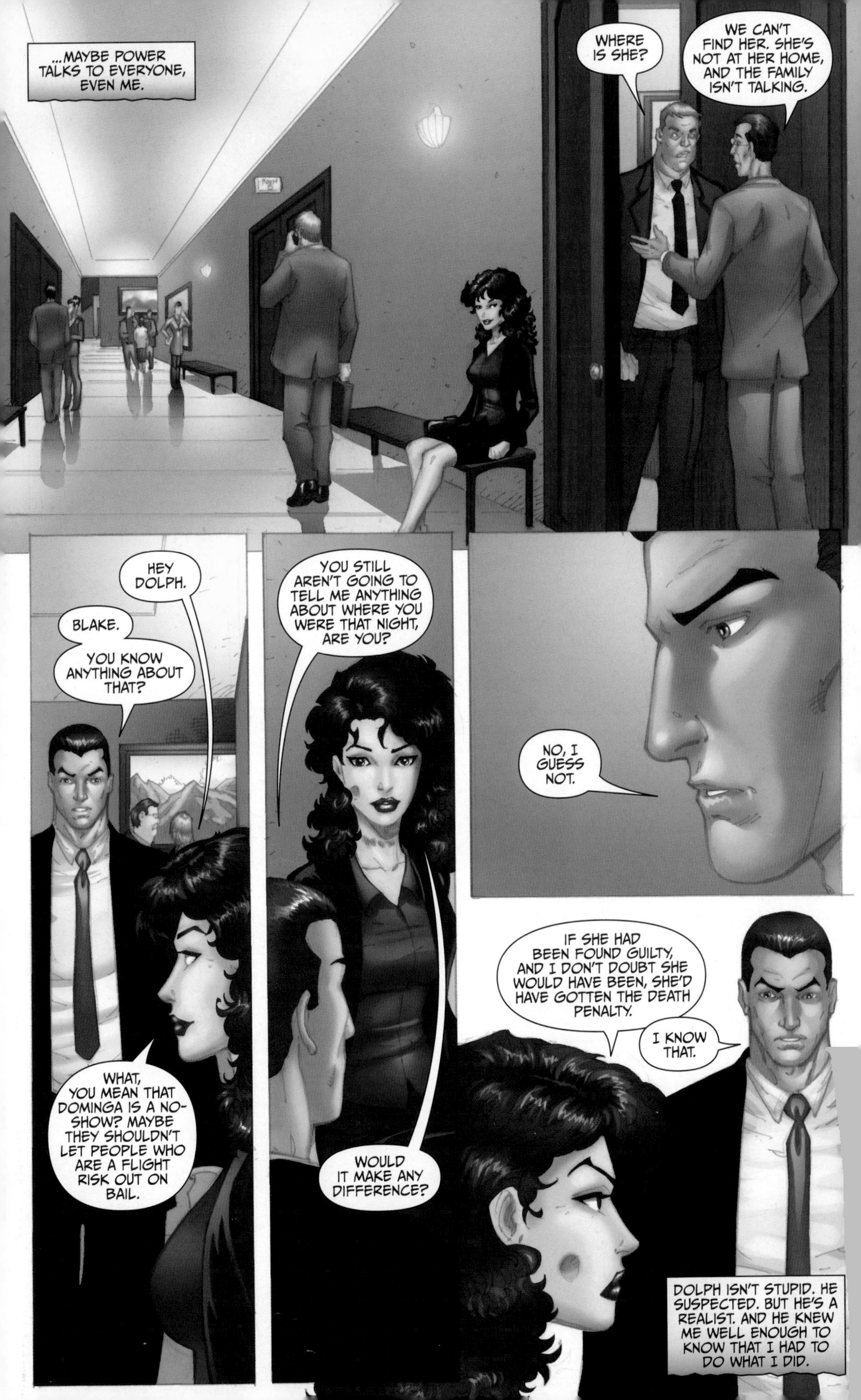
...MAYBE POWER TALKS TO EVERYONE, EVEN ME.
WHERE IS SHE?
WE CAN'T FIND HER. SHE'S NOT AT HER HOME, AND THE FAMILY ISN'T TALKING.
HEY DOLPH.
BLAKE.
YOU KNOW ANYTHING ABOUT THAT?
WHAT, YOU MEAN THAT DOMINGA IS A NO-SHOW? MAYBE THEY SHOULDN'T LET PEOPLE WHO ARE A FLIGHT RISK OUT ON BAIL.
YOU STILL AREN'T GOING TO TELL ME ANYTHING ABOUT WHERE YOU WERE THAT NIGHT, ARE YOU?
WOULD IT MAKE ANY DIFFERENCE?
NO, I GUESS NOT.
IF SHE HAD BEEN FOUND GUILTY, AND I DON'T DOUBT SHE WOULD HAVE BEEN, SHE'D HAVE GOTTEN THE DEATH PENALTY.
I KNOW THAT.
DOLPH ISN'T STUPID. HE SUSPECTED. BUT HE'S A REALIST. AND HE KNEW ME WELL ENOUGH TO KNOW THAT I HAD TO DO WHAT I DID.

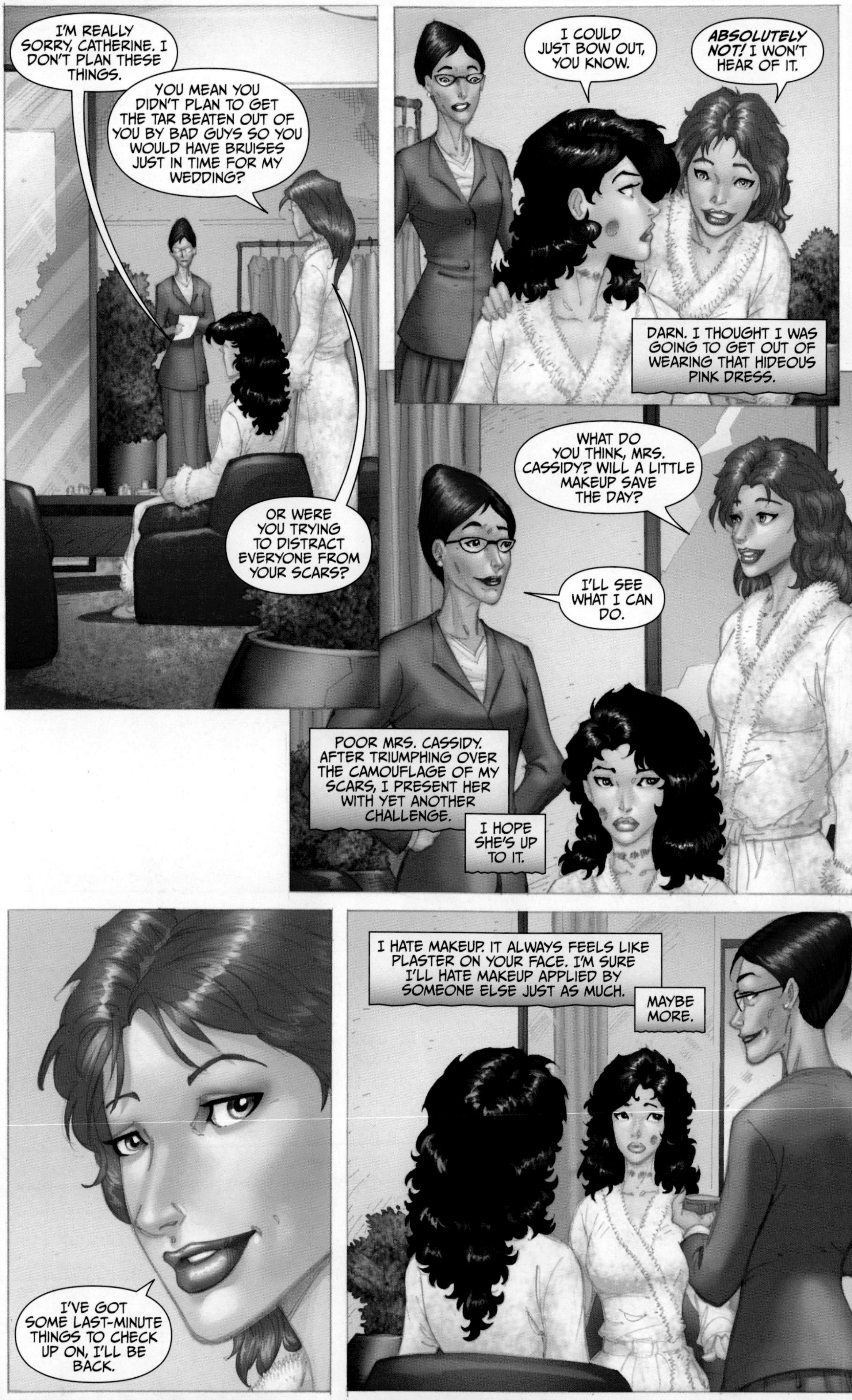
I'M REALLY SORRY, CATHERINE. I DON'T PLAN THESE THINGS.
YOU MEAN YOU DIDN'T PLAN TO GET THE TAR BEATEN OUT OF YOU BY BAD GUYS SO YOU WOULD HAVE BRUISES JUST IN TIME FOR MY WEDDING?
OR WERE YOU TRYING TO DISTRACT EVERYONE FROM YOUR SCARS?
I COULD JUST BOW OUT, YOU KNOW.
ABSOLUTELY NOT! I WON'T HEAR OF IT.
DARN. I THOUGHT I WAS GOING TO GET OUT OF WEARING THAT HIDEOUS PINK DRESS.
WHAT DO YOU THINK, MRS. CASSIDY? WILL A LITTLE MAKEUP SAVE THE DAY?
I'LL SEE WHAT I CAN DO.
POOR MRS. CASSIDY. AFTER TRIUMPHING OVER THE CAMOUFLAGE OF MY SCARS, I PRESENT HER WITH YET ANOTHER CHALLENGE.
I HOPE SHE'S UP TO IT.
I'VE GOT SOME LAST-MINUTE THINGS TO CHECK UP ON, I'LL BE BACK.
I HATE MAKEUP. IT ALWAYS FEELS LIKE PLASTER ON YOUR FACE. I'M SURE I'LL HATE MAKEUP APPLIED BY SOMEONE ELSE JUST AS MUCH.
MAYBE MORE.